Fodor's

TORONTO

D0193548

Welcome to Toronto

Cultured and cosmopolitan, Toronto nevertheless manages to remain relaxed, livable, and fun all at the same time. Canada's center of the arts and media has plenty of pleasant tree-lined streets in Yorkville for window-shopping and wandering; a host of independent galleries in West Queen West with edgy works; big-name music festivals year-round; and an adventurous, constantly evolving food scene. Toronto's impressive sights may be what pull you in, but its vibrant neighborhoods, artistic happenings, and friendly locals will make you want to return.

TOP REASONS TO GO

★ **CN Tower:** Rising 1,815 feet in the air, this icon has stupendous panoramic views.

★ **Foodie Paradise:** Sophisticated restaurants, excellent ethnic spots, and markets.

★ **Nonstop Shopping:** High-end designer flagships and a plethora of vintage shops.

★ **Festival City:** A star-studded film festival, the Nuit Blanche all-nighter, and more.

★ **Hip and Happening:** Urbanites flock to West Queen West, Old Town, and beyond.

★ **The Waterfront:** The Beach's boardwalk and car-free Toronto Islands help you unwind.

Contents

MAPS

EXPERIENCE
TORONTO

10 ULTIMATE EXPERIENCES

Toronto offers terrific experiences that should be on every traveler's list. Here are Fodor's top picks for a memorable trip.

1 Set sail for the Toronto Islands

Located just a scenic 15-minute ferry ride away from downtown, Toronto Island Park is an idyllic getaway hidden just off the shoreline of Lake Ontario. *(Ch. 3)*

2 Tour the Distillery District

Once the site of the world's largest whiskey distillery, this cobblestone-paved neighborhood still oozes Victorian industrial character. *(Ch. 4)*

3 See the city from the CN Tower

Ride the glass-bottom elevator up 1,220 feet to the observation deck, or try the EdgeWalk, where you stroll around on the top of the tower. *(Ch. 3)*

4 Soak in the city's film scene

A number of hotly anticipated movies make their debut at the Toronto International Film Festival, with stars and directors flying in to walk the red carpet and appear for panels and Q&As. *(Ch. 3)*

5 Eat your way around the globe

The city is home to a wealth of global cuisines—everything from Sri Lankan to Salvadorean to Ethiopian. Chinese, Korean, and Japanese food all have a strong foothold here. *(Ch. 5–11)*

6 Stroll along Queen West

Famously named one of the world's coolest neighborhoods in 2014 by Vogue, Queen Street West is at the heart of Toronto's cultural and independent retail scene. *(Ch. 6)*

7 Hang with dinosaurs at the ROM

The Royal Ontario Museum—the biggest museum in Canada—is a must-visit for history buffs and culture vultures alike. *(Ch. 10)*

8 Explore Kensington Market

Kensington, a bohemian, multicultural neighborhood, has fought to maintain its unique local character, including a patchwork of independent stores, grocers, and cafés. *(Ch. 6)*

9 Eat your way through St. Lawrence Market

Once home to Toronto's first city hall and then a prison, this sprawling indoor market has become one of the city's must-hit destinations for food lovers. *(Ch. 4)*

10 Take in some contemporary art

As the country's cultural capital, Toronto is home to a number of top-shelf art museums, including The Power Plant and the Art Gallery of Toronto. *(Ch. 3, 6)*

WHAT'S WHERE

1 Harbourfront, the Entertainment District, and the Financial District. Between the waterfront and Queen Street, the city's main attractions are packed in this epicenter of Canadian financial power, as well as the restaurants, theaters, and clubs of King Street West.

2 Old Town and the Distillery District. Stroll through the Old Town past Victorian buildings to the foodie paradise St. Lawrence Market. Farther east, the Distillery District offers great shopping and cafés.

3 Yonge-Dundas Square Area. The square hosts frequent performances in summer, and the surrounding neighborhood has Broadway-style theaters and department stores.

4 Chinatown, Kensington Market, and Queen West. Busy and bustling, the sidewalks here are overflowing. Wander through the much-loved hippy-punk hangout of Kensington Market and scoff dumplings in Chinatown.

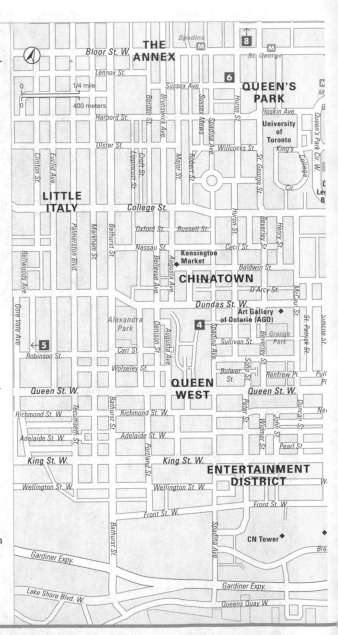

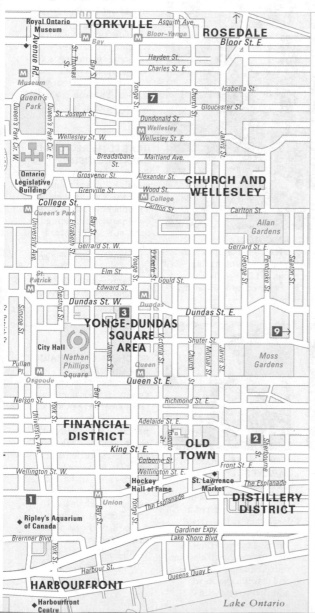

5 West Queen West, Ossington, and Parkdale. West Queen West and Ossington step up the city's hip quotient and Parkdale is North America's largest Tibetan community.

6 Queen's Park, the Annex, and Little Italy. Stately Queen's Park is home to the University of Toronto. Farther west lies Little Italy, packed with cool cafés. North of the campus you'll hit the Annex, the city's academic and artsy haunt.

7 Yorkville, Church and Wellesley, Rosedale, and Cabbagetown. Yorkville itself is refined and classy. North of here is the moneyed residential neighborhood of Rosedale. A nudge east and south is Toronto's gay-friendly Church and Wellesley neighborhood.

8 Leslieville, Greektown, Little India, and The Beaches. Here, the leafy residential streets and boardwalk of The Beaches beckon, while funkified Leslieville offers boho shopping and great brunch spots.

9 Greater Toronto. Top attractions such as Canada's Wonderland and the Toronto Zoo lure visitors from downtown.

Top Multicultural Foodie Experiences in Toronto

SPICE THINGS UP WITH INDIAN CUISINE

If you find yourself craving a good tikka masala while in Toronto, your first stop should be Banjara, which offers a broad, universally delicious menu. In Little India, the raucous, always-busy Lahore Tikka House specializes in grilled kebabs and tandoori chicken.

BROWSE THE WORLD'S CULTURES IN KENSINGTON MARKET

The bohemian Kensington Market is one of Toronto's most unique and vibrant neighborhoods, with a diversity that's reflected in its mix of shops and restaurants. You'll find established Latin and rising Japanese influences in the shops here.

SAMPLE THE LATEST IN JAPANESE SNACKS

Toronto has enjoyed a Japanese food boom in recent years, spurred in large part by the arrival (and viral success) of Uncle Tetsu's Japanese Cheesecake in 2015. You'll also find fluffy Japanese pancakes and matcha snacks in addition to Michelin-starred ramen.

EXPERIENCE INDIGENOUS CUISINE

In recent years, Toronto has become home to several restaurants serving traditional dishes from the area's First Nations peoples, which serve an important dual function as local hubs for Indigenous culture. The longest-running is Tea N Bannock, a Little India café with a menu that puts staples like bison, frybread, and arctic char front and center.

GRAB SOME REGIONAL CHINESE CUISINE

Toronto is home to a sizeable Chinese population, so it's no surprise that a number of China's local cuisines are represented. Start at Yueh Tung for a variety of Hakka dishes. In Chinatown, Rol San is an always-busy, no-frills spot for Cantonese. Mother's Dumplings has Northeastern eats like pork and chive dumplings and scallion pancakes.

GO ON A MOMO CRAWL IN PARKDALE

The west-end stretch of Queen Street is home to a large Tibetan population, which is reflected in the proliferation of eateries serving momos, Tibetan dumplings stuffed with a variety of meats and veggies and served steamed or fried. If you want to sample the whole local smorgasbord, Students For A Free Tibet hosts a Momo Crawl food event every summer.

Northern Thai at Pai

DIVE INTO NORTHERN THAI AT PAI

The family behind Pai runs several of Toronto's most beloved Thai joints, including tried-and-true Sukhothai, snack bar Sabai Sabai and genteel, marble-swathed Kiin. You can't go wrong with a meal at any of them – but Pai just might be the most memorable.

STOP BY MARKET 707 FOR AN INTERNATIONAL SMORGASBORD

It might not look like much, but Market 707, a row of shipping-container food stalls on a quiet stretch of Dundas, is an incubator for some of Toronto's most interesting new food businesses, playing host to everything from Zimbabwean to Jamaican food.

The offerings change as businesses come and go.

FEEL THE HEAT WITH CARIBBEAN EATS

Toronto's thriving Caribbean population fuels a vibrant dining scene. Many of the old-school Caribbean roti joints have fallen victim to rising rents, but mom and pops like Ali's Roti in Parkdale are still holding strong. Most of the best Caribbean dining is in the suburbs these days.

TRY JAMAICAN-CHINESE FUSION AT PATOIS

The Chinese-Jamaican-Southern mishmash you see at hip Dundas West joint Patois is unlike any other in town. The party-ready spot is fueled by dishes from the chef's Jamaican-Chinese upbringing, with plenty of tropical cocktails to wash it all down.

Best Bars and Nightlife in Toronto

BIRRERIA VOLO

Though it only opened in 2016, this narrow Little Italy bar feels like it's been there forever, with its weathered exposed brick, walled-off courtyard space, and beer hall-style tables and benches. You'll find 26 beers and ciders on tap here—including rare and limited-edition brews.

THE DRAKE HOTEL

The Drake (no relation to the rapper) packs in an underground club, a loungey ground-floor bar and restaurant, and a dynamic rooftop patio decked out with ever-changing art installations. On any given night, there could be DJs, a hip-hop show, cooking competitions, readings or dance parties happening on the premises, and the food and cocktails are some of the best in the city.

BARCHEF

There's no shortage of bars making artful drinks in this city, but the creations at Barchef are on another level entirely. Housemade bitters and infusions like sage pisco and fig rum form the backbone of the adventurous cocktail menu, which features gels, foams, and smoke alongside your usual syrups and spirits. Simpler cocktails—and with a half-dozen ingredients each, we mean that loosely—clock in at around $16 and go (way) up from there.

COCKTAIL BAR

Restaurateur Jen Agg is a household name in Toronto, and the drinks are never an afterthought at her restaurants. The proof is in the pudding at Cocktail Bar in Dundas West, where the ceiling is covered in pressed tin tiles and bottles gleam behind glass-paned cabinet doors. The drinks menu takes some delicious left turns from classic cocktails, including the Steamboat Rickey, which melds cachaça and aquavit with celery, dill, and lime.

COLD TEA

It's essentially a Toronto rite of passage: walk into a lifeless-looking Kensington Market strip mall in the dead of night, look for the door illuminated with a single red light bulb, and step into dive bar Narnia. Named for the possibly-apocryphal Chinatown practice of ordering a teapot full of beer in unlicensed restaurants, Cold Tea is a modern, neon-lit spot where DJs spin and bartenders will invent something for you on the spot depending on what you feel like drinking.

BAR RAVAL

It takes its cues from a classic pintxos bar, but you'd be hard pressed to find another place in Toronto (or anywhere) quite like Bar Raval. The compact interior, cloaked entirely in sculpted waves of mahogany, could be best described as a hobbit hole designed by Antonio Gaudí—a dramatic, elegant backdrop for noshing and

Bar Raval

drinking liberal amounts of sherry and vermouth, both poured solo and as star ingredients in cocktails. The food is just as good.

REPOSADO

Reposado, a dimly lit shrine to tequila and mezcal, still pulls them in night after night, providing a romantic, slightly transgressive backdrop for sampling flights of premium tequila (there isn't much shot-pounding going on here).

MAHJONG BAR

Mahjong Bar doesn't look like much from the outside; in fact, it looks just like a little pink-walled convenience store, complete with boxes of Kraft Dinner, bags of Cheetos, and a few vintage girly magazines for effect. The real magic happens behind a smoke-gray vinyl curtain, which

opens up to a massive back room with a lush jungle mural, cozy booths, and a checkerboard dance floor. Cocktails are tropical-inspired and delicious.

THE BAR AT ALO

Alo needs no introduction among Canadian foodies—the downtown restaurant has been named the top spot in the country multiple times, with reservations slots that fill as quickly as they become available. Happily, the restaurant's adjoining bar space takes no reservations, and it's a top-flight experience in its own right. Service at the wraparound bar is impeccable and knowledgeable, with drinks tailored to customer preference. The bar food, which includes seafood crudo and sumptuous desserts, absolutely holds a candle to the stuff being served next door.

BELLWOODS

Toronto has enjoyed a beer boom in recent years, but even with new breweries popping up monthly, Bellwoods is still the reigning champ. The two-floor flagship on Ossington is still a hot destination nearly a decade in, largely due to the industrial-cool atmosphere, sunny front patio, and tasty bar snacks. But the main draw, naturally, is a line-up of creative seasonal beers, many of which are produced in ultra-limited amounts.

The Best Thing to Do in Every Toronto Neighborhood

HARBOURFRONT

One of downtown Toronto's best experiences isn't in the downtown core at all, but a short, skyline-filled ferry ride away. The Toronto Islands are a conveniently located getaway just off the shore of Lake Ontario, offering peaceful beaches (including the notorious clothing-optional section of Hanlan's Point) and beautiful parks. Families will enjoy the Centreville amusement park; if you're hungry, stop on the giant patio at Island Cafe or grab a pint at Toronto Island BBQ and Beer.

QUEEN WEST

Queen West has become increasingly corporate as the years pass and rents rise, but this mazelike array of back alleys is a homegrown outdoor shrine to street art. The result of a city revitalization project launched in 2011, Graffiti Alley (sometimes referred to as Rush Lane) serves as an ever-changing museum of work by some of the city's foremost street artists, and is a perennially popular setting for music videos and photo shoots. Once you've walked up an appetite, head around the corner to Queen and grab some great cheap eats at Banh Mi Boys, Saffron Spice Kitchen, or Burger's Priest.

ENTERTAINMENT DISTRICT

This downtown district's biggest draw is its collection of theaters. The Royal Alexandra, built in 1907, has played host to major touring musicals like *Kinky Boots*; down the street is sister theater the Princess of Wales, a modern glass-walled space that's hosted *Mamma Mia* and *Book of Mormon*. Across the street is Roy Thomson Hall, home to the Toronto Symphony Orchestra. If film is more your speed, check out what's screening at the TIFF Bell Lightbox, which serves as the main hub for the Toronto International Film Festival in September but spotlights both classics and indie flicks year-round.

FINANCIAL DISTRICT

Unsurprisingly, Toronto's main office district is home to a lot of top-shelf restaurants ready to give those expense accounts a hearty workout. Canoe, one of the city's best-known fine dining destinations, could coast on the views from its 54th-floor perch—but instead, it offers a vibrant menu that highlights Canada's seasonal bounty. Down at street level in the same building, Bymark specializes in luxe comfort foods like lobster grilled cheese sandwiches. Richmond Station and Drake One Fifty are slightly more laid-back, but no less impressive.

THE DANFORTH

This east-end neighborhood is more broadly known by its other name, Greektown, and the area is filled with no shortage of places—from hole-in-the-wall bakeries to sit-down spots with live entertainment—to get your feta fix. On the take-out side, there's quick and reliable spots like Messini or the slightly grungy Alexandros (which stays open until 4 am). For something more elaborate, there's Christina's, home to some great Greek dips, plus belly dancers and a Greek band on weekends, and Mezes, a lively spot with a heated patio. Summer festivals like Thrill of the Grill and Taste of the Danforth bring the party outdoors.

QUEEN'S PARK

To locals, Queen's Park refers to not only the neighborhood, but the historic Ontario Legislative Building that serves as the seat of the provincial government. Built in 1893, the pink sandstone building takes its cues from British architecture, with a hefty collection of artwork from Canada and abroad. Just a few blocks west, you'll hit the edge of the University of Toronto's sprawling campus, which is packed with stately buildings, including the neo-Gothic Hart House. Bibliophiles won't want to miss the Thomas Fisher

Rare Book Library, which is home to a Babylonian cuneiform tablet and one of the few surviving copies of Shakespeare's First Folio.

CHURCH-WELLESLEY

The Village, as the locals call it, is the epicenter of gay life in Toronto. Glad Day, the world's oldest LGBTQ bookstore, is a must-visit; you can check out the latest voices in queer lit while sipping on a coffee or digging into brunch at the on-site café. Crews & Tangos hosts dancing and drag shows, while Woody's is home to some very fun events (the weekly "Best Butt" contest is a favorite) and nightly DJs. If you're around in June, the Pride festivities are among some of the biggest in the world; don't miss the Pride parade at the end of the month.

OLD TOWN

A must-visit for history buffs and foodies alike, the St. Lawrence Market started its storied life as Toronto's first city hall, then as a prison. Now, the sprawling space is jammed with vendors offering all manner of meats, cheeses, breads, produce, and artisanal foods. Be sure to pick up a peameal (aka Canadian) bacon sandwich at Carousel Bakery, and check out the farmers' market on Saturday and flea market on Sunday.

THE DISTILLERY DISTRICT

Once the site of the biggest distillery in the world, this historic neighborhood's industrial Victorian architecture has been carefully preserved; instead of pumps and stills, the rows of rough-hewn brick buildings now hold cute boutiques and cafés. Be sure to stop at Balzac's for a coffee or Mill Street for a pint; pick up chocolates at Soma and scout for fashions at Gotstyle or John Fluevog.

YONGE-DUNDAS SQUARE AREA

Referred to (accurately, if somewhat quaintly) as Toronto's answer to Times Square, Dundas Square is best known as a busy shopping area, flanked by the Eaton Centre—but its array of stores, with few exceptions, can be found in most big U.S. cities. Be sure to take a little time to check out the square itself, which frequently plays host to outdoor shows (including bigger names during Canadian Music Week in May and Pride in June), cultural events, food festivals and more. Even if nothing's going on, it's a good place to take a breather and people-watch.

CHINATOWN

Toronto's largest Chinatown has been going strong since a wave of Chinese immigration in the 1960s, and though rents are rising and hip cafés and streetwear boutiques have been creeping into the area, this stretch of Spadina Avenue is still home to some of the city's best Chinese food. Among your options: dumplings at Mother's and Dumpling House, frills-free dim sum at Rol San, seafood specialties at Taste of China, and late-night eats at New Ho King. If you're craving something else, there's all-night Vietnamese at Pho Pasteur and modernized bar snacks at R&D.

KENSINGTON MARKET

Kensington Market is an oasis of bohemian weirdness in the heart of downtown, a neighborhood of colorful homes, ramshackle shops, and often-inexpensive (and delicious) multicultural eats. Vintage hounds should stop into the shops that line Kensington Avenue for all manner of leather jackets and vintage Levi's, while foodies can dig into Indigenous cuisine (Pow Wow Cafe), jerk chicken (Rasta Pasta), amazing Baja-style fish tacos (Seven Lives), and even artistic small plates and natural wines (Grey Gardens).

WEST QUEEN WEST

This hip district is home to a wealth of boutiques that walk the line between quirky artfulness and practical wearability. Hunt for locally made leather bags at Zane, browse the Canadiana-themed gifts at Drake General Store, invest in a special piece at Horses Atelier, or give your wardrobe a burst of pattern at Coal Miner's Daughter, Hayley Elsaesser, or Birds Of North America. If you've got time to spare, head up to Dundas West for more indie boutiques, including Easy Tiger and Comrags.

PARKDALE

Queen West used to be Toronto's gallery central, but rising rents have pushed many west and north into farther reaches of the city. A number have settled in Parkdale, a gradually gentrifying neighborhood with a large immigrant population. You'll find Margin of Eras, a gallery dedicated to marginalized artists; contemporary-focused Elaine Fleck Gallery, and the wide-ranging Northern Contemporary, which doubles as an art studio. Pop up to Dundas West to find the photography-focused Stephen Bulger Gallery and Hashtag, a space focused on emerging artists.

OSSINGTON

If your Toronto travel plans include a bar crawl, odds are you'll end up on the Ossington strip, which has become one of the city's hottest nightlife destinations in recent years. Bellwoods is a low-key brewery that does the most sought-after beers in town, while Reposado is a candlelit shrine to tequila and mescal. Where Ossington meets Dundas, you'll find the Dakota Tavern, a bar that hosts folk, country, and bluegrass shows, while the Communist's Daughter is a tiny booze-can stuffed with locals. Veer just off Ossington to find neon-lit club and restaurant SoSo Food Club and Mahjong Bar, a gorgeous secret club hidden behind a bodega.

LESLIEVILLE

This low-key neighborhood has plenty of hidden-gem restaurants, stores, and cafés, but it's also become an epicenter of the city's recent brewery boom. Eastbound and Radical Road are low-key brewpubs with some unusual specialties, while Avling is a gorgeous, pastel-washed new space with a rooftop garden that fuels the kitchen. Veer north to Gerrard for Left Field, a baseball-themed brewery that turns out some of the city's finest sours and IPAs, and Godspeed, which offers a novel mash-up of Japanese and German styles.

LITTLE INDIA

Largely off the tourist beaten path, this east-end neighborhood is still lined with mom and pop businesses selling saris, bangles, and delicious eats. Lahore Tikka House, which splits its menu between North Indian and Pakistani, is the undisputed go-to for tandoori, kebabs, and biryani, while Udupi Palace has the market cornered on vegetarian eats, and Bombay Chowpatty offers fresh Indian snacks alongside an impressive selection of Bollywood DVDs. If you're not in the mood for Indian, pop by watering hole Eulalie's Corner Store or Lake Inez, a modern pan-Asian snack bar with a mosaic mural of Kate Bush and Virginia Woolf.

THE BEACHES

The sandy shores that lend this largely residential east-end neighborhood its name are without a doubt its top selling point for visitors. The beach, which is quite clean and certified safe for swimming, is divided into two main chunks. Woodbine, a long, sandy stretch that plays host to volleyball courts, paddleboards, and canoe rentals, is popular with families and beach partiers alike. Meanwhile, a ten-minute boardwalk stroll to the east, Kew-Balmy is rockier and less-crowded, the perfect spot for a quiet beach read or a dip in the lake.

THE ANNEX

Tucked north of the student strip on Bloor West is the sprawling Casa Loma, a Gothic Revival-style mansion built in the 1910s as the home of ultra-wealthy financier Henry Pellatt, at a cost of $3.5 million (yep, that's in 1913 dollars). The lushly decorated 98-room estate now serves as a museum and event venue, complete with stables, 60-foot-tall ballroom, pipe organ, collection of vintage cars, and five-acre gardens.

LITTLE ITALY

Little Italy has had its share of identities—first a stronghold for Portuguese and Italian families, then a burgeoning nightclub district—and now, finally, it seems to have found a way to balance the two. There are plenty of classic dining destinations like Cafe Diplomatico, an Italian spot known for its popular side patio. But a new generation of Italian restaurants like the imaginative, fine dining-influenced Il Covo and sleekly modern Giulietta have also settled in. Of course, it's not all checkered tablecloths: you can also get a serious fried chicken sandwich at P.G. Clucks, hunker down with some Vietnamese-inspired snacks at Pinky's Ca Phe, or try some Belgian brews at Birreria Volo.

YORKVILLE

Toronto's "mink mile" is home to some excellent cultural institutions (the Royal Ontario Museum and the Bata Shoe Museum, to name a couple) — but what the area is really known for is its shopping. Hermès, Prada, Gucci, and many, many other boldface names maintain storefronts along Bloor Street; you can find even more at Holt Renfrew, Canada's fanciest department store, which packs in bags, clothing, shoes, and beauty products and has a separate men's store down the block. Head north into the heart of the neighborhood to find the Yorkville Village mall and a number of independent boutiques catering to the well-heeled.

ROSEDALE

Though it's no less moneyed, Rosedale is a lot less splashy than Yorkville, and the shopping is a lot more subdued. Stock up on skincare products at Gee Beauty; pick up sleek, sumptuous leather goods at WANT Les Essentiels De La Vie; grab a cute, homespun-looking beanie or throw pillow at Tuck Shop Trading Co.; or stock up on fancy condiments at Summerhill Market. If your souvenir-shopping tastes run toward hard-to-find wines and spirits, the Summerhill location of the provincially-run LCBO liquor store—located inside a historic train station—is a must-visit; things appear on the shelves here that you just can't find anywhere else.

What's New in Toronto

It can be hard to define a city like Toronto. It's culturally diverse, to be sure, but that's not exactly a unifying characteristic. So what exactly is Toronto all about? Americans call Torontonians friendly and the city clean, while other Canadians say its locals can be rude and egocentric. Toronto is often touted simply as a "livable" city, a commendable but dull virtue. Toronto might not be quite as exciting as New York City, as quaint as Montréal, as outdoorsy as Vancouver, or as historic as London, but instead it's a patchwork of *all* these qualities. And rest assured that Toronto *is* clean, safe, and just all-around nice. Torontonians say "sorry" when they jostle you. They recycle and compost. They obey traffic laws. For many, Toronto is like the boy next door you eventually marry after fooling around with New York or Los Angeles. Why not cut the charade and start the love affair now?

DIVERSITY

Toronto is one of the most immigrant-friendly cities on the planet, and the city's official motto, "Diversity Our Strength," reflects this hodgepodge of ethnicities. More than half its population is foreign-born, and half of all Torontonians are native speakers of a foreign language. (The "other" national language of French, however, is not one of the most commonly spoken languages here, trailing Chinese, Portuguese, Punjabi, and Tagalog.) In a few hours in Toronto you can travel the globe, from Little India to Little Italy, Koreatown to Greektown, or at least eat your way around it, from Polish pierogi to Chinese dim sum to Portuguese salt-cod fritters.

NEIGHBORHOODS

Every city has neighborhoods, but Toronto's are particularly diverse, distinctive, and walkable. Some were once their own villages, and many, such as the Danforth (Greektown), Little Portugal, and Chinatown, are products of the ethnic groups who first settled there. For the most part, boundaries aren't fixed and are constantly evolving: on a five-minute walk down Bloor Street West you can pass a Portuguese butcher, an Ethiopian restaurant, a hip espresso bar, and a Maltese travel agency. In the 1970s and '80s, areas such as Yorkville and Queen West were transformed by struggling-artist types and have since grown into downright affluent, retail powerhouses. In the last decade once run-down neighborhoods, including West Queen West and Leslieville, have blossomed into funky, boho areas with enviable shopping and eating options with housing prices to match. Barring a change in fortune, gentrification is set to continue to more areas.

CULTURE

The Toronto International Film Festival, the Art Gallery of Ontario, Canada's center for magazine and book publishing, national ballet and opera companies, the Toronto Symphony Orchestra—these are just a handful of the many reasons Toronto attracts millions of arts and culture lovers each year to live, work, and play. On any given day or night, you'll find events to feed the brain and the spirit: art gallery openings, poetry readings, theatrical releases, film revues, dance performances, and festivals showcasing the arts, from the focused Toronto Jazz Festival and the North by Northeast indie rock extravaganza to events marrying visual and performing arts, like Nuit Blanche and Luminato.

THE WATERFRONT

Lake Ontario forms Toronto's very obvious southern border, but residents who live out of its view often forget it's there until they attend an event at the Canadian National Exhibition or the Harbourfront Centre. It's one of the city's best features, especially in the summer, providing opportunities for boating, ferrying to the Toronto Islands, or strolling, biking, or jogging beside the water. The lakeshore is more of an attraction than ever, with ongoing initiatives to revitalize the waterfront and create more parks, beaches, and walkways.

FOOD

There's no shortage of amazing restaurants in this city, and local and fresh produce is all the rage. Celebrity chefs like Lynn Crawford, Mark McEwan, and Jamie Kennedy give locavores street cred, while Toronto's cornucopia of cultures means you can sample almost any cuisine, from Abyssinian to Yemeni. Nowhere is the Toronto love of food more apparent, perhaps, than at St. Lawrence Market, where you can pick up nonessentials like fiddlehead ferns, elk burgers, truffle oil, and mozzarella *di bufala*. In warm weather, farmers' markets bring the province's plenty to the city.

What's Hot in Toronto Now?

After years of continuous condo construction and a recent building boom that included a bevy of luxury hotels, Toronto's distinctive skyline is becoming a blur of glossy high-rise buildings. The CN Tower still stretches above it all, making the loftiest architecture appear pretty insignificant.

A newer addition to the ever-changing skyline is the L Tower, a curvaceous glass building located downtown by Union Station, where the UP Express train now runs to Pearson International Airport—a much needed direct link from downtown to the city's main airport.

And speaking of airports and shoreline, the controversial Toronto Island Airport (also known as Billy Bishop Airport), squeezed between the edge of Toronto Island and the harborfront, is pushing to add more flights and bigger planes. That would provide local jet setters even greater convenience, but annoy the lakeshore's residents to no end.

The subway has been extended into the northern suburbs where so many Torontonians live, and a light rail line is under construction along Eglinton, through uptown Toronto's cosmopolitan hub.

Top Sports Experiences

Toronto has a love–hate relationship with its professional sports teams, and fans can sometimes be accused of being fair-weather, except when it comes to hockey, which has always attracted rabid, sell-out crowds whether the Maple Leafs win, lose, or draw. In other words, don't count on getting Leafs tickets but take heart that sports bars will be filled with fired-up fans. It can be easier, however, to score tickets to Blue Jays (baseball), Raptors (basketball), Argos (football), and Toronto FC (soccer) games—depending on who they play.

Ticketmaster. This outlet is a good resource for game tickets. ☎ *416/345–9200* ⊕ *www.ticketmaster.ca.*

If you prefer to work up a sweat yourself, consider golf at one of the GTA's courses, ice-skating at a city rink in winter, or exploring the many parks and beaches.

BASEBALL

Toronto Blue Jays. Toronto's professional baseball team plays late March through September. They won consecutive World Series championships in 1992 and 1993, and playoff runs in 2015 and 2016. The spectacular Rogers Centre (formerly the SkyDome) has a fully retractable roof; some consider it one of the world's premier entertainment centers. ✉ *Rogers Centre, 1 Blue Jays Way, Harbourfront* ☎ *416/341–1234 ticket line, 888/654–6529 toll-free ticket line* ⊕ *www.bluejays.com* Ⓜ *Union.*

BASKETBALL

Toronto Raptors. The city's NBA franchise, this team played its first season in 1995–96. For several years they struggled mightily to win both games and fans in this hockey-mad city, but the Raptors have finally come into their own, particularly after winning the 2019 NBA Championship. Single-game tickets are available

beginning in September; the season is from October through May. ✉ *Scotiabank Arena, 40 Bay St., at Gardiner Expwy., Harbourfront* ☎ *416/366–3865* ⊕ *www.nba.com/raptors* Ⓜ *Union.*

FOOTBALL

Toronto Argonauts. The Toronto Argonauts Canadian Football League (CFL) team has a healthy following. American football fans who attend a CFL game often discover a faster, more unpredictable and exciting contest than the American version. The longer, wider field means quarterbacks have to scramble more. Tickets for games (June–November) are usually a cinch to get. ✉ *BMO Field, Harbourfront* ☎ *416/341–2746* ⊕ *www.argonauts.ca* Ⓜ *Union.*

GOLF

The golf season lasts only from April to late October. Discounted rates are usually available until mid-May and after Canadian Thanksgiving (early October). All courses are best reached by car.

Angus Glen Golf Club. This club has remained one of the country's best places to play since it opened in 1995, hosting the Canadian Open in 2002 and 2007 on its par-72 South and North courses, respectively, and the 2015 Pan Am Games. It's a 45-minute drive north of downtown. ✉ *10080 Kennedy Rd., Markham* ☎ *905/887–0090, 905/887–5157 reservations* ⊕ *www.angusglen.com.*

Don Valley Golf Course. About a 20-minute drive north of downtown, this is a par-72, 18-hole municipal course. Despite being right in the city, it's a lovely, hilly course with water hazards and tree-lined fairways. ✉ *4200 Yonge St., North York* ☎ *416/392–2465* ⊕ *www.toronto.ca/parks/golf.*

Glen Abbey Golf Club. This Jack Nicklaus–designed 18-hole, par-73 club is considered to be Canada's top course. It's in the affluent suburb of Oakville, about 45 minutes west of the city. ⊠ *1333 Dorval Dr., just north of QEW, Oakville* ☎ *905/844-1800* ⊕ *glenabbey.clublink.ca.*

HOCKEY

Toronto Maple Leafs. Hockey is as popular as you've heard here, and Maple Leafs fans are particularly ardent. Even though the Leafs haven't won a Stanley Cup since 1967, they continue to inspire fierce devotion in Torontonians. If you want a chance to cheer them on, you'll have to get on the puck. No matter the stats, Leafs tickets are notoriously the toughest to score in the National Hockey League. The regular hockey season is October–mid-April. ■**TIP➜ Buy tickets at least a few months in advance or risk the game's being sold out.** ⊠ *Scotiabank Arena, 40 Bay St., at Gardiner Expwy., Harbourfront* ☎ *416/703-5623* ⊕ *www.mapleleafs.com* Ⓜ *Union.*

Toronto Marlies. If you're keen to see some hockey while you're in town, go to a Toronto Marlies game at Coca-Cola Coliseum. The level of play is very high, and tickets are cheaper and easier to come by than those of the Marlies' NHL affiliate, the Toronto Maple Leafs. ⊠ *Coca-Cola Coliseum, 45 Manitoba Dr., Harbourfront* ☎ *416/597-7825* ⊕ *www. marlies.ca* Ⓜ *Union or Bathurst.*

SOCCER

Toronto's British roots combined with a huge immigrant population have helped make the Toronto Football Club (TFC), the newest addition to the city's pro sports tapestry, a success. And during events like the FIFA World Cup, UEFA European Championship, and Copa América (America Cup), sports bars and cafés with TVs are teeming.

Toronto FC. Canada's first Major League Soccer team and Toronto's first professional soccer team in years, Toronto FC kicked off in 2006 in a stadium seating more than 25,000 fans. They get seriously pumped up for these games, singing fight songs, waving flags, and throwing streamers. Games sometimes sell out; single-game tickets go on sale a few days before the match. The season is March–October. ⊠ *BMO Field, 170 Princes' Blvd.* ☎ *855/985-5000 Ticketmaster* ⊕ *www. torontofc.ca* Ⓜ *Union.*

ICE-SKATING

Nathan Phillips Square Rink. This tiny rink is surrounded by towering skyscrapers in the heart of the Financial District. ⊠ *100 Queen St. W* ☎ *311 Toronto Parks, Forestry & Recreation rink hotline* ⊕ *nathanphillipssquareskaterentals.com* Ⓜ *Queen or Osgoode.*

Natrel Rink. This spacious, outdoor rink at Harbourfront Centre is often voted the best in the city due to its lakeside location and DJ'd skate nights. Skate rentals are C$8. ⊠ *235 Queens Quay W, Harbourfront* ☎ *416/973-4866* ⊕ *www. harbourfrontcentre.com* Ⓜ *Union.*

If You Like

WINING AND DINING

Those in search of haute cuisine are pampered in Toronto, where some of the world's finest chefs vie for the attention of the city's sizable foodie population. Toronto's range of exceptional eateries, from creative Asian fusion to more daring molecular gastronomy, offers wining and dining potential for every possible palate. Aromas of finely crafted sauces and delicately grilled meats emanate from eateries in Yorkville, where valet service and designer handbags are de rigueur, and the strip of bistros in the Entertainment District gets lively with theater-going crowds. Weekdays at lunch, the Financial District's Bay Street is a sea of Armani suits, crisply pressed shirts, and clicking heels heading to power lunches to make deals over steak frites.

Sassafraz. The staff here is sure to be attentive—they're used to serving celebrities and power-wielding bigwigs who fill the Yorkville hot spot.

Bymark. An ultramodern and ultracool spot primed for the Financial District set; chef-owner Mark McEwan aims for perfection with classy contemporary fare.

Canoe. Toronto's most famous "splurge" place. Sit back, enjoy the view, and let the waiter pair your dish with a recommended local Ontario wine.

The Hogtown Vegan. Popular, ultratrendy vegan nouvelle cuisine with a menu to rival any steak house.

COOL NEIGHBORHOODS

Toronto's coolness doesn't emanate from a downtown core or even a series of town centers. The action is everywhere in the city. Dozens of neighborhoods, each with its own scene and way of life, coexist within the vast metropolitan area.

West Queen West. As Queen Street West (to Bathurst Street or so) becomes more commercial and rents increase, more local artists and designers have moved farther west; it's also home to a burgeoning night scene and experimental restaurants.

Kensington Market. This well-established bastion of bohemia for hippies of all ages is a grungy and multicultural several-block radius of produce, cheese, by-the-gram spices, fresh empanadas, used clothing, head shops, and funky restaurants and cafés.

The Annex. The pockets of wealth nestled in side streets add diversity to this scruffy strip of Bloor, the favorite haunt of the intellectual set, whether starving student or world-renowned novelist.

The Beaches. This bourgeois-bohemian neighborhood (also called The Beach) is the habitat of young professionals who frequent the yoga studios and sushi restaurants along Queen Street East and walk their pooches daily along Lake Ontario's boardwalk.

PERFORMING ARTS

Refurbished iconic theaters such as the Royal Alexandra and Ed Mirvish theaters host a number of big-ticket shows in elegant surroundings. More modern venues such as the Princess of Wales Theatre highlight local and Broadway performances. The Four Seasons Centre is home to both the National Ballet of Canada and the Canadian Opera Company, which shares the music scene with the Toronto Symphony Orchestra and mainstream concerts at Meridian Hall and Massey Hall. Indie artists are attracted to the bars and grimy music venues on Queen Street West. (True theater buffs will also want to leave Toronto to hit the festivals of Stratford and Niagara-on-the-Lake.)

Massey Hall. Since 1894, this has been one of Toronto's premier concert halls. British royals have been entertained here and legendary musicians have performed: Charlie Parker, Dizzy Gillespie, George Gershwin, Bob Dylan, and Luciano Pavarotti, to name a few. Orchestras, musicals, dance troupes, and comedians also perform at this palpably historic venue.

Rivoli. In this multifaceted venue, you can dine while admiring local art, catch a musical act, or watch stand-up. Before they were famous, Beck, the Indigo Girls, Iggy Pop, Janeane Garofalo, and Tori Amos all made appearances here.

Elgin and Winter Garden Theatre Centre. These two 1913 Edwardian theaters, one stacked on top of the other, provide sumptuous settings for classical music performances, musicals, opera, and Toronto International Film Festival screenings.

The Second City. The comedic troupes here always put on a great performance. Photo collages on the wall display the club's alumni, including Mike Myers, Dan Aykroyd, and Catherine O'Hara.

ARCHITECTURE

A series of high-rises topping 50 stories is changing the skyline of the city forever. At one point, Toronto's only celebrated icon was the CN Tower, but architects have been working hard to rejuvenate the cityscape in the new millennium—at a dizzying pace. In the past 15 years, the city has unveiled the transparent-glass-fronted Four Seasons Centre for the Performing Arts (Jack Diamond), the wood-and-glass Art Gallery of Ontario (Frank Gehry), the ROM's deconstructed-crystal extension, and a redesign of Meridian Hall with attached residential 58-story, all-glass, swooping L Tower (both by Daniel Libeskind).

Philosopher's Walk. This scenic path winds through the University of Toronto, from the entrance between the ROM and the Victorian Royal Conservatory of Music, past Trinity College's Gothic chapel and towering spires. Also look for University College, an 1856 ivy-covered Romanesque Revival building, set back from the road across Hoskin Avenue.

ROMwalks. From May through October, free themed walks organized by the ROM tour some of the city's landmark buildings, such as the Church of the Redeemer, the St. Lawrence Market, and the Royal York Hotel.

Art Gallery of Ontario. The Frank Gehry–designed building and its wooden facades, glass roofs, and four-story blue titanium wing are spectacular to admire from the outside or within.

Sharp Centre for Design. Locals are split by Will Alsop's salt-and-pepper rectangle held aloft by giant colored-pencil-like stilts standing above the Ontario College of Art and Design (OCAD).

Toronto With Kids

Toronto is one of the most livable cities in the world, with many families residing downtown and plenty of activities to keep them busy. *Throughout this guide, places that are especially appealing to families are indicated by FAMILY in the margin.*

Always check what's on at **Harbourfront Centre,** a cultural complex with shows and workshops for all ages. On any given day you could find a circus, clown school, musicians, juggling, storytelling, or acrobat shows. Even fearless kids' (and adults') eyes bulge at the 1,465-foot glass-elevator ride up the side of the **CN Tower,** and once they stand on the glass floor, their minds are officially blown.

Kids won't realize they're getting schooled at the **ROM,** with its Bat Cave and dinosaur skeletons, or the **Ontario Science Centre,** with interactive exhibits exploring the brain, technology, and outer space; documentaries are shown in the massive OMNIMAX dome. Out at the eastern end of the suburb of Scarborough, the well-designed **Toronto Zoo** is home to giraffes, polar bears, and gorillas. Less exotic animals hang at **Riverdale Farm,** in the more central Cabbagetown: get nose-to-nose with sheep, cows, and pigs.

Spending a few hours on the **Toronto Islands** is a good way to decompress. The Centreville Amusement Park and petting zoo is geared to the under-12 set, with tame rides, such as the log flume and an antique carousel. Alternatively, pile the whole family into a surrey to pedal along the carless roads, or lounge at the beach at Hanlan's Point (warning: clothing-optional) or Ward's Island (clothes generally worn). The **Canadian National Exhibition (CNE),** aka "the Ex," is a huge three-week fair held in late August with carnival rides and games, puppet shows, a daily parade, and horse, dog, and cat shows.

Kids can also pet and feed horses at the horse barn or tend to chickens and milk a cow on the "farm." But the mother of all amusement parks is a half-hour drive north of the city at **Canada's Wonderland,** home of Canada's tallest and fastest roller coaster. In winter, **ice-skating** at the Harbourfront Centre is the quintessential family activity.

Young sports fans might appreciate seeing a **Blue Jays** (baseball), **Maple Leafs** (hockey), **Raptors** (basketball), or **Toronto FC** (soccer) game. To take on hockey greats in a virtual game and see the original Stanley Cup, head to the **Hockey Hall of Fame.**

Intelligent productions at the **Young People's Theatre** don't condescend to kids and teens, and many are just as entertaining for adults.

For the latest on upcoming shows and events, plus an overwhelming directory of stores and services, go to the website Toronto4Kids (⊕ *www.toronto4kids.com*).

Chapter 2

TRAVEL SMART TORONTO

Updated by
Natalia Monzocco

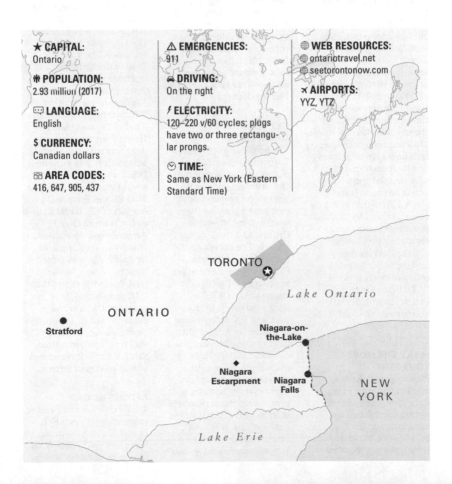

★ **CAPITAL:**
Ontario

⚭ **POPULATION:**
2.93 million (2017)

💬 **LANGUAGE:**
English

$ **CURRENCY:**
Canadian dollars

☎ **AREA CODES:**
416, 647, 905, 437

⚠ **EMERGENCIES:**
911

🚗 **DRIVING:**
On the right

⚡ **ELECTRICITY:**
120–220 v/60 cycles; plugs
have two or three rectangu-
lar prongs.

🕐 **TIME:**
Same as New York (Eastern
Standard Time)

⊕ **WEB RESOURCES:**
⊕ ontariotravel.net
⊕ seetorontonow.com

✈ **AIRPORTS:**
YYZ, YTZ

TORONTO

Lake Ontario

ONTARIO

Stratford

Niagara-on-
the-Lake

Niagara
Escarpment   Niagara
Falls

NEW
YORK

Lake Erie

What You Need to Know Before You Go

To get a sense of Toronto's culture, start by familiarizing yourself with the rituals of daily life. Decide on your priorities, and don't overbook. Allow time for wandering. Schedule coffee (or Ontario microbrew) breaks, and be realistic about your sightseeing style. Plan your days geographically.

CONSIDER WEATHER AND SEASON

Toronto is most pleasant from late spring through early fall, when there are outdoor concerts, frequent festivals, and open-air dining. On the other hand, some hotels drop their prices up to 50% during the off-season. Fall through spring is prime viewing time for dance, opera, theater, and classical music. The temperature frequently falls below freezing from late November into March, when snowstorms can wreak havoc on travel plans, although Toronto's climate is mild by Canadian standards thanks to the regulating properties of Lake Ontario. A few underground shopping concourses, such as the PATH in the Financial District downtown, allow you to avoid the cold in the winter months.

MAKE THE MOST OF YOUR TIME

Planning is the key to maximizing your experience. First, book a hotel near the activities that most interest you. If you're here to see a Broadway-style show, get the view from the CN Tower, stroll the lakefront, stomp your feet at a Raptors game, or soak up some culture at the ballet, opera, or symphony, then you should look for a room in or near Harbourfront. If food, shopping, or museums are your passion, affluent Yorkville might be better suited.

GET YOURSELF ORIENTED

The boundaries of what Torontonians consider downtown, where most of the city sights are located, are subject to debate, but everyone agrees on the southern cutoff—Lake Ontario and the Toronto Islands. The other coordinates of the rectangle that compose the city core are roughly High Park to the west, the DVP (Don Valley Parkway) to the east, and Eglinton Avenue to the north. A few sights beyond these borders make excellent half- or full-day excursions. Most city streets are organized on a grid system: with some exceptions, street numbers start at zero at the lake and increase as you go north. On the east–west axis, Yonge (pronounced "young") Street, Toronto's main north–south thoroughfare, is the dividing line: you can expect higher numbers the farther away you get from Yonge.

PLAN YOUR ROUTE INTO THE CITY IN ADVANCE

Getting from the airport to the downtown core can be tricky, but not so much if you plan your route in advance. Most flights arrive and depart from Toronto Pearson International Airport (YYZ), about a 30-minute drive northwest of downtown. Cabs, Ubers, and Lyfts are a C$50–C$75 flat rate (varies by destination) for most downtown locations. The Toronto Transit Commission (TTC) operates the 192 Airport Rocket, a shuttle bus to Kipling subway station; the TTC fare of C$3.25 applies. The UP Express train to Union Station downtown connects with the Bloor–Danforth subway line near Dundas West station and also to Weston Station. The Billy Bishop Toronto City Airport (YTZ), better known as the Toronto Island Airport, right downtown, is served almost entirely by Porter Airlines, which flies to Chicago, Newark (NJ), Boston, Washington, D.C., and several cities in northern Ontario and in eastern Canada, including Montréal. Amtrak and VIA Rail trains pull into Union Station, at the intersection of Bay and Front streets.

DITCH THE CAR

Traffic is dense and parking expensive within the city center. If you have a car, leave it at your hotel. A car is helpful to access some

Getting Here and Around

Air

AIRPORTS

Most flights into Toronto land at Terminals 1 and 3 of Lester B. Pearson International Airport (YYZ), 32 km (20 miles) northwest of downtown. The automated LINK cable-line shuttle system moves passengers almost noiselessly between Terminals 1 and 3 and Viscount Station, which is close to Value Park Garage and ALT Hotel.

Porter Airlines—which flies to destinations in eastern Canada and the northeastern United States, including Boston, Chicago, Halifax, Montréal, Newark, Ottawa, Québec City, and Washington, D.C.—is the primary airline operating from Billy Bishop Toronto City Airport (YTZ), often called Toronto Island Airport, which offers easy, quick access to downtown Toronto.

GROUND TRANSPORTATION

The drive from Pearson can take well over an hour during weekday rush hours from 6:30 to 9:30 am and 3:30 to 6:30 pm. The most time-efficient and cost-efficient way to get downtown from Pearson is the Union Pearson Express train (also referred to as the UP Express), which connects Pearson's Terminal 1 with Union Station, making stops at the Bloor (a quick transfer to the Dundas West subway station) and Weston GO stations. A trip from Pearson to Union Station takes only 25 minutes and costs C$12.35. Trains run every 15 minutes from 4:55 am (from Union Station) or 5:30 (from Pearson) until 1 am. Buy tickets at the terminal or online at ⊕ *upexpress.com.*

Taxis from Pearson have various fixed rates; most downtown destinations will cost roughly C$56. (Check the rate maps at ⊕ *www.torontopearson. com.*) It's illegal for city cabs to pick up passengers at the airport, unless they're called. Likewise, airport taxis can't pick up passengers going to the airport; only regular taxis can be hailed or called to go to the airport.

From the arrivals levels at Pearson, GO Transit interregional buses transport passengers to the Yorkdale, Sheppard-Yonge, and Finch subway stations. Departures are at least once an hour, and luggage space limited, but at C$7 it's one of the least expensive ways to get to the city's northern sections.

Two Toronto Transit Commission (TTC) buses run from Pearson to the subway system. Bus 192 connects to the Kipling subway station; Bus 52A links to the Lawrence West station. Luggage space is limited, but the price is only C$3.25 in exact change.

From Toronto Island Airport, an underground pedestrian tunnel with moving sidewalks connects the airport to the terminal at the foot of Bathurst Street. The airport also operates a free ferry from the Island to the mainland; both options take less than 10 minutes. Porter Airlines runs a free shuttle from the ferry terminal to Union Station.

Boat

Frequent ferries connect downtown Toronto with the Toronto Islands. In summer, ferries leave every 30 to 60 minutes for Ward's Island, every hour for Centre Island, and every 30 to 45 minutes for Hanlan's Point. Ferries begin operation between 6:30 and 9 am and end between 10 and 11:30 pm. Fares are C$8.19 round-trip.

farther-flung destinations, but in the city, take taxis or use the excellent TTC subway, streetcar, and bus system. Taxis here are easy to hail, or you can call ☎ 416/829–4222 for pickup. The meter starts at C$4.00 and you are charged C$2.00 for each additional km (roughly 6/10 mile) after the first 0.143 km. Ubers and Lyfts are also an option. As for public transit, the Toronto Transit Commission (TTC) operates the subway, streetcars, and buses that easily take you to most downtown attractions. The subway is clean and efficient, with trains arriving every few minutes; streetcars and buses are a bit slower. A single transferable fare is C$3.25; day (C$13) and week (C$64.95) passes are available.

HAVE AN INTERNATIONAL OUTLOOK

Almost half of Toronto's inhabitants were born outside Canada, and even more have foreign roots. Ethnic enclaves—Little Portugal, Greektown, Corso Italia (the "other Little Italy," on St. Clair West), and Koreatown—color downtown. Explore Toronto's multiculturalism in its food or its many international festivals: the glittering Toronto Caribbean Carnival (aka Caribana) along the waterfront; the Krinos Taste of the Danforth (Greece); the raucous celebration of Mexican Independence Day in Nathan Phillips Square; and the annual Festival of India.

EXPLORE THE GREAT OUTDOORS

You don't need a car to escape Toronto's bustle and summer heat and indulge in a calm, cool day by the lake. A rite of passage for every Torontonian is a warm-weather trip to the islands—a 15-minute ferry trip from downtown—for a barbecue, picnic, bike rides, or the Centreville Amusement Park. Or head to the east side of the city for strolls along the boardwalk in The Beaches neighborhood.

ORDER A COFFEE

You need to experience (or at least observe) the ritual of caffeine and sugar intake at Tim Hortons, a coffee chain with a distinctly Canadian image and affordable prices. Go for a "double-double" (two cream, two sugar) and a box of Timbits (doughnut holes). But plenty of Torontonians eschew "Tim's" for more quality brews, and the city has no shortage of independently owned cafés with stellar espresso and exquisitely steamed milk, especially along Queen Street (east of Broadview or west of Spadina) and in the Annex and Little Italy.

BE PREPARED TO CHEER

Leafs fans—or "Leafs Nation" as they are known collectively—are accustomed to jokes, rooting as they do for a team that hasn't won the Stanley Cup since 1967. If the opportunity arises to attend a game (though nearly every one has been sold out for six decades), count yourself luckier than most Torontonians. If not, try for a Marlies AHL game at th Coca Cola Coliseum. For hockey fans, the Hockey Hall of Fame is a must. Seeing a hockey game at a sports bar is a true Canadian pastime: grab a brewski and join locals in heckling the refs on bad calls. When the Leafs score, the mirth is contagious. If hockey isn't your thing, check out a basketball game (the Raptors won the 2019 NBA Championship), baseball (Blue Jays), soccer (Toronto FC), or Canadian football (Argos).

SAVE A BUCK

Not everything in this large city has to be expensive. The Toronto CityPASS saves money and time as it lets you bypass ticket lines. Admission fees to the CN Tower, Casa Loma, the ROM, Ripley's Aquarium, and the Ontario Science Centre or the Toronto Zoo are included for a onetime fee of C$92 plus tax—a savings of C$48, valid for nine days. Many events listed on the city's website are free. Harbourfront Centre hosts numerous free cultural programs and festivals year-round. Some museums and art collections have free (or Pay What You Can) admission all the time. Even the major museums, including the ROM, the Bata Shoe Museum, the Gardiner Museum, Textile Museum of Canada, and Art Gallery of Ontario, have one or two free, Pay What You Can, and/or half-price evening(s) per week, usually Wednesday or Friday, and usually beginning after 4 pm.

Bus

ARRIVING AND DEPARTING

Most buses arrive at the Toronto Coach Terminal, which serves a number of lines, including Greyhound (which has regular service to Toronto from all over the United States), Megabus, and Coach Canada. The trip takes 11 hours from Chicago and New York City. During busy times, border crossings can add an hour or more to your trip. A low-cost bus company, Megabus, runs service to and from Buffalo, Niagara Falls, New York City, and Montréal.

WITHIN TORONTO

Toronto Transit Commission buses and streetcars link with every subway station to cover all points of the city.

Car

Don't rent a car unless you are driving to sites and attractions outside the city, such as the Niagara Wine Region, Niagara Falls, Stratford, or Niagara-on-the-Lake. In Canada your own driver's license is acceptable for a stay of up to three months.

CAR RENTAL

In Ontario, you must be 21 to drive a rental car. There may be a surcharge of C$10–C$30 per day if you are under 25. Rates in Toronto begin at C$30 a day and C$150 a week for an economy car with unlimited mileage. If you prefer a manual-transmission car, check whether the rental agency of your choice offers it. All the major chains have branches both downtown and at Pearson International Airport.

FROM THE UNITED STATES

Expect waits of up to an hour or more at major border crossings. If you can, avoid crossing on weekends and holidays at Detroit–Windsor, Buffalo–Fort Erie, and Niagara Falls, New York–Niagara Falls, Ontario.

Highway 401 is the major link between Windsor, Ontario (and Detroit), and Montréal, Québec. There are no tolls anywhere along it, but between 6:30 and 9:30 each weekday morning and from 3:30 to 6:30 each afternoon, the 401 can become very crowded; plan your trip to avoid rush hours. A toll highway, the 407, offers quicker travel; there are no tollbooths, but cameras photograph license plates and the system bills you. The 407 runs roughly parallel to the 401 for a 65-km (40-mile) stretch immediately north of Toronto.

If you're driving from Niagara Falls (U.S. or Canada) or Buffalo, New York, take the Queen Elizabeth Way (QEW), which curves along the western shore of Lake Ontario and eventually turns into the Gardiner Expressway, which flows right into downtown.

Public Transportation

The Toronto Transit Commission operates the buses, streetcars, and subways. There are three subway lines, with 75 stations along the way: the Bloor–Danforth line, which crosses Toronto about 5 km (3 miles) north of the lakefront, from east to west; the Yonge–University line, which loops north and south like a giant "U," with the bottom of the "U" at Union Station; and the Sheppard line, which covers the northeastern section of the city. A light rapid transit (LRT) line extends service to Harbourfront along Queen's Quay.

Buses and streetcars link with every subway station to cover all points of the city. Service is generally excellent, with buses and streetcars covering major city

Getting Here and Around

thoroughfares about every 10 minutes; suburban service is less frequent.

FARES

The single fare for subways, buses, and streetcars is C$3.25; children under 12 ride for free. You can get change for your fare at subway turnstiles, but buses and streetcars typically require exact change. An all-day unlimited use day pass (valid until 5:30 am the next day) costs C$12 and can be purchased at TTC stations. On weekends and holidays, up to two adults and four youths under 19 can use the day pass.

Depending on the length of your stay, you may want to pick up a reloadable PRESTO fare card that can be purchased at stations for C$6. A major bonus to PRESTO is that fares paid with the card are valid for two hours, so you can hop on and off without paying twice. The PRESTO card also works on inter-city GO trains and buses and the UP Express airport train.

Subway trains run from 6 am to 1:30 am Monday through Saturday and from 8 am to 1:30 am Sunday; trains arrive every two to five minutes. Most buses and streetcars run on similar hours. On weekdays, the subways get very crowded from 8 to 10 am and 4 to 7 pm—avoid if possible.

Late-night buses along Bloor and Yonge streets, and as far north on Yonge as Steeles Avenue, run from 1 am to 5:30 am. Streetcars that run 24 hours include those on King Street, Queen Street, College Street, and Spadina Avenue, though late-night service is much less frequent. All-night transit-stop signs are marked with blue bands.

STOPS AND INFORMATION

Streetcar stops have a red pole with a picture of a streetcar on it. Bus stops usually have shelters and gray poles

with bus numbers and route maps. Both buses and streetcars have their final destination and their number on the front, back, and side windows. The drivers are generally helpful and can answer questions.

The TTC's free *Ride Guide* is available in most subways, buses, and streetcars. The guide shows nearly every major place of interest in the city and how to reach it by public transit.

 Taxi

Taxis can be hailed on the street, but outside of the city center it's smart to call ahead. Taxi fares are C$3.25 for the first 0.143 km and C25¢ for each 29 seconds not in motion and for each additional 0.143 km. A C$2 surcharge is added for each passenger in excess of four. The average fare to take a cab across downtown is C$10 to C$12, plus a 15% tip. The largest companies are Beck, Co-op, Diamond, and Royal. Ridesharing apps Uber and Lyft are also popular options.
■TIP→ **Call 416/829–4222 to be connected to taxi companies via a free automated system.**

 Train

Amtrak has service from New York to Toronto (12 hours), providing connections between its own network and VIA Rail's Canadian routes. VIA Rail runs trains to most major Canadian cities. Amtrak and VIA Rail operate from Union Station on Front Street between Bay and York streets.

GO Transit is the Greater Toronto Area's commuter rail. The double-decker trains are comfortable and have restrooms.

Essentials

🌐 Embassy/Consulate

All international embassies are in Ottawa; there are some consulates in Toronto, including a U.S. consulate. The consulate offers services between 8:30 am and noon by appointment.

What it Costs in Canadian Dollars			
$	$$	$$$	$$$$
FOR TWO PEOPLE			
under C$150	C$150– C$250	C$251– C$350	over C$350

➕ Health and Safety

Toronto does not have any unique health concerns. Pollution in the city is generally rated Good to Moderate on the international Air Quality Index. Smog advisories are listed by the Ontario Ministry of the Environment at ⊕ *www.airqualityontario. com.*

As in the United States, the phone number for emergency services is 911. The Dental Emergency Clinic operates from 8 am to midnight. Many branches of Shoppers Drug Mart are open until 10 pm, with some open 24 hours. Select Rexall drugstores are open until midnight.

🛏 Hotels

Much of Toronto's downtown hotel market is geared toward business travelers. But these same chain hotels are close to tourist attractions, so they are good picks for all kinds of travelers. There are also upscale boutique hotels, such as the Hotel Le Germain, and ultraluxe chains like the Shangri-La and Ritz-Carlton. Within a 15-minute drive of downtown are High Park and the Humber River, served by B&Bs and the lovely Old Mill Inn. West Queen West has some unique places to stay, such as the restored Gladstone and Drake hotels. Lester B. Pearson International Airport is 29 km (18 miles) northwest of downtown; staying in this area means quick connections to areas beyond.

💲 Money

ATMS AND BANKS

ATMs are available in most bank, trust company, and credit union branches across the country, as well as in many convenience stores, malls, and gas stations. The major banks in Toronto are Scotiabank, CIBC, HSBC, Royal Bank of Canada, the Bank of Montréal, and TD Canada Trust.

CREDIT CARDS

It's a good idea to inform your credit card company before you travel, especially if you're going abroad and don't travel internationally very often. Otherwise, the credit-card company might put a hold on your card owing to unusual activity—not a good thing halfway through your trip. Record all your credit-card numbers—as well as the phone numbers to call if your cards are lost or stolen—in a safe place, so you're prepared should something go wrong. Both MasterCard and Visa have general numbers you can call (collect if you're abroad) if your card is lost, but you're better off calling the number of your issuing bank as MasterCard and Visa usually just transfer you to your bank; your bank's number is usually printed on your card.

If you plan to use your credit card for cash advances, you'll need to apply for a PIN at least two weeks before your trip. Although it's usually cheaper and safer to use a credit card abroad for large purchases (so you can cancel payments or be reimbursed if there's a problem), note

Essentials

that some credit-card companies *and* the banks that issue them add substantial percentages to all foreign transactions, whether they're in a foreign currency or not. Check on these fees before leaving home so there won't be any surprises when you get the bill.

Before you charge something, ask the merchant whether he or she plans to do a dynamic currency conversion (DCC). In such a transaction the credit-card processor (shop, restaurant, or hotel, not Visa or MasterCard) converts the currency and charges you in dollars. In most cases you'll pay the merchant a 3% fee for this service in addition to any credit-card company and issuing-bank foreign-transaction surcharges.

Dynamic currency conversion programs are becoming increasingly widespread. Merchants who participate in them are supposed to ask whether you want to be charged in dollars or the local currency, but they don't always do so. And even if they do offer you a choice, they may well avoid mentioning the additional surcharges. The good news is that you *do* have a choice. And if this practice really gets your goat, you can avoid it entirely thanks to American Express; with its cards, DCC simply isn't an option.

CURRENCY AND EXCHANGE

U.S. dollars are sometimes accepted—more commonly in the Niagara region close to the border than in Toronto. Some hotels, restaurants, and stores are skittish about accepting Canadian currency over $20 due to counterfeiting, so be sure to get small bills when you exchange money or visit an ATM. Major U.S. credit cards and debit or check cards with a credit-card logo are accepted in most areas. Your credit-card-logo debit card will be charged as a credit card.

The units of currency in Canada are the Canadian dollar (C$) and the cent, in almost the same denominations as U.S. currency ($5, $10, $20, 1¢, 5¢, 10¢, 25¢, etc.). The $1 and $2 bill are no longer used; they have been replaced by $1 and $2 coins (known as a "loonie," because of the loon that appears on the coin, and a "toonie," respectively). The exchange rate is currently US77¢ to C$1, but, of course, this fluctuates often.

Even if a currency-exchange booth has a sign promising no commission, rest assured that there's some kind of huge, hidden fee. (Oh … that's right. The sign didn't say no *fee*.) And as for rates, you're almost always better off getting foreign currency at an ATM or exchanging money at a bank.

Google does currency conversion. Just type in the amount you want to convert and an explanation of how you want it converted (e.g., "14 Swiss francs in dollars"), and voilà. Oanda.com also allows you to print out a handy table with the current day's conversion rates. XE.com is another good currency conversion website.

⬤ Packing

The weather is often unpredictable in Toronto, so make sure to pack a lot of layers. Summers tend to be sweltering, so pack loose-fitting clothing, sunscreen, and a hat. A light sweater for cooler evenings isn't a bad idea. Rain gear is a good idea, especially in spring and fall. A parka, hat, and gloves are a must in winter, as is warm, waterproof footwear for navigating snowdrifts piled up by the city's plows.

Jeans are as popular in Toronto as they are elsewhere and are perfectly acceptable for most eateries. Men will need a jacket and tie for the better restaurants and many of the nightspots.

🆅 Passport and Visa

Anyone who is not a Canadian citizen or Canadian permanent resident must have a passport to enter Canada. Passport requirements apply to minors as well. Anyone under 18 traveling alone or with only one parent should carry a signed and notarized letter from both parents or from all legal guardians authorizing the trip. It's also a good idea to include a copy of the child's birth certificate, custody documents if applicable, and death certificates of one or both parents, if applicable.

Non-Canadian citizens or permanent residents and non-U.S. citizens flying into Canada are now asked to acquire a temporary visa, called an Electronic Travel Authorization (or eTA), online through the Government of Canada website. The authorization costs C$7 and applications generally take up to 72 hours to approve (with most being approved in just a few minutes), but applications are still encouraged in advance in case of any unforeseen issues. After approval, the eTA is valid for six months. To learn more and apply, visit ⊕ *www.cic.gc.ca/english/ visit/eta-start.asp.*

🍴 Restaurants

Toronto's calling card—its ethnic diversity—offers up a potent mix of cuisines. The city's chefs are now pushing into new territory, embracing trends from all over the world. Top-notch Spanish tapas, Japanese ramen, and Korean fusion fare have all enjoyed trend status, and farm-to-table dining is a staple. The city's growing cachet has lured in world-famous chefs such as Daniel Boulud and David Chang, who have landed in Toronto with Café Boulud and Momofuku. And as locals will tell you, first come the chefs, then come the foodie travelers, always snapping photos at the city's newest hot spots.

What it Costs in Canadian Dollars			
$	$$	$$$	$$$$
AT DINNER			
under C$12	C$12–C$20	C$21–C$30	over C$30

💲 Tipping

Tips and service charges aren't usually added to a bill in Toronto. In general, tip 15% to 20% of the total bill. This goes for food servers, barbers and hairdressers, and taxi drivers. Porters and doormen should get about C$2 a bag. For maid service, leave C$2 to C$5 per person a day.

Best Tours in Toronto

GENERAL TOURS

Tourism Toronto. Tourism Toronto can provide further tour information. ✉ *Toronto* ☎ *416/203–2600, 800/363–1990* ⊕ *www. seetorontonow.com.*

BOAT TOURS

If you want to get a glimpse of the skyline, try a boat tour. There are many boat-tour companies operating all along the boardwalk of Harbourfront.

Great Lakes Schooner Company. To further your appreciation for man-made beauty, this company lets you see Toronto's skyline from the open deck of the 165-foot three-mastered *Kajama.* Two-hour tours are available early May to the end of September. ✉ *Harbourfront* ☎ *416/203–2322* ⊕ *www.greatlakesschooner.com* 🎫 *From C$27.*

BUS TOURS

For a look at the city proper, take a bus tour around the city. If you want the freedom to get on and off the bus when the whim strikes, take a hop-on, hop-off tour.

Toronto Bus Company. Two-hour guided tours are offered in 24-passenger buses. ✉ *Toronto* ☎ *416/945–3414* ⊕ *www. torontobusco.com* 🎫 *From C$25.*

Gray Line Sightseeing Bus Tours. Gray Line has London-style double-decker buses. It also runs tours to Niagara Falls. ✉ *610 Bay St., north of Dundas St., Dundas Square Area* ☎ *800/594–3310* ⊕ *www. grayline.ca* 🎫 *From C$43.*

SPECIAL-INTEREST TOURS

Toronto Field Naturalists. More than 150 guided tours are scheduled throughout the year, each focusing on an aspect of nature, such as geology or wildflowers, and with starting points accessible by public transit. ✉ *Toronto* ☎ *416/593–2656* ⊕ *www.torontofieldnaturalists.org* 🎫 *Free.*

Toronto Bruce Trail Club. This hiking club arranges day and overnight hikes around Toronto and its environs. ✉ *Toronto* ☎ *416/763–9061* ⊕ *www.torontobrucetrailclub.org* 🎫 *From C$30.*

WALKING TOURS

Heritage Toronto. To get a feel for Toronto's outstanding cultural diversity, check out one of about 65 walking tours offered from May to early October. They last 1½ to 2 hours and cover one neighborhood or topic, such as music history on Yonge Street or historical architecture downtown. ✉ *Toronto* ☎ *416/338–0682* ⊕ *www.heritagetoronto.org* 🎫 *Free, some starting at C$20.*

Royal Ontario Museum. The museum offers 1½- to 2-hour walks on such topics as Cabbagetown, a now-trendy, heritage neighborhood with many houses dating to the 1850s. Several free walks are given weekly. ✉ *Toronto* ☎ *416/586–5799* ⊕ *www.rom.on.ca/en/whats-on/rom-walks* 🎫 *Free.*

A Taste of the World. Food, literary, and ghost-themed tours of various lengths are offered in several neighborhoods. Reservations are essential. ✉ *Toronto* ☎ *416/923–6813* ⊕ *www.torontowalks-bikes.com* 🎫 *From C$25.*

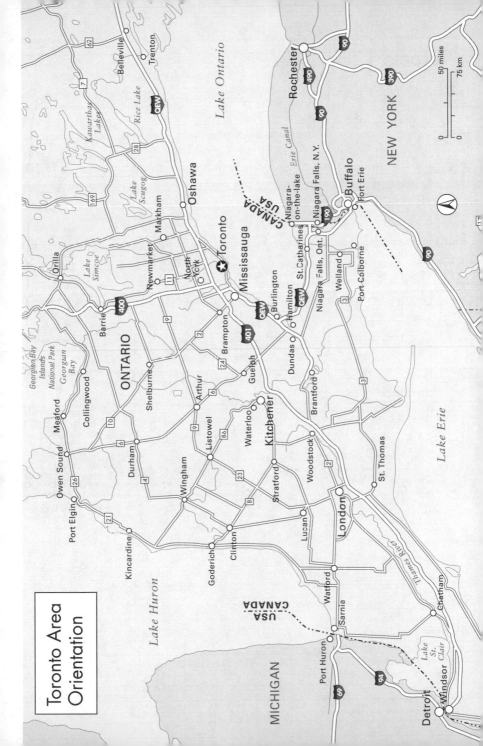

Toronto Area Orientation

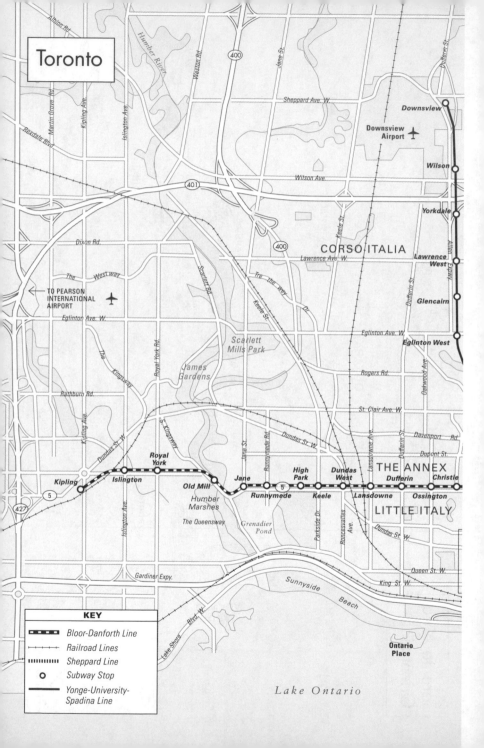

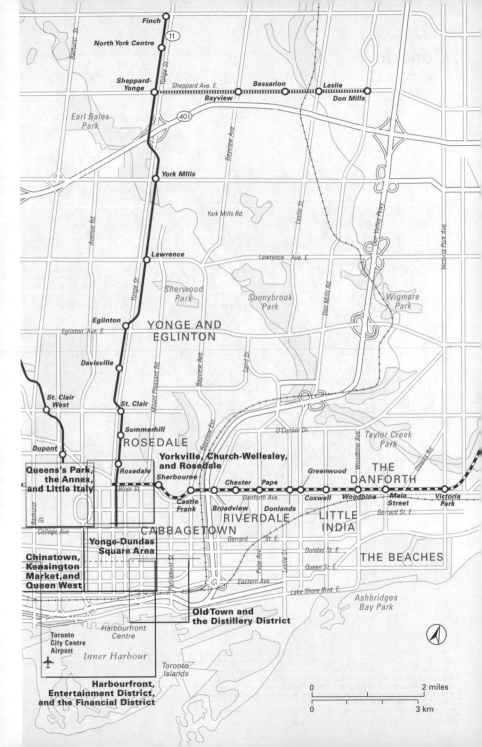

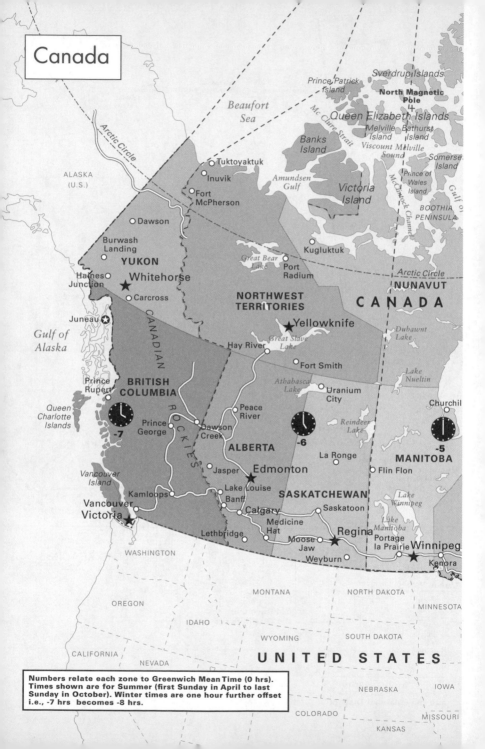

Canada

Beaufort
Sea

Arctic Circle

ALASKA
(U.S.)

Prince Patrick
Island

Sverdrup Islands

**North Magnetic
Pole**

Queen Elizabeth Islands

Mc Clure Strait

Banks
Island

Melville
Island

Bathurst
Island

Viscount Melville
Sound

Somerset
Island

Amundsen
Gulf

Victoria
Island

Prince of
Wales
Island

BOOTHIA
PENINSULA

Gulf of

Tuktoyaktuk

Inuvik

Fort
McPherson

Dawson

Burwash
Landing

YUKON

Haines
Junction

Whitehorse

Juneau

Carcross

Gulf of
Alaska

Kugluktuk

Great Bear
Lake

Port
Radium

Arctic Circle

NUNAVUT

**NORTHWEST
TERRITORIES**

C A N A D A

Dubawnt
Lake

Yellowknife

Hay River

Great Slave
Lake

Fort Smith

Lake
Nueltin

C
A
N
A
D
I
A
N

Athabasca
Lake

Uranium
City

Churchill

Prince
Rupert

**BRITISH
COLUMBIA**

R
O
C
K
I
E
S

Peace
River

Reindeer
Lake

Queen
Charlotte
Islands

Prince
George

Dawson
Creek

-7

-6

-5

MANITOBA

ALBERTA

La Ronge

Flin Flon

Vancouver
Island

Jasper

Edmonton

SASKATCHEWAN

Kamloops

Lake Louise
Banff

Vancouver

Victoria

Calgary

Lethbridge

Medicine
Hat

Moose
Jaw

Saskatoon

Lake
Winnipeg

Regina

Lake
Manitoba

Portage
la Prairie

Winnipeg

WASHINGTON

Weyburn

Kenora

OREGON

MONTANA

NORTH DAKOTA

MINNESOTA

IDAHO

CALIFORNIA

NEVADA

WYOMING

SOUTH DAKOTA

U N I T E D   S T A T E S

NEBRASKA

IOWA

COLORADO

KANSAS

MISSOURI

**Numbers relate each zone to Greenwich Mean Time (0 hrs).
Times shown are for Summer (first Sunday in April to last
Sunday in October). Winter times are one hour further offset
i.e., -7 hrs becomes -8 hrs.**

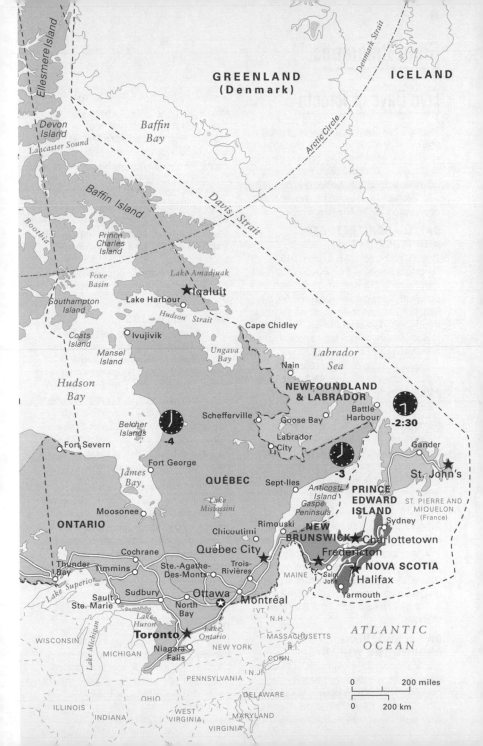

Great Itineraries

Five Days in Toronto

To really see Toronto, a stay of at least one week is ideal. However, these itineraries are designed to inspire thematic tours of some of the city's best sights, whether you're in town for one day or five. We've also included a two- to three-day escape to the Niagara region.

DAY 1: ARCHITECTURE AND MUSEUMS

There's no better spot to begin your Toronto adventure than Finnish architect Viljo Revell's **City Hall,** at Queen and Bay, with its regal predecessor, **Old City Hall,** right across the street. Take a stroll through the **Financial District,** looking up to admire the skyscrapers above you, and then head west along Front Street. You'll see your next destination before you reach it: the spectacular **CN Tower.** Take a trip to the top to experience its glass floor and amazing views.

Next, grab a streetcar going east to Parliament, then head south toward the water to find the **Distillery District,** filled with restored Victorian industrial buildings. Here's a great place to stop for lunch, with plenty of delicious restaurants and bistros.

After lunch, head to the **Royal Ontario Museum**—even if you just admire the still controversial modern Crystal gallery from the outside. Across the street is the smaller **Gardiner Museum,** filled with gorgeous ceramics, and down the street is a shoe-lover's dream, the **Bata Shoe Museum.**

DAY 2: SHOPPING AROUND THE WORLD

Brave shoppers should begin in **Chinatown,** at the wonderfully chaotic intersection of Spadina Avenue and Dundas Street, for shops and stalls overflowing with exotic vegetables, fragrant herbs, and flashy Chinese baubles. Go all out with a heaping bowl of steaming noodles, or just grab a snack at an empanada stand in nearby **Kensington Market** (head west on Dundas to Augusta and turn right). Take your time browsing the market; quirky grocery stores, modern cafés, and funky clothing boutiques all beckon. Then grab the College streetcar across town to Gerrard Street (between Coxwell and Greenwood) to see the **Gerrard India Bazaar** and shop for some bejeweled saris and shiny bangles. Finish the day with a spicy madras curry washed down with a soothing mango lassi (yogurt drink).

DAY 3: WITH KIDS

Get an early start at the **Toronto Zoo,** where 700-plus acres of dense forests are home to 5,000 animals and 460 species, including two giant panda cubs—Canada's first pandas. Little science enthusiasts might prefer the equally exciting (and indoor air-conditioned) exhibits at the **Ontario Science Centre.** Sports fans can see the original Stanley Cup at the **Hockey Hall of Fame,** right downtown at Yonge and Front.

Kid-friendly adventures vary by season. In the sweltering summer, Harbourfront Centre is full of activities and performances along the cooler waterfront. In winter, bundle kids up for a skate on the Centre's ice rink. **Ripley's Aquarium of Canada** is a great way for kids to stay warm or stay cool in any season, and get to learn about 450-plus species of sea creatures.

DAY 4: ISLAND LIFE

Start with picnic supplies from **St. Lawrence Market** (closed Sunday and Monday) for a cornucopia of imported delicacies. It's a short walk from the market to catch the ferry, at the foot of Bay Street and Queen's Quay, to the **Toronto Islands.** There, besides a city skyline you can't get anywhere else, beaches include **Hanlan's Point** (infamous for its nudists, so be warned) and **Ward's Island,** with its sandy beach and sprawling patio at the Riviera restaurant. Island life has an alluring slow pace, but anyone who'd rather cover more ground can rent a bicycle at the pier on **Centre Island.** Winter options include cross-country skiing, snowshoeing, and skating on the frozen streams.

DAY 5: NEIGHBORHOOD EXPLORING

Window-shoppers should begin along the rows of restored Victorian homes of **Yorkville**—in the 1960s, a hippie haven of emerging Canadian artists like Joni Mitchell and Gordon Lightfoot. These days, the country's most exclusive shops and hottest designers have all moved in and spilled over onto Bloor Street West, between Yonge Street and Avenue Road, which is so swanky it's sometimes called Toronto's Fifth Avenue. But in traditional Torontonian style, walk a few blocks west for a stark contrast in the grungy shops along Bloor in crumbling turn-of-the-20th-century homes. Take a rest to recharge at **Future Bistro,** a student favorite for affordable comfort food, or splurge at **Sotto Sotto** or at **Cafe Boulud.** In the evening, catch a play, concert, or comedy show downtown at **Second City.**

DAYS 6–7: NIAGARA GETAWAY

If you have a few days to spare, don't miss the glory of **Niagara Falls,** about 80 miles south of Toronto. It's easiest to get there by car, or else hop on a VIA train (or seasonal GO train) from Union Station. When you arrive, see the Falls best via a ride on the **Maid of the Mist.** In the afternoon, and especially if you've got energetic kids to tire out, try the kitschy **Clifton Hill** for the skywheel and glow-in-the-dark mini putt. For a more relaxing day, try the **Botanical Gardens** or **White Water Walk** along the scenic Niagara

Parkway. Get dressed up for dinner at the **Skylon Tower** or another restaurant overlooking the falls and tuck in for a night at the slots. Look to the skies for fireworks at 10 pm every night from June to Labor Day (and on weekends and holidays in May, September, and October) from either your falls-view hotel room or the **Table Rock Center.** The next day, a good breakfast is essential to prepare for a day of wine-tasting and strolling in bucolic **Niagara-on-the-Lake.** You'll need a car to follow the beautiful Niagara Parkway north to Niagara-on-the-Lake's **Queen Street** for shopping. Wine and dine the day away along the **Wine Route,** which follows Highway 81 as far west as Grimsby. Dinner at one of the wineries or excellent area restaurants, then a night in a boutique hotel or luxurious B&B is a great way to end your trip. If you're lucky enough to visit during the **Shaw Festival,** running between April and October, be sure to book a theater ticket.

Toronto's Best Festivals

Festivals keep Toronto lively even when cold winds blow in off Lake Ontario in winter. Themes range from art to food, Caribbean culture to gay pride. Most national championship sports events take place in and around Toronto.

THROUGHOUT THE YEAR

Shaw Festival. Held from late spring until fall in quaint Niagara-on-the-Lake, this festival presents plays by George Bernard Shaw and his contemporaries. Niagara-on-the-Lake is a two-hour drive south of Toronto. ☎ *905/468–2172, 800/511–7429* ⊕ *www.shawfest.com.*

Stratford Festival. One of the best known Shakespeare festivals in the world, this event was created in the 1950s to revive a little town two hours west of Toronto that happened to be called Stratford (and its river called the Avon). The festival includes at least three Shakespeare plays as well as other classical and contemporary productions. Respected actors from around the world participate. ☎ *519/273–1600, 800/567–1600* ⊕ *www.stratfordfestival.ca.*

JANUARY AND FEBRUARY

Winterlicious. A winter culinary event offering discount prix-fixe menus at top restaurants as well as themed tastings and food-prep workshops. ⊕ *winterlicious.ca.*

APRIL AND MAY

Contact Photography Festival. Sponsored by Scotiabank, this photography festival features more than 250 exhibits in art spaces and galleries across the city throughout the month of May. ⊠ *Toronto* ☎ *416/539–9595* ⊕ *www.scotiabankcontactphoto.com.*

Hot Docs. North America's largest documentary film fest, Hot Docs takes over independent cinemas for two weeks. ☎ *416/203–2155* ⊕ *www.hotdocs.ca.*

JUNE

Luminato Festival. Running for two weeks, this citywide arts festival combines visual arts, music, theater, dance, literature, and more in hundreds of events, many of them free. ☎ *416/368–4849* ⊕ *www.luminatofestival.com.*

Pride Toronto. Rainbow flags fly high during Pride Toronto, the city's best-known gay and lesbian event. It includes cultural and political programs, concerts, a street festival, and a few parades (including the massive closing parade on the final Sunday of the festival), and is centered around the Church–Wellesley area. ⊠ *Church–Wellesley* ☎ *416/927–7433* ⊕ *www.pridetoronto.com.*

Toronto Jazz Festival. For 10 days this festival brings big-name jazz artists to city jazz clubs and other indoor and outdoor venues. ⊠ *Toronto* ☎ *416/928–2033* ⊕ *torontojazz.com.*

JULY

Beaches International Jazz Festival. In the east-end Beach (aka Beaches) neighborhood, this event is a free jazz, blues, and Latin music event and street festival that runs throughout July. ⊠ *The Beach* ☎ *416/698–2152* ⊕ *www.beachesjazz.com.*

Honda Indy. At this summer fixture, cars speed around an 11-turn, 1.77-mile track that goes through the Canadian National Exhibition grounds and along Lake Shore Boulevard. ⊠ *Toronto* ☎ *416/588–7223* ⊕ *hondaindy.com.*

Summerlicious. Each summer, around 200 restaurants in Toronto create prix-fixe menus—some at bargain prices—for this two-week culinary event. ⊠ *Toronto* ⊕ *summerlicious.ca.*

Toronto Fringe Festival. This 10-day event is the city's largest theater festival. It features new and developing plays by emerging artists. ✉ *Toronto* ☎ *416/966–1062* ⊕ *www.fringetoronto.com.*

JULY AND AUGUST

Toronto Caribbean Carnival. One of the largest carnival festivals in North America, the Toronto Caribbean Carnival (commonly called Caribana) is a three-week celebration featuring calypso, steel pan, soca, and reggae music, along with fiery cuisine and plenty of revelry. It culminates with a massive parade on the first Saturday of August. ✉ *Toronto* ☎ *416/391–5608* ⊕ *torontocarnival.ca.*

AUGUST

Canadian National Exhibition. With carnival rides, concerts, an air show, a dog show, a garden show, inventive carnival eats, and a "Mardi Gras" parade, this 2½-week-long fair is the biggest in Canada. Also known as "The Ex," it's been held at the eponymous fairgrounds on the Lake Ontario waterfront since 1879. ✉ *Harbourfront* ☎ *416/263–3330* ⊕ *www.theex.com.*

Rogers Cup. Founded in 1881, this is an ATP Masters 1000 event for men and a Premier event for women. It's held at Aviva Centre on the York University campus, with the men's and women's events alternating between Toronto and Montréal each year. ✉ *Toronto* ☎ *416/665–9777* ⊕ *rogerscup.com.*

SummerWorks Performance Festival. Plays, concerts, and performances are mounted at local theaters during this 11-day festival. ✉ *Toronto* ☎ *416/628–8216* ⊕ *summerworks.ca.*

Toronto International BuskerFest. No ordinary street festival, aerialists, fire-eaters, dancers, contortionists, musicians, and more perform here in Woodbine Park at the end of the summer. ✉ *The Beach* ⊕ *www.torontobuskerfest.com.*

SEPTEMBER

Toronto International Film Festival. Renowned worldwide, this festival is considered more accessible to the public than Cannes, Sundance, or other major film festivals. A number of films make their world or North American premieres at this 11-day festival each year, some at red-carpet events attended by Hollywood stars. ✉ *Toronto* ☎ *416/599–2033, 888/258–8433* ⊕ *tiff.net.*

OCTOBER

Nuit Blanche. Concentrated in Toronto's downtown, this all-night street festival has interactive contemporary art installations and performances. ✉ *Toronto* ⊕ *nbto.com.*

NOVEMBER

Royal Agricultural Winter Fair. Held since 1922 at the Ex, this 10-day fair is a highlight of Canada's equestrian season each November, with jumping, dressage, and harness-racing competitions. ✉ *Toronto* ☎ *416/263–3400* ⊕ *royalfair.org.*

NOVEMBER–DECEMBER

Toronto Christmas Market. Taking over the Distillery District from late November until just before Christmas, this festive outdoor market features local vendors and dazzling light displays. ✉ *Distillery District* ⊕ *tochristmasmarket.com.*

Contacts

Air

**AIRLINE SECU-
RITY ISSUES Canadian
Transportation Agency.**
☎ 888/222–2592 ⊕ www.
otc-cta.gc.ca. **Transportation Security Administration.**
⊕ www.tsa.gov.

AIRLINES Air Canada.
☎ 888/247–2262, ⊕ www.
aircanada.com. **Air Transat.**
☎ 877/872–6728, ⊕ www.
airtransat.ca. **American
Airlines.** ☎ 800/433–7300
⊕ www.aa.com. **Delta Airlines.** ☎ 800/221–1212 for
U.S. and Canadian reser-
vations, 800/241–4141 for
international reservations
⊕ www.delta.com. **Porter
Airlines.** ☎ 888/619–8622,
416/619–8622 ⊕ www.fly-
porter.com. **United Airlines.**
☎ 800/864–8331 ⊕ www.
united.com. **WestJet.**
☎ 888/937–8538 ⊕ www.
westjet.com.

**AIRPORT INFORMATION
Billy Bishop Toronto City
Airport.** ☎ 416/203–6942
⊕ billybishopairport.com.
**Lester B. Pearson Interna-
tional Airport.** ☎ 416/247–
7678, 866/207–1690
⊕ www.torontopearson.
com.

**GROUND TRANSPOR-
TATION GO Transit.**
☎ 416/869–3200,
888/438–6646 ⊕ www.
gotransit.com. **Toronto
Transit Commission (TTC).**
☎ 416/393–4636 ⊕ www.
ttc.ca. **Union Pearson**

Express. ☎ 416/869–3300,
844/438–6687 ⊕ www.
upexpress.com.

⊙ Boat

**BOAT INFORMATION
Toronto Islands Ferry.**
☎ 416/392–8193 ⊕ www.
toronto.ca/parks/island.

⊕ Bus

**BUS INFORMATION Coach
Canada.** ☎ 866/488–4452
⊕ www.coachcanada.
com. **Greyhound Lines of
Canada.** ☎ 800/661–8747
⊕ www.greyhound.ca.
Megabus. ☎ 866/488–4452
⊕ ca.megabus.com.

⊕ Emergencies

**DOCTORS AND DENTISTS
Dental Emergency Clinic.**
✉ 1650 Yonge St., Greater
Toronto ☎ 416/485–7121
⊕ dentalemergencyser-
vices.ca.

**FOREIGN CONSULATES
Consulate General of the
United States.** ✉ 360
University Ave., Queen
West ☎ 416/595–1700,
416/595–6506 emergency
line, 416/201–4056 after
hrs ⊕ ca.usembassy.gov.

**GENERAL EMERGENCIES
Ambulance, fire, and police.**
☎ 911.

Taxi

TAXI COMPANIES Beck.
☎ 416/751–5555 ⊕ www.
becktaxi.com. **Co-op.**
☎ 416/504–2667 ⊕ www.
co-opcabs.com. **Diamond.**
☎ 416/366–6868 ⊕ www.
diamondtaxi.ca.

⊙ Visitor Information

**VISITOR INFORMA-
TION Canadian Tourism
Commission.** ⊕ www.
canadatourism.com.
City of Toronto. ⊕ www.
toronto.ca. **Ontario Travel.**
☎ 800/668–2746 ⊕ www.
ontariotravel.net. **Tourism
Toronto.** ☎ 416/203–2500,
800/499–2514 ⊕ www.
seetorontonow.com.

Chapter 3

HARBOURFRONT, ENTERTAINMENT DISTRICT, AND THE FINANCIAL DISTRICT

Updated by
Jennifer Foden

◉ Sights   🍴 Restaurants   🛏 Hotels   🛍 Shopping   🍸 Nightlife
★★★★★   ★★★★☆   ★★★★★   ★★★★☆   ★★★★★

HARBOURFRONT AND THE ISLANDS

The Harbourfront area is appealing for waterfront strolls or bike rides, and its myriad recreational and amusement options make it ideal for first-timers getting to know the lay of the land or longtime residents looking to get reacquainted with the city. The nearby Toronto Islands provide a perfect escape from the sometimes stifling summer heat of downtown.

One of downtown Toronto's most special experiences isn't in the downtown core at all, but a short, skyline-filled ferry ride away. The Toronto Islands are a conveniently located getaway just off the shore of Lake Ontario, offering peaceful beaches (including the notorious clothing-optional section of Hanlan's Point) and beautiful parks.

BEST TIME TO GO

If it's sun and sand you're looking for, you'll want to aim for a visit in June, July, or August. The cool breeze coming off Lake Ontario can be the perfect antidote to one of Toronto's hot and humid summer days, but in the off-season it can make things a little chilly if you aren't wearing an extra layer.

WAYS TO EXPLORE

BOAT

The best way to enjoy the waterfront is to get right onto Lake Ontario. There are many different boat tours—take your pick from the vendors lining the Harbourfront's lakeside boardwalk—but most offer the same deal: a pleasant, hour-long jaunt around the harbor for about C$25. Sunset dinner cruises are also offered.

To soak up the sun and skyline views, use the public ferry to head for the **Toronto Islands.** The best beaches are those on the southeast tip of Ward's Island, Centre Island Beach, and Hanlan's Point Beach. This last one is the most secluded, natural beach on the islands, backed by a small dunes area, a portion of which is clothing-optional. Most families with kids head for Centre Island Beach.

BIKE AND STROLL

To get away from busy downtown and stretch your legs, the Toronto Islands are the perfect destination. This car-free open space has paved trails for biking or strolling; miles and miles of green space to explore; and picture-perfect vistas of the surrounding lake and skyline.

Bicyclists, power-walkers, and Sunday strollers all enjoy the **Martin Goodman Trail,** the Toronto portion of the 450-km (280-mile) Lake Ontario Waterfront Trail. The string of beaches along the eastern waterfront (east of Coxwell Avenue) is connected by a continuous boardwalk that parallels the path. At the western end of the walking and biking trail is **Sunnyside Park Beach,** a favorite place for a swim in the "tank" (a huge heated pool) or a snack at the small restaurant inside the handsomely restored 1923 Sunnyside Bathing Pavilion.

FESTIVALS AND EVENTS

The **Canadian National Exhibition** (better known as "the Ex") takes place the last two weeks of August and Labor Day weekend, attracting more than 1.5 million people each year. It began in 1879 primarily as an agricultural show and today is a collection of midway rides and games, carnival food, free concerts, horticultural and technological exhibits, and parades. It also hosts the Canadian International Air Show

Throughout the year, **Harbourfront Centre** hosts a dizzying array of festivals, covering cultural celebrations such as Kuumba (February) and the Mexican Day of the Dead (November); foodie-friendly fetes like the Hot & Spicy Festival (August) and Vegetarian Food Fair (September); and literary events such as the International Festival of Authors (October).

NEIGHBORHOOD SNAPSHOT

TOP EXPERIENCES

■ **Hit the Trail:** Walk or bike the edge of Lake Ontario along the Martin Goodman Trail, the Toronto portion of the 450-km (280-mile) Lake Ontario Waterfront Trail.

■ **Explore the Waterfront:** If you want to take in the most marvelous views of the city skyline, hop aboard one of the public ferries to the beautiful Toronto Islands.

■ **Cheer the Home Team:** This is a great city for sports fans. Depending on the time of year, catch a Jays (baseball), Raptors (basketball), or Leafs (hockey) game.

■ **Head Straight to the Top:** It's a thrilling ride to the observation deck of the CN Tower, the tallest freestanding tower in the Western Hemisphere.

■ **Go Out on the Town:** They call it the Entertainment District for a reason: you can't beat this neighborhood for after-dark excitement.

GETTING HERE

To get to the Harbourfront, take the 509 Queens Quay streetcar from Union Station. The Entertainment District is around St. Andrew and Osgoode subway stations. The Financial District is at Queen, King, and Union stations. There is parking in these areas, but parking is expensive and traffic is congested. Try taking transit whenever possible.

PLANNING YOUR TIME

If you have kids in tow, plan on spending a whole day in the Harbourfront area. If you're going to the Toronto Islands, add 45 minutes total traveling time each way just to cross the bay by ferry. Depending on what you're planning at the TIFF Bell Lightbox, you could spend an hour browsing an exhibit or several hours taking in a few movies. The Hockey Hall of Fame and the Design Exchange are each good for about an hour.

QUICK BITES

■ **BeaverTails.** Try the famed Canadian Beaver Tail pastry: fried dough, with the topping of your choice. Nutella or cinnamon sugar are popular options. ⊠ *145 Queens Quay W, Harbourfront* ⊕ *beavertails.com*

■ **Burrito Boyz.** For casual, inexpensive Mexican eats, you can't go wrong at this local favorite. ⊠ *224 Adelaide St. W, Entertainment District* ⊕ *www.burritoboyz.ca* Ⓜ *St. Andrew*

■ **Marché.** The atrium under the glass canopy at Brookfield Place makes a lovely place to enjoy lunch or coffee and a pastry from Marché, a bustling food market. ⊠ *181 Bay St., Financial District* ⊕ *www.marche-movenpick.ca* Ⓜ *Union Station*

In the last 20 years, Toronto's Harbourfront has been completely transformed. Cranes dot the skyline as condominium buildings seemingly appear overnight. Some of the area's best chefs have made this a culinary destination, and trendy boutique retail establishments have drawn shoppers of all types. Outdoors lovers head to the lakefront to take in the expansive views. Suddenly everyone wants to be overlooking, facing, or playing in Lake Ontario.

During the day, the warehouses in the Entertainment District might look deserted, but when the sun goes down, this neighborhood is party central. The bustle and excitement generated by Toronto's clubbers, theatergoers, and night owls keep the show alive until the wee hours of the morning. Meanwhile, while the sidewalks of the Financial District are brimming with suits and cell phones during the day, after the sun sets, the area really quiets down. Still, there are a few notable attractions here, such as the Hockey Hall of Fame and the Design Exchange. As for the Harbourfront area, many of its most popular attractions are outdoors, so it's especially appealing during warm weather.

Should a sudden downpour catch you off guard, shelter can be found in the area's museums and the network of underground shopping.

Harbourfront

In fair weather, the Harbourfront area is appealing for strolls, and myriad recreational and amusement options make it ideal for those traveling with children. The nearby Toronto Islands provide a perfect escape from the sometimes stifling summer heat of downtown.

 Sights

★ CN Tower

OBSERVATORY | FAMILY | The tallest free-standing tower in the Western Hemisphere, this landmark stretches 1,815 feet and 5 inches high and marks Toronto with its distinctive silhouette. The CN Tower is so tall for a reason: prior to the opening of this telecommunications tower in 1976, so many buildings had been

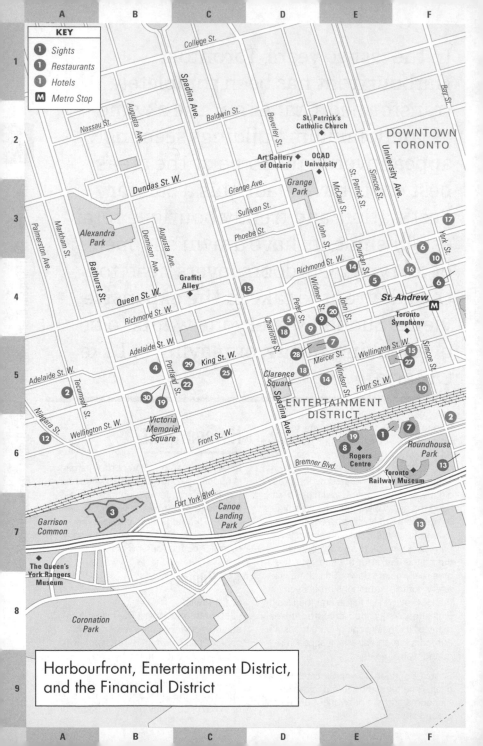

Sights ▼

1 CN Tower F6
2 Design Exchange G4
3 Fort York B7
4 Harbourfront Centre.... G7
5 Hockey Hall of Fame ... H4
6 PATH F4
7 Ripley's Aquarium
    of Canada................ F6
8 Rogers Centre........... E6
9 TIFF Bell Lightbox........ E4
10 Toronto-Dominion
    Centre.................... G4
11 Toronto Island Park..... G9
12 Union Station........... G5

Restaurants ▼

1 Against the Grain
    Urban Tavern.............. I6
2 Beast..................... A5
3 Beer Bistro H3
4 Buca...................... B5
5 Burrito Boyz E4
6 Bymark.................... G4
7 Cactus Club Cafe G4
8 Canoe G4
9 The Chase G3
10 Drake One Fifty.......... F3
11 e11even.................. G6
12 Edulis.................... A6
13 Evviva F6
14 The Fifth Grill E4
15 Fresh on Spadina D4
16 The Gabardine G3
17 Harbour Sixty
    Steakhouse............. H6
18 Khao San Road.......... D4
19 Lee....................... B5
20 Luma E4
21 Pearl Diver............... I3
22 Pizzeria Libretto.......... C5
23 Real Sports
    Bar & Grill G6
24 Reds Wine Tavern G3
25 Rodney's
    Oyster House............. C5
26 Terroni H3
27 TOCA..................... F5
28 Victor.................... D5
29 Wilbur Mexicana C5
30 WVRST.................. B5

Hotels ▼

1 Cambridge Suites....... H3
2 Delta Hotel Toronto...... F6
3 Executive Hotel
    Cosmopolitan........... H4
4 Fairmont Royal York G5
5 Hilton Garden Inn
    Downtown.............. D4
6 Hilton Toronto F4
7 Hôtel Le Germain
    Toronto.................. D5
8 Hotel Victoria........... G4
9 Hyatt Regency
    Toronto.................. D4
10 InterContinental
    Toronto Centre F5
11 Le Germain Hotel
    Maple Leaf Square G6
12 One Key West Hotel
    & Residence............. H4
13 Radisson Hotel Admiral
    Toronto-Harbourfront ... F7
14 Residence Inn Toronto
    Downtown............... E5
15 The Ritz-Carlton,
    Toronto.................. F5
16 Shangri-La
    Toronto.................. F4
17 Sheraton Centre F3
18 SoHo Metropolitan
    Hotel.................... D5
19 Toronto Marriott
    City Centre.............. E6
20 Westin Harbour
    Castle H6

Harbourfront, Entertainment District, and the Financial District HARBOURFRONT

erected over the previous decades that lower radio and TV transmission towers had trouble broadcasting. It's worth a visit to the top if the weather is clear, despite the steep fee. Six glass-front elevators zoom up the outside of the tower at 15 miles per hour, and the ride takes less than a minute. Each elevator has one floor-to-ceiling glass wall—three opaque walls make the trip easier on anyone prone to vertigo—and most have glass floor panels for the dizzying thrill of watching the earth disappear before your eyes.

There are four observation decks. The **Glass Floor Level,** which is exactly what it sounds like, is 1,122 feet above the ground. This may be the most photographed indoor location in the city—lie on the transparent floor and have your picture taken from above like countless visitors before you. Don't worry—the glass floor can support more than 48,000 pounds. Above is the **LookOut Level,** at 1,136 feet; one more floor above, at 1,151 feet, is the excellent **360 Restaurant.** If you're here to dine, your elevator fee is waived. At an elevation of 1,465 feet, the **SkyPod** is the world's highest public observation gallery. All the levels provide spectacular panoramic views of Toronto, Lake Ontario, and the Toronto Islands, and on really clear days you may see the mist rising from Niagara Falls to the south. Adrenaline junkies can try the **EdgeWalk** attraction, which allows harnessed tower-goers to roam "hands free" around a 5-foot ledge outside the tower's main pod. Reservations are required.

On the ground level, the Gift Shop at the Tower has 5,000 square feet of shopping space with quality Canadian travel items and souvenirs, along with a shop selling Inuit art. Displays and exhibits throughout the building feature the story of the construction and history of the Tower; how the Tower works today, including engineering components that make it such a unique attraction; and a dynamic weather display. Peak visiting hours are 11 to 4; you may wish to work around them, particularly on weekends. ⊠ *290 Bremner Blvd., Harbourfront* ☎ *416/868–6937, 416/362–5411 restaurant, 416/601–3833 EdgeWalk* ⊕ *www.cntower.ca* ▧ *First 2 observation levels C$38, SkyPod C$15, EdgeWalk C$195* Ⓜ *Union.*

Fort York

MILITARY SITE | The most historic site in Toronto is a must for anyone interested in the city's origins. Toronto was founded in 1793 when the British built Fort York to protect the entrance to the harbor during Anglo-American strife. Twenty years later the fort was the scene of the bloody Battle of York, in which explorer and general Zebulon Pike led U.S. forces against the fort's outnumbered British, Canadian, and First Nations defenders. The Americans won this battle—their first major victory in the War of 1812—and burned down the provincial buildings during a six-day occupation. A year later British forces retaliated when they captured Washington, D.C., and torched its public buildings, including the Executive Mansion. Exhibits include restored barracks, kitchens, and gunpowder magazines, plus changing museum displays. There are guided tours, marching drills, and cannon firings daily during the summer months. The visitor center has exhibits on the founding of York, the changing harbor, and the War of 1812, plus an area displaying rare and precious artifacts related to Toronto and Fort York's history. ⊠ *250 Fort York Blvd., between Bathurst St. and Strachan Ave., Harbourfront* ☎ *416/392–6907* ⊕ *www.fortyork.ca* ▧ *C$9* Ⓜ *Bathurst.*

Harbourfront Centre

STORE/MALL | **FAMILY** | Stretching from just west of York Street to Spadina Avenue, this culture-and-recreation center is a match for San Francisco's Pier 39 and Baltimore's Inner Harbor. The original Harbourfront opened in 1974, rejuvenating more than a mile of city and today's

Harbourfront Centre, a streamlined version of the original concept, draws more than 3 million visitors to the 10-acre site each year. **Queen's Quay Terminal** at Harbourfront Centre is a former Terminal Warehouse building, where goods shipped to Toronto were stored before being delivered to shops in the city. In 1983 it was transformed into a magnificent, eight-story building with specialty shops, eateries, the 450-seat Fleck Dance Theatre, and plenty of harbor views. Exhibits of contemporary painting, sculpture, architecture, video, photography, and design are mounted at the **Power Plant,** which can be spotted by its tall red smokestack; it was built in 1927 as a power station for the Terminal Warehouse's ice-making plant. Developed by renowned cellist Yo-Yo Ma and garden designer Julie Moir Messervy, the **Music Garden** on the south side of Queen's Quay is Yo-Yo Ma's interpretation of Johann Sebastian Bach's Cello Suite No. 1 (which consists of six movements—Prelude, Allemande, Courante, Sarabande, Minuet, and Gigue). Each movement is reflected in the park's elaborate design: undulating riverscape, a forest grove of wandering trails, a swirling path through a wildflower meadow, a conifer grove, a formal flower parterre, and giant grass steps. **York Quay Centre** hosts concerts, theater, readings, and even skilled artisans. The Craft Studio, for example, has professional craftspeople working in ceramics, glass, metal, and textiles from February to December, in full view of the public. A shallow pond outside is used for canoe lessons in warmer months and as the largest artificial ice-skating rink in North America in winter. At the nearby Nautical Centre, many private firms rent boats and give sailing and canoeing lessons. Among the seasonal events at Harbourfront Centre are the Ice Canoe Race in late January, Winterfest in February, a jazz festival in June, Canada Day celebrations and the Parade of Lights in July, the Authors' Festival and Harvest Festival in October, and the Swedish Christmas Fair in November. ⊠ *235 Queen's Quay W, Harbourfront* ☎ *416/973–4000 event hotline, 416/973–4600 offices* ⊕ *www. harbourfrontcentre.com* Ⓜ *Union.*

★ Ripley's Aquarium of Canada

ZOO | North America's largest aquarium is sleek and angular, and has shapes of sharks on the roof. It contains more than 450 species of marine life spread out between 45 exhibit spaces. Maintaining their philosophy to "foster environmental education, conservation, and research," Ripley's also lives up to its reputation for providing a wow-inducing entertainment venue. One exhibit simulates a Caribbean scuba diving experience, complete with bountiful tropical fish, coral reefs, and a bright blue sky above. Sharks are a dominant theme: you can wind your way through tunnels that take you right into the almost 80,000-gallon shark tank, which houses three species of sharks and more than 5,000 other aquatic animals. The shark pattern on the roof is an unexpected treat for visitors peering down on the aquarium from the top of the CN Tower. ⊠ *288 Bremner Blvd., Harbourfront* ☎ *647/351–3474* ⊕ *www. ripleyaquariums.com/canada* ⊠ *C$30* Ⓜ *Union or St. Andrews.*

Rogers Centre

SPORTS VENUE | FAMILY | One of Toronto's most famous landmarks, the Rogers Centre is home to baseball's Blue Jays and was the world's first stadium with a fully retractable roof. Rogers Communications, the owner of the Blue Jays, bought the stadium, formerly known as the Sky-Dome, in February 2005 for a mere C$25 million. One way to see the 52,000-seat stadium is to buy tickets for a Blue Jays game or one of the many other events and concerts that take place here. You can also take a one-hour guided walking tour: the route depends on what's going on at the stadium, so you may find yourself in the middle of the field, in a press box, in the dressing rooms, or, if a roof tour is available, 36 stories above home plate on a catwalk. ✉ *1 Blue Jays Way, Harbourfront* ☎ *416/341–2770 for tours, 416/341–1234 for ticket information* 🌐 *www.rogerscentre.com* 🎟 *Tours C$17* [M] *Union.*

★ Toronto Island Park

ISLAND | **FAMILY** | These 14 narrow, tree-lined islands, just off the city's downtown, in Lake Ontario, provide a gorgeous green retreat with endless outdoor activities. The more than 230 hectares of parkland are hard to resist, especially in the summer, when they're usually a few degrees cooler than the city.

Sandy beaches fringe the islands; the best are on the southeast tip of Ward's Island, the southernmost edge of Centre Island, and the west side of Hanlan's Point. In 1999 a portion of Hanlan's Beach was officially declared "clothing-optional" by the Toronto City Council. The declaration regarding Ontario's only legal nude beach passed without protest—perhaps a testament to the city's live-and-let-live attitude. In the summer, Centre Island has bike and row boat rentals. Bring picnic fixings or something to grill in one of the park's barbecue pits, or grab a quick (but expensive) bite at one of the snack bars. (Note that the consumption of alcohol in a public park is illegal in Toronto.) There are also supervised wading pools, baseball diamonds, volleyball nets, tennis courts, and even a disc-golf course. Winter can be bitterly cold on the islands, but snowshoeing and cross-country skiing with downtown Toronto over your shoulder are appealing activities.

All transportation on the islands is self-powered; no private cars are permitted. The boardwalk from Centre Island to Ward's Island is 2½ km (1½ miles) long. Bikes are allowed on all ferries, or you can rent one for an hour or so once you get there. Bike rentals can be found south of the Centre Island ferry docks on the Avenue of the Islands.

You may want to take one of the equally frequent ferries to Ward's Island or Hanlan's Point from Jack Layton Ferry Terminal. Both islands have tennis courts and picnic and sunbathing spots. Late May through early September, the ferries run between the docks at the bottom of Bay Street and the Ward's Island dock between 6:35 am and 11:45 am; for Centre and Hanlan's islands, they begin at 8 am. Ward's Island Ferries run roughly at half-hour intervals most of the working day and at quarter-hour intervals during peak times such as summer evenings. In winter the ferries run only to Ward's Island on a limited schedule. ✉ *Ferries at foot of Bay St. and Queen's Quay, Harbourfront* ☎ *416/392–8186 for island information, 311 for ferry information* 🌐 *www.toronto.ca/parks/island* 🎟 *Ferry C$8 round-trip* [M] *Union.*

🍴 Restaurants

The vibe here in summer is decidedly beachy; take a stroll along the lake, stopping for lunch on one of the breezy patios. If you brought your bathing suit, head to Sugar Beach—an urban oasis where locals sunbathe. Or work off that lunch by renting one of the city's public bikes and pedal around until you're ready for dinner.

Against the Grain Urban Tavern

$$$ | **CANADIAN** | Making the most of its proximity to Sugar Beach, Against the Grain is a sunbathing destination minutes from downtown, with a stellar patio in full sunny view of the lake. Shareable apps like nachos and wings, plus a great craft beer selection, capitalize on the laid-back vibe. Sink your teeth into comfort food mains like the fried chicken, Beyond Meat burger, or the *naan* chicken club. **Known for:** great water views; popular with the after-work crowd; diverse comfort food menu. [$] *Average main: C$21* ✉ *Corus Bldg., 25 Dockside Dr., Corus Bldg., Harbourfront* ☎ *647/344–1562* 🌐 *corusquay.atgurbantavern.ca* [M] *Union.*

E11even

$$$ | **AMERICAN** | By day, E11even presents steak-house fare for the downtown business crowd; by night, concertgoers and sports fans slide into wooden booths for a refined meal or nightcap. The menu of North American classics includes savory-sweet maple-glazed bacon, salads flanked with seared tuna, steak frites, and casual fare like kosher beef dogs and lobster rolls. The wine list is also impressive. **Known for:** 3,200-bottle-long wine list; refined atmosphere; the steak, of course. [$] *Average main: C$30* ✉ *15 York St., Harbourfront* ☎ *416/815–1111* 🌐 *www.e11even.ca* ⏲ *Closed Sun. No lunch Sat.* [M] *Union.*

Harbour Sixty Steakhouse

$$$$ | **STEAKHOUSE** | Bucking the trend toward relaxed fine dining, Harbour Sixty goes for sheer opulence, the drama of which is apparent from the get-go as you walk up stone steps to the grand entrance of the restored Harbour Commission building. The kitchen rises to the occasion with starters like the zesty shrimp cocktail and mains like a bone-in rib steak. The fluffy coconut cream pie is a must-eat dessert. **Known for:** extravagant interior; extensive wine list; authentic fine dining experience. [$] *Average main: C$60* ✉ *60 Harbour St., Harbourfront* ☎ *416/777–2111* 🌐 *www.harboursixty.com* ⏲ *No lunch weekends* [M] *Union.*

Real Sports Bar & Grill

$$ | **AMERICAN** | This is an out-size shrine to the world of sports. No matter what game you want to catch—baseball, football, basketball, hockey, or tennis—you'll be able to pull up a seat near a television (the two-story HDTV that dominates the space, if you're lucky) and take in the action. While you're here, nosh on outside-the-box bar eats like smoked ribs braised in soy sauce and lime juice. **Known for:** intense sports crowd vibe; packed with 200 television screens; more than 100 beer taps. [$] *Average main: C$19* ✉ *15 York St., Harbourfront* ☎ *416/815–7325* 🌐 *www.realsports.ca* [M] *Union.*

🛏 Hotels

Staying around here is convenient for exploring the greatest concentration of Toronto's must-see attractions—especially the kid-friendly ones—like the Rogers Centre, Ontario Place, and the CN Tower.

Delta Hotel Toronto

$$$ | **HOTEL** | Just steps from the Rogers Centre, CN Tower, and Ripley's Aquarium (as well as the waterfront), the Delta Toronto has rooms with great views. **Pros:** connected to the PATH, convention center, and Union Station; modern decor and clean, spacious rooms; attentive staff. **Cons:** rooms can fill up quickly; parking is expensive; no mini-refrigerator. [$] *Rooms from: C$309* ✉ *75 Lower Simcoe St., Harbourfront* ☎ *416/849–1200, 888/890–3222* 🌐 *www.deltatoronto.com* 🛏 *541 rooms* 🍴 *Free breakfast* [M] *Union.*

Le Germain Hotel Maple Leaf Square

$$$ | **HOTEL** | Inside the Maple Leaf Square complex, this ultrastylish hotel is perfectly poised to receive traffic from the Scotiabank Arena across the street and the Rogers Centre just minutes away. **Pros:** near Billy Bishop Toronto City Airport; attached to PATH network; great service. **Cons:** area is boisterous when events are happening at nearby Scotiabank Arena; limited equipment in fitness center; very basic continental breakfast. [$] *Rooms from: C$296* ✉ *75 Bremner Blvd., Harbourfront* ☎ *416/649–7575, 888/940–7575* 🌐 *www.germainmapleleafsquare.com* 🛏 *167 rooms* 🍴 *Free breakfast* [M] *Union.*

Radisson Hotel Admiral Toronto–Harbourfront

$$$ | **HOTEL** | **FAMILY** | You can't get much closer to Toronto's waterfront than this hotel, where unobstructed Lake Ontario and Toronto Islands vistas come standard. **Pros:** easy access to local attractions;

beautiful outdoor pool; excellent views. **Cons:** neighborhood seems out of the way; pool is open to the public; rates are pricey. $ *Rooms from: C$309* ✉ *249 Queen's Quay W, at York St., Harbourfront* ☎ *416/203–3333, 800/395–7046* ⊕ *www.radisson.com* ⇌ *157 rooms* ⦿ *No meals* Ⓜ *Union.*

Westin Harbour Castle
$$$ | HOTEL | FAMILY | On a clear day you can see the skyline of Rochester, New York, across the sparkling blue Lake Ontario from most rooms at this midrange, kid-friendly hotel. **Pros:** very comfortable beds; great kids' programs; pet-friendly. **Cons:** not right in downtown; hotel can feel overwhelmingly large; decor is rather dated. $ *Rooms from: C$349* ✉ *1 Harbour Sq., at Bay St., Harbourfront* ☎ *416/869–1600, 866/716–8101* ⊕ *www.marriott.com/yyzwi* ⇌ *977 rooms* ⦿ *No meals* Ⓜ *Union.*

🌙 Nightlife

In general, this area is quiet after dark, but a nightlife scene is slowly emerging as more condos are built and the waterfront gets more and more developed. Waterfront concerts take place here in summer, and dinner cruises leave from the Harbourfront.

BARS
Real Sports Bar & Grill
BARS/PUBS | No hole-in-the-wall sports bar, this sleek 25,000-square-foot space adjacent to the Scotiabank Arena lights up with almost 200 high-definition flat-screen TVs and amazing sightlines from every club-style booth, table, or stool at one of the three bars. Head to the second floor to watch a game on the biggest TV, an HDTV screen two stories high. For popular sporting events, or any day or night the Leafs or Raptors play, it's best to make a reservation (accepted up to three weeks in advance), though the bar does keep a third of its seats for walk in traffic an hour before face-off. ✉ *15 York St., at Bremner Blvd., Harbourfront* ☎ *416/815–7325* ⊕ *www.realsports.ca* Ⓜ *Union.*

BREWERIES
Amsterdam BrewHouse
BREWPUBS/BEER GARDENS | This brewpub features two massive bars with more than 10 brews on tap, an open-concept kitchen with an imported Italian wood-burning pizza oven, and a sprawling patio with stunning views of the Toronto Islands. The building, a former 1930s boathouse, also houses a brewery; tours and beer tastings are available daily. Tours are free, but book in advance. ✉ *245 Queens Quay W., Harbourfront* ☎ *416/504–1020* ⊕ *www.amsterdambeer.com* Ⓜ *Union.*

🎭 Performing Arts

MAJOR VENUES
Harbourfront Centre
ARTS CENTERS | When looking for cultural events in Toronto, make sure to check the schedule at the Harbourfront Centre. A cultural playground, it has two art galleries (The Power Plant and Artport), a music garden (where summertime concerts happen) co-designed by Yo-Yo Ma, as well as many festivals and cultural events, some especially for kids and many of them free. The campus has two theaters for dance and a renowned dance series called Torque. The **Fleck Dance Theatre** was built specifically for modern dance in 1983. The outdoor Concert Stage hosts some of the best local and Canadian modern and contemporary companies, in addition to some international acts. The **Harbourfront Centre Theatre** welcomes these same types of dance performances as well as plays and concerts. The theaters are small (under 500 seats) so you're never far from the stage. ✉ *235 Queen's Quay W, at Lower Simcoe St., Harbourfront* ☎ *416/973–4000* ⊕ *www.harbourfrontcentre.com* Ⓜ *Union, then 510 streetcar.*

Rogers Centre

CONCERTS | Toronto's largest performance venue, with seating for up to 52,000, is the spot for the biggest shows in town—the Rolling Stones, Bruce Springsteen, Justin Bieber—though the acoustically superior Scotiabank Arena is the more widely used arena venue. ✉ *1 Blue Jays Way, at Spadina Ave., Harbourfront* ☎ *855/985–5000 concert and event tickets* ⊕ *https://www.mlb.com/bluejays/ ballpark* Ⓜ *Union.*

Scotiabank Arena

CONCERTS | Most arena shows are held here rather than at the larger Rogers Centre due to superior acoustics. Past performances at the nearly 20,000-capacity arena have included Beyoncé, Rod Stewart, American Idol Live!, and Nine Inch Nails. ✉ *40 Bay St., at Gardiner Expressway, Harbourfront* ☎ *416/815–5500* ⊕ *www.scotiabankarena.com* Ⓜ *Union.*

Activities

BIKING
Martin Goodman Trail

BICYCLING | The Martin Goodman Trail is a part of a larger Waterfront Trail route that spans over 3,000 km (1,850 miles) across Southern Ontario. You can walk (or cycle) the entire length of the city or just stick to the Harbourfront neighborhood, where you'll have nice views of the Toronto Islands and airplanes flying into Billy Bishop Toronto City Airport to your south and the city skyline to your north. Bike Share Toronto offers a convenient way to bike the trail (or the city) with 5,000 bicycles parked at various locations across the city. You can buy a day pass or get a discounted rate for longer periods. ✉ *Harbourfront* ⊕ *waterfronttrail.org/ places/communities/toronto.*

Shopping

Shopping in the Harbourfront area is somewhat limited, but the Harbourfront Centre complex can be a good place to find interesting items.

SPECIALTY GIFTS
Harbourfront Centre Shop

CRAFTS | You'll find plenty of locally made crafts and clever design objects here, including textiles, jewelry, ceramics, wood carvings, and glass pieces blown in Harbourfront Centre's own studios. The shop also carries quirky design items from outside Canada, too, including vases by Finnish designer Alvar Aalto and gadgets for the kitchen or office from around the world. ✉ *Harbourfront Centre, 235 Queens Quay W, Harbourfront* ☎ *416/973–4993* ⊕ *www.harbourfront-centre.com* Ⓜ *Union.*

Entertainment District

This downtown district's biggest draw is its collection of theaters. The Royal Alexandra, built in 1907, has played host to major touring musicals. Down the street is sister theater the Princess of Wales, a modern glass-walled space. Across the street is Roy Thomson Hall, home to the Toronto Symphony Orchestra. If film's more your speed, check out what's screening at the TIFF Bell Lightbox, which serves as the main hub for the Toronto International Film Festival in September but spotlights both classics and indie flicks year-round.

Sights

TIFF Bell Lightbox

ARTS VENUE | A five-story architectural masterpiece in the city's center, this glass-paneled building houses the year-round headquarters of the internationally acclaimed, wildly popular Toronto International Film Festival, which takes place in September. Throughout the year

The TIFF Bell Lightbox is the focal point for the annual Toronto International Film Festival.

visitors can attend film-related lectures, watch screenings, and enjoy smaller film festivals, including the TIFF Next Wave Film Festival, a film festival with free movies for anyone under 25 that takes place in February. A stellar educational program includes summer camps and ongoing workshops—on how to produce a stop-motion movie, for example. The TIFF Cinematheque, open to the public, plays world cinema classics and contemporary art house films all year. ⊠ *Reitman Square, 350 King St. W, at John St., Entertainment District* ☎ *416/599–8433, 888/599–8433* ⊕ *www.tiff.net* Ⓜ *St. Andrew station.*

🍴 Restaurants

The Entertainment District tends to be pretty laid-back during the day, but it comes to life at night and on weekends when throngs of well-dressed people head to the theater and out for dinner or drinks.

★ Beast

$$ | **INTERNATIONAL** | In a quiet dining room tucked into the first floor of a house just off King West, this carnivore's mecca serves inventive dishes such as succulent pork hocks with kimchi and roasted peanuts or duck breast with sheep's milk feta cheese. Pescatarians are well-served, too, with mains like grilled squid tostadas and smoked trout. Brunch means the restaurant's signature beastwich: fried chicken, pork sausage gravy, egg, and cheese on a biscuit. **Known for:** cozy interior; menu celebrates local producers and farmers; innovative brunch options. ⓢ *Average main: C$14* ⊠ *96 Tecumseth St., King West* ☎ *647/352–6000* ⊕ *www.thebeastrestaurant.com* ⊗ *Closed Mon. and Tues. No lunch Wed.–Fri. No dinner Sun.* Ⓜ *St. Andrew.*

★ Buca

$$$ | **ITALIAN** | With its refreshing roster of Italian classics, stylish Buca was a pioneer on this stretch of King Street, and its influence continues today. Tucked into an alley just off the main drag, the repurposed boiler room has exposed brick walls, metal columns, and wooden tables that reflect the philosophy behind the menu. Start with a selection of cheeses and cured meats and perhaps an order of *nodini*, warm bread knots seasoned with rosemary and sea salt. **Known for:** consistently voted one of the best Italian restaurants in Toronto; wines are meticulously chosen from Italian vinters; trendy decor. $ Average main: C$28 ⊠ 604 King St. W, Entertainment District ☎ 416/865–1600 ⊕ www.buca.ca ⊗ No lunch Ⓜ Osgoode.

Burrito Boyz

$ | **MEXICAN** | One of the best places to stuff yourself silly, Burrito Boyz answers the call for rice-filled tortillas stuffed with succulent halibut or hearty steak. And vegetarians also have options, like soy or sweet potato. The casual eatery is always busy, but it's the most alive in the wee hours of the morning with the postclubbing crowd looking to refuel and sleep soundly on a full stomach. **Known for:** perfect late-night destination; inexpensive eatery; 17 toppings. $ Average main: C$8 ⊠ 224 Adelaide St. W, Entertainment District ☎ 647/439–4065 ⊕ www.burritoboyz.ca Ⓜ St. Andrew.

★ Edulis

$$$$ | **EUROPEAN** | European bistro meets local forager is the theme at Edulis, where the five- and seven-course tasting menus are devoted to classic rustic dishes. Rough-hewn wood walls and burlap breadbaskets evoke a farmhouse feel, and the soft lighting adds to the intimate atmosphere. **Known for:** affordable lunchtime specials on weekends; standout seafood dishes; truffle menu. $ Average main: C$75 ⊠ 169 Niagara St., King West ☎ 416/703–4222 ⊕ www.edulisrestaurant.com ⊗ Closed Mon. and Tues. No lunch Wed.–Sat. Ⓜ St. Andrew.

Evviva

$ | **CANADIAN** | Don't let the opulent interior at this busy breakfast spot fool you: the meals here are affordable (and yummy). It's one of the closest brunch restaurants to the Rogers Centre, so a good place to grab a cup of coffee and some pancakes before an afternoon Jays game. **Known for:** velvet chairs and grand chandeliers; small but cozy side patio; extensive brunch menu. $ Average main: C$12 ⊠ 25 Lower Simcoe St., Entertainment District ☎ 416/351–4040 ⊕ evviva.ca ⊗ No dinner Ⓜ Union Station.

The Fifth Grill

$$$ | **FRENCH** | Enter through the Fifth Social Club, a main-floor dance club, and take a freight elevator to this semiprivate dining club and loft space with just the right balance of formality and flirtation. The menu is a French-inspired chef's tasting menu that changes seasonally. In winter, you can relax on a sofa in front of the huge fireplace; in summer, there's a gazebo terrace for dining. **Known for:** luxurious dining rooms; romantic atmosphere; intimate rooftop setting. $ Average main: C$30 ⊠ 225 Richmond St. W, Entertainment District ☎ 416/979–3005 ⊕ fifthrestaurant.thefifth.com ⊗ Closed Sun.–Wed. No lunch Ⓜ Osgoode.

Fresh on Spadina

$$ | **VEGETARIAN** | **FAMILY** | This delicious vegan restaurant will make even the most die-hard meat eaters happy. The menu is lengthy and full of everything from tacos and rice bowls to flatbreads and burgers. **Known for:** tasty homemade sodas and smoothies; casual atmosphere; young, lively crowd. $ Average main: C$17 ⊠ 147 Spadina Ave., Entertainment District ☎ 416/599–4442 ⊕ freshplantpowered.com Ⓜ St. Andrew or Osgoode.

★ Khao San Road

$$ | **THAI** | Named for a street in Bangkok bursting with nightlife and excellent street eats, Khao San Road lives up to its moniker. The garlic tofu with a sweet-and-sour tamarind dip might just be the vegetarian equivalent of chicken nuggets. For heartier dishes, try for the *khao soi*, a dish of egg noodles in a rich coconut milk

sauce, or try the warming *massaman*, a tamarind-infused curry with peanuts, potatoes, and deep-fried shallots. **Known for:** ingredients sourced directly from Thailand; busy, vibrant atmosphere; all of the noodle dishes are standouts. $ *Average main: C$14* ✉ *11 Charlotte St., Entertainment District* ☎ *647/352–5773* ⊕ *www.khaosanroad.ca* ⊘ *No lunch Sun.* Ⓜ *St. Andrew.*

Lee

$$$ | **ASIAN** | Everyone looks beautiful here, on the red velvet barstools or surrounded by abacus-like copper screens hung around the dining room. Famed Toronto chef Susur Lee's creations mix Asian and European sensibilities and small, perfect dishes like the Peking and *char siu* duck with steamed pancake and foie gras tickle all the senses. **Known for:** great dishes from China and Hong Kong; the crowd couldn't be more chic; addictive sweet-and-sour ribs. $ *Average main: C$30* ✉ *601 King St. W, Entertainment District* ☎ *416/504–7867* ⊕ *www.susur.com/lee* ⊘ *No lunch* Ⓜ *St. Andrew.*

★ Luma

$$$ | **CANADIAN** | Duck out of a double-feature at the TIFF Bell Lightbox to grab a meal at Luma. Within the bustling glass-paneled film festival and film education venue, the restaurant is a mini oasis on the second floor. Even if you're not going to a film, it's a great restaurant, complete with a patio overlooking the lively Entertainment District and the CN Tower. Start with steak with truffle-parm fries and finish things off with a lemon tart topped with sour cream ice cream. **Known for:** great spot for people-watching; globally inspired menu; fresh seafood dishes. $ *Average main: C$30* ✉ *330 King St. W, Entertainment District* ☎ *647/288–4715* ⊕ *www.lumarestaurant.com* ⊘ *No lunch Sat. Closed Sun.* Ⓜ *St. Andrew.*

Toronto's Poutine

The Québécois classic, traditionally made from french fries, cheese curds, and gravy, tends to get dressed up in Toronto. Modern takes might include pulled pork and other meats, as well as different sauces and ethnic spices. Poutini's House of Poutine (⊕ *www.poutini. com*) and Smoke's Poutinerie (⊕ *www.smokespoutinerie.com*) are restaurants dedicated to it.

Pizzeria Libretto

$$ | **ITALIAN** | If you love Italian cuisine, this Toronto institution serves popular Neapolitan pizzas and a selection of pastas to discerning locals. It caters to all dietary restrictions, including gluten-free, dairy-free, nut free, vegetarian, and vegan. The King Street location is a go-to date spot, too. **Known for:** lunchtime specials; family-style menu options; outstanding negroni selection. $ *Average main: C$18* ✉ *545 King St. W, Entertainment District* ☎ *647/352–1200* ⊕ *www.pizzerialibretto. com* Ⓜ *504 streetcar.*

Rodney's Oyster House

$$$ | **SEAFOOD** | A den of oceanic delicacies, this playful basement raw bar is frequented by solo diners and showbiz types. Among the options are soft-shell steamer clams, a variety of smoked fish, and "Oyster Slapjack Chowder," plus a rotating list of more than 20 varieties of oysters (including perfect Malpeques from owner Rodney Clark's own oyster beds on Prince Edward Island). A zap of Rodney's in-house line of condiments or a splash of vodka and freshly grated horseradish are eye-openers. **Known for:** impressive wine list; maritime hospitality; fun, vibrant vibe. $ *Average main: C$28* ✉ *469 King St. W, Entertainment District*

☎ 416/363–8105 ⊕ www.rodneysoysterhouse.com ⊘ Closed Sun. Ⓜ St. Andrew.

TOCA

$$$$ | **CANADIAN** | The swanky Ritz-Carlton dining experience comes to Toronto in the form of TOCA, where the menu of elevated Italian food takes advantage of local ingredients. To really up the ante you can reserve seats at the chef's table, at a private dining nook in the kitchen. **Known for:** there is a 30-minute "express" lunch option on weekdays for business diners; the Sunday Market Brunch; the cheese cave. $ Average main: C$44 ⊠ 181 Wellington St. W, Entertainment District ☎ 416/572–8008 ⊕ www.tocarestaurant. ca Ⓜ St. Andrew.

Victor

$$$ | **CANADIAN** | Just off King Street in the Hôtel Le Germain, Victor presents a seafood-forward menu, in a swanky atmosphere with plate-glass walls, wood floors, and lively yellow banquettes. Carnivores can opt for hearty dishes like short-rib strozzapreti pasta, panko-crusted veal, or brick chicken with a comforting side of mac and cheese. **Known for:** great spot for a pretheater dinner or romantic date night; quiet location, unlike other busy spots in this neighborhood; carefully curated wine, beer and cocktail list. $ Average main: C$25 ⊠ Hôtel Le Germain Toronto, 30 Mercer St., Entertainment District ☎ 416/883–3431 ⊕ www.victorrestaurant.com ⊘ No lunch Ⓜ St. Andrew.

Wilbur Mexicana

$ | **MEXICAN** | This fun, lively counterservice joint serves up Southern California–style Mexican street food like burritos and tacos. It's more than the average fast-food joint, though, and patrons like to linger with friends over beers. **Known for:** the hot sauce bar; great value; outstanding guacamole. $ Average main: C$10 ⊠ 552 King St. W, Entertainment District ☎ 416/792–1878 ⊕ wilburmexicana.com Ⓜ 504 streetcar, or St. Andrew and a 15-minute walk.

WVRST

$ | **GERMAN** | You don't need to wait around until Oktoberfest to drink great German beer and indulge in delicious bratwurst; just walk into WVRST, a modern beer hall on King West. Choose amid the selection of sausages, from the traditional pork to vegetarian, or get a little wild with selections such as pheasant, duck, or bison. **Known for:** dozens of craft beers and ciders on tap; the double-fried duck fat fries are outstanding; German beer-hall vibe. $ Average main: C$10 ⊠ 609 King St. W, King West ☎ 416/703–7775 ⊕ www.wvrst.com Ⓜ St. Andrew.

Hotels

Hilton Garden Inn Downtown

$$$ | **HOTEL** | Like the downtown entertainment hub that surrounds it, this hotel pulses with activity. **Pros:** location in the heart of downtown; excellent service; lots of amenities. **Cons:** some rooms can get noisy due to nearby nightclub; pool and gym on the small side; unmemorable decor. $ Rooms from: C$329 ⊠ 92 Peter St., Entertainment District ☎ 416/593–9200 ⊕ hiltongardeninn.hilton.com ⮑ 224 rooms ⦿ No meals Ⓜ Osgoode, St. Andrew.

Hilton Toronto

$$$ | **HOTEL** | If you want to be close to the Entertainment and Financial districts, this hotel offers one of the area's best locations, and its lobby restaurant, Tundra, serves stellar Canadian cuisine. **Pros:** across the street from the Four Seasons Centre for the Performing Arts; popular on-site steak house; connected to PATH. **Cons:** rooms can be small; service lags at times; Wi-Fi not free for everyone. $ Rooms from: C$289 ⊠ 145 Richmond St. W, at University Ave., Entertainment District ☎ 416/869–3456, 800/267–2281 ⊕ www.hilton.com ⮑ 600 rooms ⦿ No meals Ⓜ Osgoode.

Local Chains Worth a Taste

For those times when all you want is a quick bite, consider these local chains where you're assured of fresh, tasty food and good value.

Burger's Priest: The junk-food faithful flock to this local chain for old-school burgers, fries, and shakes. Their not-so-secret secret menu (find it on their website) features awe-inspiring items like the Four Horsemen of the Apocalypse: a double cheeseburger with two veggie patties, all stacked between two grilled-cheese sandwiches. ⊕ www.theburgerspriest. com.

Freshii: This is a healthier choice where baseball-capped salad artists get through the lunch rush like a championship team. The interior is all steely white and blond wood, and designer greens and custom-made sandwiches clearly appeal to the masses. The Cobb is a standout. ⊕ www.freshii.com.

Harvey's: Harvey's says it makes a hamburger a beautiful thing, and we agree—whether it's a beef, chicken, or veggie burger. You get to choose your toppings, which is a boon for picky kids. The fries are a hit, too. ⊕ www. harveys.ca.

Milestones: Duck into the cool comfort of these happening spots for crispy breaded shrimp or spinach and artichoke dip. The steak and the prime rib are among the kitchen's best options. ⊕ www.milestonesrestaurants.com.

Second Cup: You'll find coffee plain and fancy, as well as flavored hot chocolates, a variety of teas, Italian soft drinks, and nibbles that include muffins, bagels, and raspberry–white chocolate scones. ⊕ www.secondcup. com.

Spring Rolls: Appealing soups and spiced salads, savory noodle dishes, and spring rolls all satiate lunchtime hunger pangs here. ⊕ www.springrolls. ca.

Swiss Chalet Rotisserie and Grill: This Canadian institution is well-known for its rotisserie chicken and barbecued ribs, in portions that suit every family member. ■ TIP→ Ask for extra sauce for your french fries. ⊕ www. swisschalet.ca.

Tim Horton's: Most locations never close, and coffee is made fresh every 20 minutes. Check out the variety of fresh doughnuts, muffins, bagels, and soup-and-sandwich combos. The Canadian Maple doughnut is an obvious front-runner. ⊕ www.timhortons.com.

★ **Hôtel Le Germain Toronto**

$$$$ | HOTEL | The retro, redbrick exterior of this chic hotel—conveniently located near the TIFF Bell Lightbox, site of the Toronto International Film Festival—blends seamlessly with the historic architecture of the surrounding theater district. **Pros:** complimentary continental breakfast; attentive staff goes above and beyond; outdoor terrace on 11th floor.

Cons: popular hotel fills up fast; neighborhood can get noisy on weekends; some rooms have views of alleys. Ⓢ *Rooms from: C$375* ⊠ *30 Mercer St., at John St., Entertainment District* ☎ *416/345–9500, 866/345–9501* ⊕ *www.germain-toronto.com* ⤶ *122 rooms* ℀ *Free breakfast* Ⓜ *St. Andrew.*

Hyatt Regency Toronto

$$$ | **HOTEL** | Request views of the CN Tower at this luxury hotel smack in the middle of the pulsating Entertainment District. **Pros:** closest large hotel to King Street West theaters; dozens of excellent restaurants and cinemas nearby; outdoor swimming pool and 24-hour fitness center. **Cons:** rooms can be small; guest rooms on lower floors facing King Street may be noisy; hotel could use a renovation. [$] *Rooms from: C$269* ✉ *370 King St. W, Entertainment District* ☎ *416/343–1234, 800/633–7313 in U.S.* 🌐 *www.hyatt.com* 🛏 *426 rooms* 🍴 *No meals* [M] *St. Andrew.*

InterContinental Toronto Centre

$$$ | **HOTEL** | Attached to the Metro Toronto Convention Centre, this large but unassuming hotel is a good bet for visiting business executives, and vacationers can often find deals on weekends. **Pros:** not as stuffy as your usual business hotel; bright and airy lobby restaurant; near theaters and dining. **Cons:** no shopping nearby; expensive parking; busy during conferences. [$] *Rooms from: C$280* ✉ *225 Front St. W, west of University Ave., Entertainment District* ☎ *416/597–1400, 877/660–8550* 🌐 *www.torontocentre.intercontinental.com* 🛏 *576 rooms* 🍴 *No meals* [M] *Union.*

★ Residence Inn Toronto Downtown

$$$$ | **HOTEL** | **FAMILY** | A big hit with families and extended-stay visitors to the city, the modern suites at the Residence Inn Toronto Downtown come with full kitchens, spacious living and dining rooms, and comfortable bedrooms. **Pros:** close to Toronto's major attractions; a smart choice for families; pool, gym, and other amenities. **Cons:** breakfast buffet gets extremely crowded during peak season; can get very crowded on game days; valet parking only. [$] *Rooms from: C$359* ✉ *255 Wellington St. W, at Windsor St., Entertainment District* ☎ *416/581–1800* 🌐 *www.residenceinn.marriott.com* 🛏 *256 suites* 🍴 *Free breakfast* [M] *Union.*

★ Shangri-La Toronto

$$$$ | **HOTEL** | The Shangri-La Toronto combines the attention to service for which the Shangri-La brand is known while putting an art-focused twist on its traditional East-meets-West aesthetic. **Pros:** stellar ambience; noted art collection; luxurious amenities. **Cons:** pricey rates; standard rooms are small; service can be inconsistent. [$] *Rooms from: C$455* ✉ *188 University Ave., Entertainment District* ☎ *647/788–8888* 🌐 *www.shangri-la.com/toronto/shangri-la* 🛏 *202 rooms* 🍴 *No meals* [M] *Osgoode, St. Andrew.*

Sheraton Centre

$$$ | **HOTEL** | Views from this hotel in the city center are marvelous—to the south are the CN Tower and the Rogers Centre; to the north, both new and old city halls. **Pros:** underground access to PATH network; swimming pool is open late; walk to Four Seasons Centre. **Cons:** expensive parking and online access; hotel is overwhelmingly large; not all rooms have complimentary breakfast. [$] *Rooms from: C$309* ✉ *123 Queen St. W, at Bay St., Entertainment District* ☎ *416/361–1000, 866/716–8101* 🌐 *www.sheratontoronto.com* 🛏 *1377 rooms* 🍴 *No meals* [M] *Osgoode.*

SoHo Metropolitan Hotel

$$$$ | **HOTEL** | Saturated in pampering detail, the SoHo Met conjures luxury with Frette linens, down duvets, walk-in closets, marble bathrooms with heated floors, and Molton Brown bath products. **Pros:** high-tech touches like electronic do-not-disturb signs; stylish but not showy; spa is excellent. **Cons:** lap pool only 3-feet deep; construction noise; can be pricey. [$] *Rooms from: C$435* ✉ *318 Wellington St. W, east of Spadina Ave., Entertainment District* ☎ *416/599–8800, 866/764–6638* 🌐 *www.soho.metropolitan.com* 🛏 *91 rooms* 🍴 *No meals* [M] *St. Andrew.*

Did You Know?

The Toronto Caribbean Festival was created in 1967 as a community heritage project to celebrate Canada's centennial and was such a success that it's been held every year since. This 2½-week summer celebration highlights the food, costumes, music, and art of Caribbean cultures, and attracts more than 2 million visitors each year.

★ Toronto Marriott City Centre

$$ | HOTEL | FAMILY | This hotel completely integrated into the Rogers Centre, the sports and entertainment dome that serves as the home of the Toronto Blue Jays, and 70 of the choicest rooms overlook the stadium itself. **Pros:** best place to watch Blue Jays baseball games; reasonable parking fee; good restaurant. **Cons:** little natural light in guest rooms overlooking field; the best rooms book up fast on game days; pick somewhere else if you're not a sports fan. $ *Rooms from: C$229* ✉ *1 Blue Jays Way, at Front St. W, Entertainment District* ☎ *416/341–7100, 800/237–1512* ⊕ *www.marriott.com/yyzcc* ⇴ *346 rooms* ❍ *No meals* Ⓜ *Union.*

🌙 Nightlife

Traditionally this was Toronto's center for dance clubs cranking out house music. A few of the more popular clubs are still going strong (especially along Richmond Street), but the area is becoming less ostentatious as condos are erected and professionals in their thirties and forties move in. It's also home to three of the big Broadway-style theaters and tourist-oriented preshow restaurants with bars. The King West neighborhood has experienced a surge of swanky lounges, bars, and restaurants since the Toronto International Film Festival moved its headquarters to the area from Yorkville.

BARS

Lobby Lounge at the Shangri-La Hotel

BARS/PUBS | The Shangri-La Hotel's spacious Lobby Lounge serves up trendy cocktails, delicious bar bites, and live music. ✉ *Shangri-La Hotel, 188 University Ave., Entertainment District* ☎ *647/788–8888* ⊕ *www.shangri-la.com* Ⓜ *Osgoode.*

Steam Whistle Brewery

BREWPUBS/BEER GARDENS | The Steam Whistle Brewery makes an authentically crafted pilsner, and offers daily tours

(C$12) of its historic premises. There's a tasting room with a full food menu, and the brewery hosts special events, like Oktoberfest and the twice-a-year (winter and summer) Roundhouse Craft Beer Festival. It's a great place to stop before or after a Blue Jays game. ✉ *The Roundhouse, 255 Bremner Blvd., Entertainment District* ☎ *416/362–2337* ⊕ *www.steamwhistle.ca* Ⓜ *Union.*

COMEDY CLUBS

★ The Second City

COMEDY CLUBS | Since it opened in 1973, Toronto's Second City—the younger sibling of the Second City in Chicago—has been showcasing some of the best comedy in Canada. Regular features include sketch comedy, improv, and revues. Seating is cabaret-style with table service and is assigned on a first-come, first-served basis. ■ **TIP→ Arrive 30 minutes prior to showtime.** Weekend shows tend to sell out. Tickets usually run between C$14 and C$35. Note that the Second City is set to relocate at the end of 2020. ✉ *51 Mercer St., 1 block south of King, Entertainment District* ☎ *416/343–0011* ⊕ *www.secondcity.com* Ⓜ *St. Andrew.*

Yuk Yuk's

COMEDY CLUBS | Part of a Canadian comedy franchise, this venue headlines stand-up comedians on the rise (Jim Carrey and Russell Peters performed here on their way up), with covers usually between C$11 and C$25. Admission is C$5 on Tuesday for amateur night. The small space is often packed; getting cozy with your neighbors and sitting within spitting distance of the comedians is part of the appeal. Booking a dinner-and-show package guarantees better seats. ✉ *224 Richmond St. W, 1½ blocks west of University Ave., Entertainment District* ☎ *416/967–6431* ⊕ *www.yukyuks.com* Ⓜ *Osgoode.*

With its circular shape and striking glass canopy, Roy Thompson Hall is a classic of Toronto architecture.

🎭 Performing Arts

CLASSICAL MUSIC

★ Toronto Symphony Orchestra

MUSIC | Since 1922 this orchestra has achieved world acclaim with music directors such as Sir Ernest MacMillan, Seiji Ozawa, and Sir Andrew Davis. Canadian-born Peter Oundjian reinvigorated the ensemble and significantly strengthened its presence in the world when he was musical director from 2004 until 2018. Guest performers have included pianist Lang Lang, violinist Itzhak Perlman, and singer-songwriter Rufus Wainwright. Each season the orchestra screens a classic film, such as *Star Wars* or *Singin' in the Rain,* and plays the score as it runs. The TSO also presents about three concerts weekly at Roy Thomson Hall from September through June. ⊠ *Roy Thomson Hall, 60 Simcoe St., Entertainment District* ☎ *416/593–1285 TSO information and tickets, 416/593–4828 Roy Thomson Hall ticket line* ⊕ *www.tso.ca* Ⓜ *St. Andrew.*

MAJOR VENUES

★ Roy Thomson Hall

CONCERTS | Toronto's premier concert hall, home of the Toronto Symphony Orchestra (TSO), also hosts visiting orchestras, popular entertainers, and Toronto International Film Festival red-carpet screenings. The 2,630-seat auditorium opened in 1982 and is named after Roy Thomson, who was born in Toronto and founded the publishing empire Thomson Corporation (now Thomson Reuters). ⊠ *60 Simcoe St., at King St., Entertainment District* ☎ *416/872–4255 tickets, 416/593–4822 tours* ⊕ *www.roythomson.com* Ⓜ *St. Andrew.*

THEATERS

Factory Theatre

THEATER | This is the country's largest producer of exclusively Canadian plays. Many of the company's shows are world premieres that have gone on to tour Canada and win prestigious awards. ⊠ *125 Bathurst St., at Adelaide St.,*

Entertainment District ☎ *416/504–9971* ⊕ *www.factorytheatre.ca.*

Princess of Wales

THEATER | State-of-the-art facilities and wonderful murals by American artist Frank Stella grace this 2,000-seat theater, built by father-and-son producer team Ed and David Mirvish in 1993 to accommodate the technically demanding musical *Miss Saigon.* Big-budget musicals like *Lion King* and *The Book of Mormon* and plays such as *War Horse* are showcased. ⊠ *300 King St. W, at John St., Entertainment District* ☎ *416/872–1212 tickets, 800/461–3333 tickets* ⊕ *www.mirvish. com* Ⓜ *St. Andrew.*

Royal Alexandra

THEATER | The most historic of the Mirvish theaters, the "Royal Alex" has been the place to be seen in Toronto since 1907 and is the oldest continuously operating legitimate theater in North America. The restored and reconfigured theater features 1,244 plush red seats, gold plasterwork, and baroque swirls and flourishes that make theatergoing a refined experience. Charleston Heston made his debut here and Lawrence Olivier, Edith Piaf, Mary Pickford, Alan Bates, and John Gielgud have also graced the stage. Programs are a mix of blockbuster musicals and dramatic productions, some touring before or after Broadway appearances. ⊠ *260 King St. W, Entertainment District* ☎ *416/872–1212 tickets, 800/461–3333 tickets* ⊕ *www.mirvish. com* Ⓜ *St. Andrew.*

🛍 Shopping

While there aren't a ton of shops between the theaters and restaurants of King Street West between Bay and Spadina, those that are here are some of the city's best.

ANTIQUES

★ **Toronto Antiques on King**

ANTIQUES/COLLECTIBLES | The 6,000 square feet of this shop provides ample

opportunity for browsing pre- or post-show (the Princess of Wales Theatre is next door) among the cabinets, shelves, and bins overflowing with porcelain, silver tea sets, Majolica pottery, Lalique vases, collectibles, and antique maps. It's also Toronto's leading purveyor of vintage and estate jewelry, making it a popular stop for those seeking out engagement rings. ⊠ *284 King St. W (2nd fl.), at John St., Entertainment District* ☎ *416/260–9057* ⊕ *www.cynthiafindlay. com* ☾ *Closed Mon.* Ⓜ *St. Andrew.*

OUTDOOR EQUIPMENT AND CLOTHING

★ **Mountain Equipment Co-op**

SPORTING GOODS | MEC (rhymes with "check"), the much-beloved Toronto spot for anyone remotely interested in camping, sells wares for minor and major expeditions. It's also a go-to spot for cycling gear. The vast assortment of backpacks means you can shop here for anything from a schoolbag to something that will accompany you on travels around the world. For C$5, you get lifetime membership to the co-op. ⊠ *300 Queen St. W, Entertainment District* ☎ *416/340–2667* ⊕ *www.mec.ca.*

SPAS

Hammam Spa

SPA/BEAUTY | At Hammam Spa devoted Entertainment District clients come to soak up eucalyptus-scented steam in a 500-square-foot marble-tile Turkish bath following a massage or detoxifying algae wrap. ⊠ *602 King St. W, at Portland, Entertainment District* ☎ *416/366–4772* ⊕ *www.hammamspa.ca* Ⓜ *Spadina or St. Andrew.*

SPECIALTY GIFTS

★ **TIFF Shop**

GIFTS/SOUVENIRS | This sleek little gift shop at the TIFF Bell Lightbox, the cinematic HQ of the Toronto International Film Festival, stocks an ever-changing selection of cinematic paraphernalia linked to TIFF's current programming. The exhaustive inventory of film books includes many difficult-to-find titles, biographies of just about every director you can think of, and studies of even the most obscure film movements. There are also unusual gift items and cute items for children. ⊠ *TIFF Bell Lightbox, 350 King St. W, at John St., Entertainment District* ☎ *416/934–7959* ⊕ *shop.tiff.net* Ⓜ *St. Andrew.*

Financial District

Toronto's Financial District has a wonderful architectural variety of skyscrapers. Most of the towers have bank branches, restaurants, and retail outlets on their ground floors and are connected to the PATH, an underground city of shops and tunnels. Unsurprisingly, Toronto's main office district is home to a lot of top-shelf restaurants ready to give those expense accounts a hearty workout.

◉ Sights

Design Exchange
MUSEUM | The Design Exchange (or DX as it's now commonly known) is a museum of Canadian culture and design, with fun exhibits that cover furniture, home decor, and electronics. The building itself is a delightful example of streamlined modern design (a later and more austere version of art deco), clad in polished pink granite and smooth buff limestone, with stainless-steel doors. Between 1937 and 1983, the DX was home to the Toronto Stock Exchange. Don't miss the witty stone frieze carved above the doors—a banker in top hat marching behind a laborer and sneaking his hand into the worker's pocket. Only in Canada, where socialism has always been a strong force, would you find such a political statement on the side of a stock exchange. ⊠ *234 Bay St., at King St., Financial District* ☎ *416/363–6121* ⊕ *www.dx.org* ☾ *Closed weekends* Ⓜ *King, St. Andrew.*

★ Hockey Hall of Fame
MUSEUM | FAMILY | Even if you're not a hockey fan, it's worth a trip here to see this shrine to Canada's favorite sport. Exhibits include the original 1893 Stanley Cup, as well as displays of goalie masks, skate and stick collections, players' jerseys, video displays of big games, and a replica of the Montréal Canadiens' locker room. Grab a stick and test your speed and accuracy in the "Shoot Out" virtual experience, or strap on a goalie mask and field shots from big-name players with the "Shut Out" computer simulation. It's also telling that this museum is housed in such a grand building, worthy of any fine art collection. A former Bank of Montréal branch designed by architects Darling & Curry in 1885, the building is covered with beautiful ornamental details. Note the richly carved Ohio stone and the Hermès figure supporting the chimney near the back. At the corner of Front and Yonge streets, the impressive 17-foot bronze statue entitled "Our Game" is a good photo-op. ■**TIP→ Entrance is through Brookfield Place on the lower level.** ⊠ *Brookfield Place, 30 Yonge St., at Front St., Financial District* ☎ *416/360–7765* ⊕ *www.hhof.com* ☒ *C$20* Ⓜ *Union.*

PATH
PEDESTRIAN MALL | Though tunnels under the city date back to 1900, this subterranean universe expanded in the mid-1970s partly to replace the retail services in small buildings that were demolished to make way for the latest skyscrapers and partly to protect office workers from the harsh winter weather. As each major building went up, its developers agreed to build and connect their underground shopping areas with others and with the subway system. You can walk from beneath Union Station to the Fairmont Royal York hotel, the Toronto-Dominion Centre, First Canadian Place, the Sheraton Centre, The Bay and Eaton Centre, and City Hall without ever seeing the light of day, encountering everything from art exhibitions to buskers

(the best are the winners of citywide auditions, who are licensed to perform throughout the subway system) and walkways, fountains, and trees. There are underground passageways in other parts of the city that you can reach by subway—one beneath Bloor Street and another under College Street (both run from Yonge to Bay Street)—but this is the city's most extended subterranean network. ⊠ *Financial District* Ⓜ *Queen's Park, St. Andrew, Osgoode, St. Andrew, Union, King, Queen, Dundas.*

Toronto-Dominion Centre

BUILDING | Ludwig Mies van der Rohe, a virtuoso of modern architecture, designed a significant portion of this six-building office complex, though he died before its completion in 1992. As with his acclaimed Seagram Building in New York, Mies stripped the TD Centre's buildings to their skin and bones of bronze-color glass and black-metal I-beams. The tallest building, the Toronto Dominion Bank Tower, is 56 stories high. The only architectural decoration consists of geometric repetition. In summer, the plazas and grass are full of office workers eating lunch. Inside the low-rise square banking pavilion at King and Bay streets is a virtually intact Mies interior. ⊠ *66 Wellington St. W., Financial District* Ⓜ *St. Andrew.*

Union Station

TRANSPORTATION SITE (AIRPORT/BUS/FERRY/TRAIN) | Historian Pierre Berton wrote that the planning of Union Station recalled "the love lavished on medieval churches." Indeed, this train depot can be regarded as a cathedral built to serve the god of steam. Designed in 1907 and opened by the Prince of Wales in 1927, it has a 40-foot-high coffered Guastavino tile ceiling and 22 pillars weighing 70 tons apiece. The floors are Tennessee marble laid in a herringbone pattern (the same that's in Grand Central Terminal in New York City). The main hall, with its lengthy concourse and light flooding

in from arched windows at each end, was designed to evoke the majesty of the country that spread out by rail from this spot. The names of the towns and cities across Canada that were served by the country's two railway lines, Grand Trunk (incorporated into today's Canadian National) and Canadian Pacific, are inscribed on a frieze along the inside of the hall. As train travel declined, the building came very near to being demolished in the 1970s, but public opposition eventually proved strong enough to save it, and Union Station, a National Historic site, is now a vital transport hub. Commuter, subway, and long-distance trains stop here. ⊠ *65 Front St. W, between Bay and York Sts., Financial District* Ⓜ *Union.*

🍴 Restaurants

As one of the city's major business hubs, with plenty of hungry people at all times of the day, the Financial District has no shortage of places to eat. Venues cater to all the worker bees, from the assistant out on an espresso run to the executives with expense accounts.

Beer Bistro

$$ | EUROPEAN | A culinary tribute to beer, the creative menu here incorporates its star ingredient in every dish, but in subtle and clever ways without causing a malted-flavor overload. Start the hoppy journey with a taster flight of three draft beers, and follow that with perhaps a beer-bread pizza made with oatmeal stout or a bowl of mussels in a beer-based broth. **Known for:** cozy interior with an open kitchen; great patio in summer; there are even (delicious) beer-focused desserts. Ⓢ *Average main: C$19* ⊠ *18 King St. E, Financial District* ☎ *416/861–9872* ⊕ *www.beerbistro.com* Ⓜ *King.*

Bymark

$$$$ | CANADIAN | *Top Chef* Canada judge Mark McEwan has created a refined modern menu showcasing sophisticated

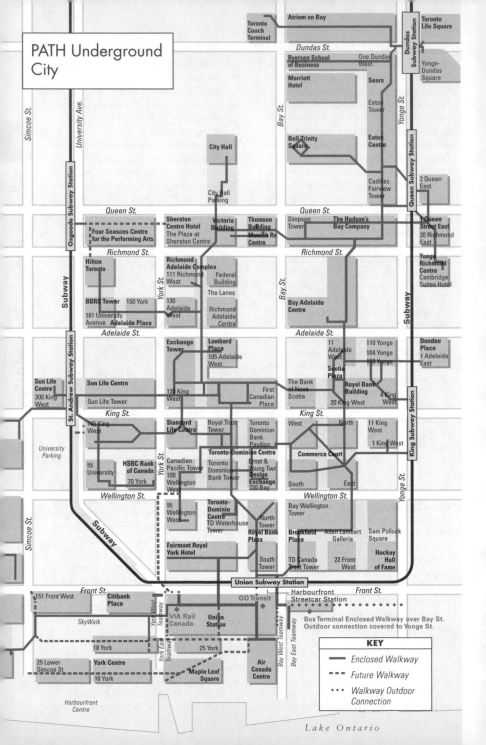

seafood dishes, like whole roasted orata, and simply prepared meats, like the signature 8-ounce burger with molten Brie de Meaux, grilled porcini mushrooms, and shaved truffles. **Known for:** 5,000-bottle wine cellar; opulent interior; swank upstairs bar. [$] *Average main: C$40* ✉ *66 Wellington St. W, Concourse Level, Financial District* ☎ *416/777–1144* 🌐 *www.mcewangroup.ca/bymark* 🕒 *Closed Sun. No lunch Sat.* [M] *St. Andrew.*

Cactus Club Cafe

$$$ | **STEAKHOUSE** | The Toronto flagship of a Vancouver-based casual fine dining chain, this massive, modern Financial District spot is one of the business district's trendiest dining destinations. Stellar dishes include butternut ravioli topped with sage, prawns, and truffle butter, and the "millionaire's cut"—a filet mignon with mashed potatoes and roasted asparagus. **Known for:** year-round patio; hip interior; fun appetizers to share. [$] *Average main: C$22* ✉ *First Canadian Pl., 77 Adelaide St. W, Financial District* ☎ *647/748–2025* 🌐 *www.cactusclubcafe.com* [M] *King.*

★ Canoe

$$$$ | **CANADIAN** | Huge dining-room windows frame breathtaking views of the Toronto Islands and the lake at this restaurant, on the 54th floor of the Toronto Dominion Bank Tower. Dishes like an appetizer of venison tartare with bannock bread and pink peppercorns and entrées like gin-cured duck with mushrooms and foie gras dumplings nod to both tradition and trend. **Known for:** classic desserts like a raisin butter tart round out exceptional meal; innovative tasting menus; food inspired by Canada. [$] *Average main: C$44* ✉ *Toronto-Dominion Centre, 66 Wellington St. W, 54th fl., Financial District* ☎ *416/364–0054* 🌐 *www.canoerestaurant.com* 🕒 *Closed weekends* [M] *King.*

Down Town

According to *Guinness World Records*, the PATH is the biggest underground shopping complex in the world. Maps to guide you through the labyrinth are available in many downtown news and convenience stores.

The Chase

$$$$ | **SEAFOOD** | On the fifth floor of the historic Dineen Building, overlooking the Financial District, the Chase's marvelous lighting fixtures and floor-to-ceiling windows are a glamorous setting for the fish-and-oyster focused menu. Dishes like a whole fish or a whole grilled octopus (also available as half) are meant for sharing, as are opulent seafood platters layered with shrimp, oysters, and king crab. **Known for:** elegant atmosphere; lovely rooftop patio; raw bar is outstanding. [$] *Average main: C$35* ✉ *10 Temperance St., 5th fl., Financial District* ☎ *647/348–7000* 🌐 *www.thechasetoronto.com* 🕒 *Closed Sun. No lunch Sat.* [M] *King.*

Drake One Fifty

$$$ | **INTERNATIONAL** | While the Drake Hotel on Queen Street West has become synonymous with Toronto's art and nightlife scene, its sister restaurant in the Financial District is more about a cool yet clubby luxury dining experience. The striking space is decked out with pop art–inspired murals and understated retro fixtures, and the kitchen turns out everything from charcuterie to oysters, and from steaks to steak tartare to short-rib burgers and a handful of pizzas. **Known for:** creative cocktails—try the brown butter maple old-fashioned; swanky vibe; great weekend brunch. [$] *Average main: C$25* ✉ *150 York*

St., Financial District 🕿 *416/363–6150*
⊕ *www.drakeonefifty.ca* Ⓜ *Osgoode.*

The Gabardine

$$$ | BRITISH | A cozy and unpretentious dining room sets the scene for gastro-pub classics like Cobb salad, chicken pot pie, and deviled eggs, plus international flourishes like skirt steak topped with piri piri. The rich mac and cheese topped with buttery herbed bread crumbs is great comfort food, as is the house-ground sirloin bacon cheeseburger with Thousand Island dressing. **Known for:** tin ceilings add a nostalgic vibe; comfort-food classics; laid-back vibe. 🛈 *Average main: C$22* ⊠ *372 Bay St., Financial District* 🕿 *647/352–3211* ⊕ *www.thegabardine.ca* ⊗ *Closed weekends* Ⓜ *Queen.*

Pearl Diver

$$$ | SEAFOOD | A rustic-chic haunt for seafood lovers steps from the Financial District, Pearl Diver specializes in a global array of oysters, all displayed on ice behind the handsome bar. If that's not enough, their excellent trout and the dry-aged beef burger will make you fall for the Pearl Diver hook, line, and sinker. **Known for:** laid-back vibe; Tuesday night seafood tower specials; famed 100 oysters for C$100 deal every Thursday. 🛈 *Average main: C$25* ⊠ *100 Adelaide St. E, Financial District* 🕿 *416/366–7827* ⊕ *www.pearldiver.to* ⊗ *Closed Mon., no lunch Tues. and Wed.* ▭ *No credit cards* Ⓜ *King.*

Reds Wine Tavern

$$$ | AMERICAN | Repurposed wine bottles and wine glasses assembled as giant chandeliers hover above the tables at Reds Wine Tavern, offering a nod to the lengthy list of international wine picks. The menu is global, skipping from seared tuna tostadas with guacamole and daily curries to comfort foods like lobster grilled cheese and a variety of steaks. **Known for:** everything here is made from scratch; bread baked right on the premises; business lunches and

after-work drinks. 🛈 *Average main: C$22* ⊠ *77 Adelaide St. W, Financial District* 🕿 *416/862–7337* ⊕ *www.redswinetavern.com* ⊗ *Closed Mon., closed for lunch Tues. and Wed.* Ⓜ *King.*

Terroni

$$ | ITALIAN | FAMILY | Open shelving lined with Italian provisions decorates this cool pizza joint, but it's the thin-crust pies, bubbled and blistered to perfection, that keep diners coming back. The menu suits all pizza lovers—from the simple Margherita to extravagant options like the Polentona, with tomato, mozzarella, fontina, speck (smoked prosciutto), and pine nuts. Daily specials can be hit-or-miss, but desserts—like a warm, oozing round of flourless chocolate cake—are universally delicious. **Known for:** in addition to the pizza, the pastas are quite popular; the secluded back patio is lovely in good weather; cool location inside a former court house. 🛈 *Average main: C$19* ⊠ *57 Adelaide St. E, Financial District* 🕿 *416/504–1992* ⊕ *www.terroni.ca* ⊗ *No lunch Sun.* Ⓜ *Queen.*

 Hotels

Cambridge Suites

$$$ | HOTEL | With just 12 suites per floor, this self-dubbed boutique hotel focuses on service: rooms are cleaned twice daily, and there's same-day dry cleaning and laundry, a rooftop gym with a view (and a whirlpool), and complimentary Wi-Fi. **Pros:** central location near many of the top attractions; social hour with discounted drinks; late checkout. **Cons:** parking is expensive; some dated decor; pets not allowed. 🛈 *Rooms from: C$297* ⊠ *15 Richmond St. E, at Victoria St., Financial District* 🕿 *416/368–1990, 800/463–1990* ⊕ *www.cambridgesuitestoronto.com* ⊷ *229 suites* ⊗ *No meals* Ⓜ *Queen.*

Executive Hotel Cosmopolitan

$$ | HOTEL | Tucked away on a side street in the heart of Toronto, this uberboutique, all-suite hotel seamlessly blends a modern Eastern aesthetic with apartment-style amenities. **Pros:** central location; hipness factor; friendly staff. **Cons:** side streets dark at night; some rooms have so-so views; no on-site parking. 💲 *Rooms from: C$234* ✉ *8 Colborne St., at Yonge St., Financial District* 📞 *416/350–2000, 888/388–3932* ⊕ *www.cosmotoronto.com* 🛏 *95 suites* 🍴 *No meals* Ⓜ *King.*

Fairmont Royal York

$$$$ | **HOTEL** | Like a proud grandmother, the Royal York stands serenely on Front Street in downtown Toronto, surrounded by gleaming skyscrapers and the nearby CN Tower. **Pros:** lots of history; excellent health club (lap pool, whirlpool, saunas, well-appointed gym, and more); steps from Union Station. **Cons:** rooms can be small; charge for in-room Internet access; expensive parking. 💲 *Rooms from: C$499* ✉ *100 Front St. W, at York St., Financial District* 📞 *416/368–2511, 866/540–4489* ⊕ *www.fairmont.com/royalyork* 🛏 *898 rooms* 🍴 *No meals* Ⓜ *Union.*

Hotel Victoria

$$$ | **HOTEL** | A local landmark built in 1909, "the Vic" is Toronto's second-oldest hotel, with a long-standing reputation for excellent service. **Pros:** gym privileges at nearby health club; stylishly decorated rooms; lobby restaurant is fantastic. **Cons:** inconvenient off-site parking; front rooms get street noise; not all rooms get newspapers. 💲 *Rooms from: C$259* ✉ *56 Yonge St., at Wellington St., Financial District* 📞 *416/363–1666, 800/363–8228* ⊕ *www.hotelvictoria-toronto.com* 🛏 *56 rooms* 🍴 *No meals* Ⓜ *King.*

One King West Hotel & Residence

$$$ | **HOTEL** | Made up entirely of suites, this 51-story tower is attached to the old Dominion Bank of Canada (circa 1914) in the city's downtown business and shopping core. **Pros:** great views from upper floors; central location; excellent service. **Cons:** not all suites have washer/dryer; parking is valet-only;

pricey rates. 💲 *Rooms from: C$309* ✉ *1 King St. W, at Yonge St., Financial District* 📞 *416/548–8100, 866/470–5464* ⊕ *www.onekingwest.com* 🛏 *340 suites* 🍴 *No meals* Ⓜ *King.*

The Ritz-Carlton, Toronto

$$$$ | **HOTEL** | This Ritz has a great location—across from Roy Thompson Hall and smack-dab in the center of the Financial District—and a solid elegance, embellished with a Canadian motif of brass maple leaves and local woods. **Pros:** reliable Ritz service; top-of-the-line amenities; expansive rooms. **Cons:** five-star prices; expensive valet parking; pricey high tea. 💲 *Rooms from: C$469* ✉ *181 Wellington St. W, Financial District* 📞 *416/585–2500* ⊕ *www.ritzcarlton.com/toronto* 🛏 *319 rooms* 🍴 *No meals* Ⓜ *St. Andrew, Union.*

Nightlife

The bars and restaurants in the Financial District tend to be tony affairs, equally suited to schmoozing clients and blowing off steam after a long day at the office. After happy hour, this business- and high-rise-dense part of town quiets down.

BARS

Oliver & Bonacini Cafe Grill

BARS/PUBS | If you want to "see and be seen" in the Financial District head to this vast restaurant and bar, which has a wraparound year-round patio that faces both Front and Yonge streets. The O&B Café Grill, as it's locally called, has become the destination for Bay Street's movers and shakers, and the neighborhood's urban dwellers. Check out the impressive cocktail menu. ✉ *33 Yonge St., Financial District* 📞 *647/260–2070* ⊕ *www.oliverbonacini.com* Ⓜ *Union.*

Shopping

Toronto's Financial District has a vast underground maze of shops underneath its office towers. The tenants of this

Underground City are mostly the usual assortment of chain stores, with an occasional surprise. Marked PATH, the walkways (the underground street system) help visitors navigate the subterranean mall, though it can be confusing for novices. The network runs roughly from the Fairmont Royal York hotel near Union Station north to the Atrium at Bay and Dundas.

CLOTHING
Moores Clothing For Men

CLOTHING | This is the place to browse thousands of discounted Canadian-made dress pants, sport coats, and suits, including many famous labels. Sizes run from extra short to extra tall and from regular to oversize; the quality is solid and the service is good. ⊠ *100 Yonge St., at King St., Financial District* ☎ *416/363–5442* ⊕ *www.mooresclothing.com* Ⓜ *King.*

SPORTING GOODS
Running Room

SPORTING GOODS | The knowledgeable staff at this chain can guide you to the perfect pair of running shoes. Running Rooms have spawned a running community, and shops have sprouted up all over the city; group runs are held every Wednesday evening and Sunday morning. ⊠ *53 Yonge St., at Wellington, Financial District* ☎ *416/867–7575* ⊕ *www.runningroom.com* Ⓜ *King.*

Chapter 4

OLD TOWN AND THE DISTILLERY DISTRICT

4

Updated by
Jennifer Foden

◉ Sights   🍴 Restaurants   🛏 Hotels   🛍 Shopping   🍸 Nightlife
★★★★☆   ★★★★☆   ★★★☆☆   ★★★★☆   ★★★☆☆

NEIGHBORHOOD SNAPSHOT

TOP EXPERIENCES

■ **Buy the Best Local Produce:** Check out the more than 100 vendors at the St. Lawrence Market, one of the world's best indoor food markets.

■ **Dive Into the Distillery District:** Stroll along the cobblestone streets and take in the restored collection of Victorian industrial buildings.

■ **Go Out on the Town:** An after-work crowd heads to atmospheric Old Town during the week, and weekends find more late-night revelry.

■ **Shop Till You Drop:** The Distillery District has become one of the city's most eclectic shopping destinations.

■ **Take in a Show:** Some of the city's best small theater companies make their home in these distinct districts.

GETTING HERE

Old Town is in the eastern reaches of downtown, with the borders of Church Street to the west, Parliament Street to the east, Queen Street to the north, and Front Street to the south. Take the subway to King or Queen subway station and walk five minutes east. You can also take the 504 King streetcar or 501 Queen streetcar. The Distillery District is just east of Old Town, south of Front Street between Parliament and Cherry streets. The area is pedestrian-only, but parking lots and street parking are available. On the TTC, take the Parliament bus south from Castle Frank subway station, the Cherry Street bus from Union station, or the 504 King streetcar to Parliament.

PLANNING YOUR TIME

Allow yourself at least two hours to wander the cobblestone streets and artisanal shops of the Distillery District. Be sure to stop to see the modern art statues along Gristmill Lane and have a drink at Mill Street Brewery. You'll need at least half a day to wander the streets of Old Town. There are plenty of cool shops, restaurants, and museums in the neighborhood.

QUICK BITES

■ **Brick Street Bakery.** Stop for a hot beverage and a delicious pastry (the maple-walnut butter tarts are highly recommended) to fuel your stroll around the historic Distillery District. ⊠ *55 Mill St., Distillery District* ⊕ *www.brickstreetbakery.com* Ⓜ *Union*

■ **St. Lawrence Market.** Whether you want to snack on Canadian bacon, fresh seafood, or a slice of pizza, St. Lawrence Market is *the* place for casual eats in the neighborhood. ⊠ *92–95 Front St. E* ⊕ *www.stlawrencemarket.com* Ⓜ *Union*

■ **Soma Chocolatemaker.** Calling all chocolate lovers! Indulge in everything from truffles to single-origin chocolate bars to creamy gelato at this sweet spot. ⊠ *32 Tank House La., Distillery District* ⊕ *www.somachocolate.com* Ⓜ *King*

Old Town was of the first neighborhoods in Toronto, getting its name in the early 1800s. Today, it's a mix of historic attractions—including Toronto's First Post Office, St. James Cathedral, and the world-famous St. Lawrence Market—and glittering new developments that bring with them some of the city's hottest restaurants and shops.

Farther east, the pedestrian-only Distillery District is one of Toronto's hottest entertainment destinations. Its cobblestone streets are filled with restored Victorian-era factories that once housed a large whiskey distillery and other businesses. The historic area is now filled with contemporary galleries, bustling pubs, and funky boutiques.

Old Town

A must-visit for history buffs and food freaks alike, the St. Lawrence Market started its storied life as Toronto's first city hall, then a prison. Now, the sprawling space is jammed with vendors offering all manner of meats, cheeses, breads, produce, and artisanal foods. Be sure to pick up a peameal (aka Canadian) bacon sandwich at Carousel Bakery, and check out the farmers' market on Saturday and flea market on Sunday.

Sights

Flatiron Building
BUILDING | One of several wedge-shape buildings scattered around North America, Toronto's Flatiron occupies the triangular block between Wellington, Scott, and Front streets. It was erected in 1892 as the head office of the Gooderham and Worts distilling company. On the back of the building, a witty trompe l'oeil mural by Derek Besant is drawn around the windows, making it appear that part of the building has been tacked up on the wall and is peeling off. ✉ *49 Wellington St. E, between Church and Scott Sts., Old Town* Ⓜ *King.*

Museum of Illusions
MUSEUM | FAMILY | While this small museum may not pack as big of a punch as the city's larger arts destinations, it's a fun spot to bring the kids on a rainy afternoon. The various illusions will mess with everyone's minds, and there's everything from holograms to an anti-gravity room to a rotating room (where it looks like you're turned upside down). It's a great spot to snap some photos. ✉ *132 Front St. E, Old Town* ☎ *416/889-2285* ⊕ *museumofillusions.ca* ✑ *C$24.*

St. James Cathedral
RELIGIOUS SITE | Bank towers dwarf it now, but this Anglican church with noble Gothic spires has the tallest steeple in

The outstanding St. Lawrence food market, one of the finest in the world, sells a huge variety of local and imported specialties.

Canada. Its illuminated clock once guided ships into the harbor. This is the fourth St. James Cathedral on the site; the third burned down in the Great Fire of 1849. As part of the church's bicentennial in 1997, a peal of 12 bells was installed. Stand near the church most Sundays after the 9 am service ends (about 10:10 am) and you'll be rewarded with a glorious concert of ringing bells. ⊠ 106 King St. E, Old Town ☎ 416/364–7865 ⊕ stjamescathedral.ca Ⓜ King.

★ St. Lawrence Market

MARKET | Both a landmark and an excellent place to sample Canadian bacon, this market was originally built in 1849 as the first true Toronto city hall. The building now has an exhibition hall upstairs—the Market Gallery—where the council chambers once stood. The food market, which began growing around the building's square in the early 1900s, is considered one of the world's best. Local and imported foods such as fresh shellfish, sausage, and cheeses are renowned. Stop for a simple sandwich of a roll with

Canadian bacon (also known as "peameal bacon") at the Carousel Bakery. The brick building across Front Street, on the north side, is open on Saturday morning for the 200-year-old farmers' market; it's a cornucopia of produce and homemade jams, relishes, and sauces from farms just north of Toronto. On Sunday the wares of more than 80 antiques dealers are displayed in the same building. ⊠ Front and Jarvis Sts., Old Town ☎ 416/392–7219 ⊕ www.stlawrencemarket.com ⊘ Closed Mon. Ⓜ Union.

St. Lawrence Hall

BUILDING | Built between 1850 and 1851 on the site of the area's first public meeting space, St. Lawrence Hall is Renaissance Revival architecture at its finest. The hall was intended for musical performances and balls, and famed opera soprano Jenny Lind sang here, but it's also the spot where antislavery demonstrations were held, and where P. T. Barnum first presented Tom Thumb. Take time to admire the exterior of this architectural gem, now used for everything from concerts to wedding receptions. If you find yourself taking part in one of the many walking tours of the area, you might get a chance to see the photos in the lounge on the third floor; the pictures feature notable figures who once performed, lectured, or were entertained here. ✉ *157 King St. E, Old Town* ☎ *416/392–7809* 🌐 *www.stlawrencemarket.com* [M] *Union.*

Toronto's First Post Office

GOVERNMENT BUILDING | **FAMILY** | This small working post office dates from 1833 and still functions with quill pens, ink pots, and sealing wax—you can use the old-fashioned equipment to send a letter for C$2. Exhibits include reproductions of letters from the 1820s and 1830s. Distinctive cancellation stamps are used on all outgoing letters. ✉ *260 Adelaide St. E, Old Town* ☎ *416/865–1833* 🌐 *www.townofyork.com* [M] *King.*

🍴 Restaurants

Irish Embassy Pub & Grill

$$ | **IRISH** | Popular both with the after-work crowd and late-night revelers, this pub is the place for hearty homemade food and a proper pint. The soaring ceilings and columns of mahogany wood make an authentic backdrop for the approachable lineup of imported beers, such as Guinness, Smithwick's, Harp, and Kilkenny. **Known for:** good variety of whiskeys and scotches; fun-loving crowd day and night; authentic pub eats. [$] *Average main: C$19* ✉ *49 Yonge St., Old Town* ☎ *416/866–8282* 🌐 *www.irishembassypub.com* [M] *King.*

PJ O'Brien

$$ | **IRISH** | This traditional pub will make you feel like you're in Dublin the second you step inside. Tuck into an authentic meal of Irish Kilkenny Ale–battered fish-and-chips, beef and Guinness stew, or corned beef and cabbage, and save room for the bread pudding steeped in whiskey and custard, just like Gran made. **Known for:** broken up into different areas for music lovers, sports fans, and other groups; dependably good pub grub; affable staff. [$] *Average main: C$15* ✉ *39 Colborne St., Old Town* ☎ *416/815–7562* 🌐 *www.pjobrien.com* 🕒 *Closed Sun.* [M] *King.*

🛏 Hotels

Novotel Toronto Centre

$$ | **HOTEL** | A good-value, modern hotel with few frills, the Novotel is in the heart of the animated, bar-lined Esplanade area, near the St. Lawrence Market, Scotiabank Arena, and Union Station. **Pros:** excellent location; solid value; great breakfast buffet. **Cons:** small in-hotel parking spaces; spotty service and housekeeping; neighborhood can get noisy. [$] *Rooms from: C$199* ✉ *45 The Esplanade, at Church St., Old Town* ☎ *416/367–8900* 🌐 *www.novotel.com* 🔑 *262 rooms* 🍽 *No meals* [M] *Union.*

The Omni King Edward Hotel

$$$ | **HOTEL** | Toronto's landmark "King Eddy" Hotel, which has hosted the well-heeled for over a century, continues to be a favorite choice for special occasions and a nod to grand hotels of the past. **Pros:** mix of historic charm with modern luxury; central location; friendly service. **Cons:** expensive parking is valet-only; charge for online access; lots of street traffics. [$] *Rooms from: C$309* ✉ *37 King St. E, east of Yonge St., Old Town* ☎ *416/863–9700, 888/444–6664* 🌐 *www.thekingedwardhotel.com* 🔑 *301 rooms* 🍽 *No meals* [M] *King.*

🍸 Nightlife

BARS

Betty's

BARS/PUBS | This laid-back dive bar has an excellent selection of draft beers and a full menu of pub fare, from tacos to pad Thai to chicken wings. It's a fun spot to watch sports. ✉ *240 King St. E, Old Town* ☎ *416/368–1300* 🌐 *www.bettysonking.com.*

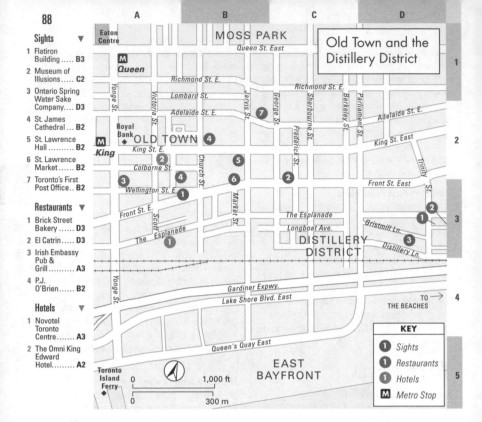

Bier Markt

BARS/PUBS | With more than 150 beers from 30 countries, including 50 on tap, this enormous restaurant/bar has a corner on the international beer market, but the best thing about it is the over-size year-round sidewalk patio on the Esplanade, ideal for an afternoon brew. ■TIP→ **The lines are ridiculous on weekends—do as the locals do and go midweek instead.** ✉ *58 The Esplanade, just west of Church St., Old Town* ☎ *416/862–7575* ⊕ *www.thebiermarkt.com* Ⓜ *Union, King.*

C'est What

BARS/PUBS | In a cozy underground setting that's part beer cellar, part library, and part pool hall, C'est What offers more than 40 taps of Canadian beer, plus a menu of globally inspired pub grub. The main room is home to a couple of pool tables and a comfy fireplace area lined with couches, while an adjoining room hosts live folk, rock, and roots acts a few times a week. ✉ *67 Front St. E, Old Town* ☎ *416/867–9499* ⊕ *www.cestwhat.com* Ⓜ *Union.*

Pravda Vodka Bar

BARS/PUBS | A deliberately faded elegance, like a Communist-era club gone rough around the edges, permeates Pravda. Huge paintings of Stalin and Lenin adorn the brick walls, and crystal chandeliers run the length of the two-story room, along with exposed ductwork. Weekday happy-hour specials draw an after-work crowd to lounge on well-worn leather sofas, around low wooden tables, or in a red-velvet-curtained VIP bottle-service area upstairs. Some 75 to 100 vodkas from around the globe are always on the menu, as are vodka flights, martinis, and Czech and Russian beers, along with

caviar, smoked fish, and pierogi. ✉ *44
Wellington St. E, between Church and
Yonge Sts., Old Town* ☎ *416/366–0303*
⊕ *www.pravdavodkabar.com* Ⓜ *King.*

The Sultan's Tent and Cafe Moroc
BARS/PUBS | Not far from the historic
St. Lawrence Market, the Sultan's Tent
and its front bar, Cafe Moroc, re-create
a traditional Moroccan banquet atmosphere, complete with plush divans and
metal lanterns. In addition to wine and
beer, they have a speciality cocktail list
that puts a North African spin on classic
drinks, like the Arabian Caesar or the
Moroccan old fashioned. There's live
music and belly dancers every evening.
✉ *49 Front St. E, Old Town* ☎ *416/961–
0601* ⊕ *www.thesultanstent.com* Ⓜ *King.*

 Performing Arts

MAJOR VENUES
Meridian Hall
ARTS CENTERS | Formerly called the Sony
Centre, this iconic 3,191-seat hall boasts
an international program of diverse yet
mostly mainstream artists such as Paul
Simon, the Just for Laughs Comedy
Festival, the Alvin Ailey American Dance
Theater, and numerous other cultural
acts that cater to the diversity of Toronto.
✉ *1 Front St. E, at Yonge St., Old Town*
☎ *855/872–7669 tickets* ⊕ *www.sonycen-
tre.ca* Ⓜ *Union, King.*

THEATERS
Canadian Stage
THEATER | Canadian Stage focuses on
cross-disciplinary works that integrate
theater, dance, film, visual arts, and
more. It stages productions at the **Bluma
Appel Theatre** (*27 Front Street East*),
which seats 868, and the more intimate
Berkeley Street Theatre (*26 Berkeley
Street*), which has a capacity of 244.
✉ *Bluma Appel Theatre, 27 Front St. E,
Old Town* ☎ *416/368–3110 box office,
877/399–2651 toll-free* ⊕ *www.canadian-
stage.com* Ⓜ *King.*

Théâtre Français de Toronto
THEATER | High-quality French-language
drama—with English subtitles—is
performed at this theater, whose French
and French-Canadian repertoire ranges from classical to contemporary. A
children's play and a teen show are part
of the season, which features about
a half dozen plays. ✉ *Berkeley Street
Theatre, 26 Berkeley St., 2nd fl., at Front
St. E, Old Town* ☎ *416/534–6604* ⊕ *www.
theatrefrancais.com* Ⓜ *King.*

Young People's Theatre
THEATER | FAMILY | Plays are contemporary,
relevant, and kid-focused at YPT, whether
a heavily interactive romp, such as *Where
the Wild Things Are,* based on Maurice
Sendak's classic book, or a dramatic
thought-provoker like *Hana's Suitcase,*
the story of a young girl living during the
Holocaust. Productions aren't conde-
scending nor do they compromise on
dramatic integrity. They are as entertaining
for adults as for kids. ✉ *165 Front St. E,
between Jarvis and Sherbourne Sts., Old
Town* ☎ *416/862–2222* ⊕ *www.youngpeo-
plestheatre.org* Ⓜ *King or Union.*

Shopping

ART AND CRAFTS GALLERIES
Feheley Fine Arts
ART GALLERIES | Browse traditional, as well
as contemporary and even avant-garde
Canadian Inuit art—a far cry from the
traditional whale carvings and stone-cut
prints you may expect—at this fami-
ly-owned gallery founded in 1964. ✉ *65
George St., at King St. E,, Old Town*
☎ *416/323–1373* ⊕ *www.feheleyfinearts.
com* Ⓜ *King.*

Distillery District

This restored collection of Victorian
industrial buildings, complete with
cobblestone lanes, has become a hub of
independent restaurants, boutiques, and
art spaces, with the carefully preserved

former Gooderham and Worts Distillery (founded in 1832) reborn as a cultural center. The 13-acre site includes 45 19th-century buildings and a pedestrian-only village that houses more than 100 tenants—including galleries, artist studios and workshops, shops, breweries, upscale eateries, bars, and cafés. Live music, outdoor exhibitions, fairs, and special events take place year-round, but summer months are the best time to visit. Hour-long walking tours take place seven days a week.

Sights

Ontario Spring Water Sake Company
WINERY/DISTILLERY | Ontario's first sake brewery uses natural spring water from the nearby town of Huntsville—known for its low mineral content—and highly polished rice from California to create its sake. The brewery has a small tasting bar and retail shop with products made with the sake *kasu* (the lees, or yeast, leftover from fermentation), such as soaps, salad dressings, and miso soup, as well as ceramics and sake glassware. You can also take tours (weekends at 1 pm and 3:30 pm) to learn about Junmai (pure rice) and Namazake (unpasteurized sake), to find out how sake is made, and to enjoy a guided tasting of four sakes. ✉ *51 Gristmill La., Bldg. 4, Distillery District* ☎ *416/365–7253* 🌐 *www.ontariosake.com* 🎫 *Tours C$15.*

Restaurants

Brick Street Bakery
$ | BAKERY | If the smell of fresh bread and buttery croissants doesn't draw you into this charming bakery, the decadent sweets on display—like the sticky ginger cake loaves, maple-walnut butter tarts, or French macarons—certainly will. For heartier appetites there are items like a pulled pork sandwich and steak-and-stout pie. **Known for:** no seating, so most people take their meals to go; handcrafted sandwiches and soups; freshest bread in the neighborhood. [$] *Average main: C$4* ✉ *55 Mill St., Bldg. 45A, Distillery District* ☎ *416/214–4949* 🌐 *www.brickstreetbakery.com* [M] *Union.*

★ El Catrin
$$ | MEXICAN | With a 5,000-square-foot patio and stunning floor-to-ceiling murals, El Catrin is the hottest place to be in the Distillery District. Delicious eats include traditional tacos *al pastor* with shaved pork and pineapple salsa, a selection of ceviches, mains like 24-hour braised short rib in mole sauce, and guacamole prepared table-side. **Known for:** adventurous diners can sample flash-fried crickets; nearly 200 types of mescal and tequila available; huge patio is open year-round. [$] *Average main: C$20* ✉ *18 Tank House La., Distillery District* ☎ *416/203–2121* 🌐 *www.elcatrin.ca* [M] *Union.*

Nightlife

BARS

Mill Street Beer Hall
BREWPUBS/BEER GARDENS | Brewing some of Toronto's most widely enjoyed craft beers, Mill Street Brewery runs a pair of adjoining brew pubs in the Distillery District. Enter off Tank House Lane to find the Brew Pub, home of dressed-up bar eats, or veer down a side alley to feast at the modern Beer Hall. Both bars have several beer taps, with choices ranging from Mill Street staples like Organic Lager and Dark Tankhouse Ale to seasonal and one-off beers. A bottle shop attached to the Brew Pub offers a selection of Mill Street offerings to go. ✉ *21 Tank House La., Distillery District* ☎ *416/681–0338* 🌐 *millstreetbrewery.com/toronto-beer-hall.*

Performing Arts

THEATERS

★ Soulpepper Theatre Company
THEATER | Established in 1998 by some of Canada's leading theater artists,

Did You Know?

The cobblestone historic Distillery District is now home to more than 100 upscale galleries, shops, and restaurants.

Soulpepper is Toronto's largest not-for-profit theater company. It produces classic and newly commissioned plays, musicals, and concerts year-round. ⊠ *Young Centre for the Performing Arts, 50 Tank House La., Distillery District* ☎ *416/866–8666* ⊕ *www.soulpepper.ca.*

Shopping

ART GALLERIES
Corkin Gallery
ART GALLERIES | With work by contemporary artists such as Barbara Astman and David Urban, this gallery is one of the most fascinating in town. They show hand-painted photos, documentary photos, fashion photography, and mixed-media art. ⊠ *7 Tank House La., Distillery District* ☎ *416/979–1980* ⊕ *www.corkingallery.com* Ⓜ *King.*

CLOTHING
★ Gotstyle
CLOTHING | This Torontonian start-up has hit the nail on the head, providing stylish men's clothes—Tiger of Sweden, Sand Copenhagen, and John Varvatos—to residents of the city's downtown condos. This huge airy branch carries ladies' clothing as well, including brands like Line, Soia & Kyo, and Hilary MaMillan. Head up to the lush purple-carpeted mezzanine level for business and eveningwear and a round on the purple pool table. ⊠ *21 Trinity St., Distillery District* ☎ *416/260–9696* ⊕ *www.gotstyle.com* Ⓜ *King or Castle Frank.*

JEWELRY AND ACCESSORIES
Corktown Designs
JEWELRY/ACCESSORIES | Most of the reasonably priced jewelry at this Distillery District shop is Canadian-designed, and all of it is unique and handmade. Pieces range from inexpensive glass-and-silver pendants to Swiss-made stainless steel rings and pricier pieces set with pearls and other semiprecious stones. ⊠ *5 Trinity St., Distillery District* ☎ *416/861–3020* ⊕ *www.corktowndesigns.com* Ⓜ *King.*

SHOES, HANDBAGS, AND LEATHER GOODS
★ John Fluevog
SHOES/LUGGAGE/LEATHER GOODS | Fluevog's funky shoes are perfectly displayed in this roughly converted high-ceilinged industrial space. The building was once the distillery boiler house, which explains the three-story brick oven that takes up a third of the floor-space, and the safety ladder leading to an overhead catwalk. Take a seat on the stunning embossed leather couch when trying on the fun, cutting-edge merchandise. ⊠ *4 Trinity St., Distillery District* ☎ *416/583–1970* ⊕ *www.fluevog.com* Ⓜ *King or Castle Frank.*

WINE AND SPECIALTY FOOD
Soma Chocolatemaker
FOOD/CANDY | You can almost satisfy your sweet tooth just by inhaling the delicate wafts of chocolate, dried fruits, and roasted nuts in this gourmet chocolate shop that specializes in fair-trade ingredients. Big sellers include truffles, mango chili and raspberry fruit bars, and gelato. For something different, try the Bicerin, a thick mixture of melted chocolate, espresso, and whipped cream. ⊠ *32 Tank House La., Distillery District* ☎ *416/815–7662* ⊕ *www.somachocolate.com* Ⓜ *King or Castle Frank.*

YONGE-DUNDAS
SQUARE AREA

Updated by
Natalia Manzocco

⊙ Sights	🍴 Restaurants	🛏 Hotels	🛍 Shopping	🍸 Nightlife
★★★☆☆	★★★★☆	★★★★★	★★★★★	★★☆☆☆

NEIGHBORHOOD SNAPSHOT

TOP EXPERIENCES

■ **The Lights Are Much Brighter There:** Take in the hustle and bustle of Yonge-Dundas Square, Toronto's answer to Times Square.

■ **The Best in Window Shopping:** Do some serious browsing at the Eaton Centre, the city's much loved (and sometimes vilified) shopping center.

■ **Two Theaters for the Price of One:** Don't miss a chance to see the world's last stacked Victorian theaters: The Elgin and the Winter Garden.

■ **Take a Trip Around the World:** Enjoy foods from around the world or lively music from street musicians at larger-than-life Dundas Square.

■ **Learn About the Fabric of Canada:** Explore fashion history at the Textile Museum of Canada, which has 13,000 artifacts from across the globe.

■ **Enjoy the Best Place for Live Music:** Near-perfect acoustics and excellent sight lines are the draw at Canada's best concert theater, Massey Hall.

GETTING HERE

The subway stations Dundas and Queen, conveniently at either end of the Eaton Centre, are the main transportation hubs for this part of the city. There are also streetcar lines running along Dundas and Queen streets, linking this area to Chinatown and Kensington Market, and Queen West, respectively. This is one of the busiest intersections in the city, so parking is tougher to find the closer you get to Yonge and Dundas, though there is a garage underneath the Eaton Centre.

PLANNING YOUR TIME

Depending on your patience and the contents of your wallet, you could spend anywhere from one to 10 hours in the colossal Eaton Centre, literally shopping until you drop. The Mackenzie House, Textile Museum of Canada, and Toronto Police Museum merit an hour each; and you could easily while away an afternoon people-watching in Yonge-Dundas Square.

QUICK BITES

■ **GB Hand-Pulled Noodles.** Watch tasty, filling Chinese noodles get stretched to order at this busy shop. ⊠ *66 Edward St., Dundas Square Area* Ⓜ *Dundas*

■ **Trinity Square Cafe.** Tucked into a courtyard outside the Eaton Centre, this not-for-profit café makes a mean bowl of soup. ⊠ *19 Trinity Sq., Dundas Square Area* ⊕ *trinitysquarecafe.ca* Ⓜ *Dundas*

■ **Tsujiri.** This matcha-focused spot dishes out green-tea flavored soft-serve ice cream, baked goods, fanciful drinks, and more. ⊠ *147 Dundas St. W, Dundas Square Area* ⊕ *tsujiri-global.com* Ⓜ *Dundas*

Yonge Street is Toronto's main artery: it starts at Lake Ontario and slices the city in half as it travels through downtown's Dundas Square and north to the suburbs. There's usually a crowd gathered below the enormous billboards and flashy lights in Dundas Square, especially in the summer, when the large public area comes alive with outdoor festivals and entertainment.

All visitors tend to end up here at some point during their trip. Usually it's the enticement of nonstop shopping in the Eaton Centre, Toronto's biggest downtown shopping mall, or the shops lining Yonge Street nearby. Others see the allure of outdoor markets, ethnic food festivals, and street concerts in the bright and lively, larger-than-life Dundas Square.

There's also a selection of intriguing niche museums. History buffs will enjoy the Mackenzie House, the former home of Toronto's first mayor; contemporary fashion and design are highlighted at the Textile Museum of Canada; and at the Toronto Police Museum, kids can learn about the exciting history of Toronto's police.

⊙ Sights

Mackenzie House
MUSEUM | Once home to journalist William Lyon Mackenzie, Toronto's first mayor (elected in 1834) and designer of the city's coat of arms, this Greek Revival row house is now a museum. Among the period furnishings and equipment preserved here is an 1845 printing press, which visitors may try. Mackenzie served only one year as mayor. In 1837, he gathered some 700 supporters and marched down Yonge Street to try to overthrow the government, but his rebels were roundly defeated, and he fled to the United States with a price on his head. When Mackenzie was pardoned by Queen Victoria years later, he returned to Canada and was promptly elected once again to the legislative assembly. By this time, though, he was so down on his luck that a group of friends bought his family this house. Mackenzie enjoyed the place for only a few years before his death in 1861. His grandson, William Lyon Mackenzie King, became the longest-serving prime minister in Canadian history. ✉ 82 Bond St., Dundas Square Area ☎ 416/392–6915 ⌨ C$8 ⊙ Closed Mon., weekdays May–Dec. Ⓜ Dundas.

★ Textile Museum of Canada
MUSEUM | With a 45-year history of exploring ideas and building cultural understanding through its collection of more than 13,000 artifacts from across the globe, this museum's exhibitions

Yonge-Dundas Square Area

Sights ▼
1 Mackenzie House **D4**
2 Textile Museum of Canada **B3**
3 Toronto Police Museum and Discovery Centre ... **C1**
4 Yonge-Dundas Square **D3**

Restaurants ▼
1 Barberian's **C3**
2 Kinka Izakaya **E2**
3 Lai Wah Heen **B3**
4 Salad King **C3**
5 The Senator **D4**
6 Uncle Tetsu's Japanese Cheesecake **C3**

Hotels ▼
1 Chelsea Hotel **C2**
2 DoubleTree by Hilton Downtown **B3**
3 Marriott Eaton Centre ... **C4**
4 Pantages Hotel **D4**
5 Saint James Hotel **D2**

and programming connect contemporary art and design to international textile traditions. Wednesday evening (after 5) admission is Pay What You Can. ✉ *55 Centre Ave., Dundas Square Area* ☎ *416/599–5321* 🌐 *www.textilemuseum.ca* 🎫 *C$15* [M] *St. Patrick.*

Toronto Police Museum and Discovery Centre

MUSEUM | FAMILY | A replica of a 19th-century police station inside the working police headquarters, this collection is devoted to the history of Toronto police and has exhibits about infamous crimes. It's quirky but entertaining. *You must call ahead to book a tour.* ✉ *40 College St., Dundas Square Area* ☎ *416/808–7020* 🌐 *www.torontopolice.on.ca/museum* 🎫 *Free* 🕒 *Closed weekends* [M] *College.*

★ Yonge-Dundas Square

PLAZA | A public square at a major downtown crossroads, Toronto's answer to New York's Times Square is surrounded by oversize billboards and bright light displays. Visitors and locals converge on the tables and chairs that are scattered across the square when the weather is fine, and kids (and the young at heart) frolic in the 20 water fountains that shoot out of the cement floor like miniature geysers. From May to October, there's something happening every weekend—it could be an artisan market, an open-air film viewing, a summertime festival, or a live musical performance. ✉ *1 Dundas St. E, Dundas Square Area* 🌐 *www.ydsquare.ca* [M] *Dundas.*

🍴 Restaurants

Dundas Square has bright neon screens beaming down the newest fashions and trends. The area is dominated by big chains and Asian franchises but also a variety of neighborhood spots.

Barberian's

$$$$ | STEAKHOUSE | A Toronto landmark where wheeling, dealing, and lots of eating have gone on since 1959, Barberian's also has a romantic history: Elizabeth Taylor and Richard Burton got engaged here (for the first time). It's one of the oldest steak houses in the city, and the menu is full of classic dishes like tomato and onion salad and jumbo shrimp cocktail. **Known for:** beautifully maintained midcentury modern decor; steaks ranging from porterhouse to filet mignon; enormous underground wine cellar. [$] *Average main: C$50* ✉ *7 Elm St., Dundas Square Area* ☎ *416/597–0335* 🌐 *www.barberians.com* 🕒 *No lunch Sat.–Mon.* [M] *Dundas.*

Kinka Izakaya

$$ | JAPANESE | When Kinka opened in 2009, it quickly defined the Japanese izakaya-style dining experience (drinks and small plates) in the minds of Torontonians: it's noisy and ultrafriendly, complete with an open space and communal tables. The Kinoko cheese *bibimbap* (rice and garlic sautéed mushrooms with seaweed sauce and cheese in a hot stone bowl) take this humble dish to new heights. **Known for:** sensational sake cocktails; snack-size Japanese eats; rowdy atmosphere. [$] *Average main: C$16* ✉ *398 Church St., Dundas Square Area* ☎ *416/977–0999* 🌐 *www.kinkaizakaya.com* [M] *College.*

Lai Wah Heen

$$$$ | CHINESE | An elegant dining room and formal service with silver serving dishes set the scene for upscale Asian food. The 100-dish inventory features excellent dishes like wok-fried shredded beef tenderloin with sundried chili peppers alongside delicacies dotted with truffle and foie gras. **Known for:** elegant setting; tableside Peking duck service; excellent lunchtime dim sum. [$] *Average main: C$40* ✉ *DoubleTree by Hilton Hotel, 108 Chestnut St., 2nd fl., Dundas Square Area* ☎ *416/977–9899* 🌐 *www.laiwahheen.com* [M] *St. Patrick.*

Salad King

$ | THAI | A long-running favorite for local students and shoppers looking for a budget-friendly meal, Salad King occupies a second-floor dining room tucked above

Did You Know?

Toronto kicks off the holiday season each year with the Cavalcade of Lights in Nathan Phillips Square. The festival includes fireworks, live music performances, and the lighting of the city's official Christmas tree.

Yonge Street. Mains hover at the C$12 mark, including a variety of curries and stir-fries. **Known for:** quirky spice scale peaks at "may cause stomach upset"; communal seating means getting to know the locals; colorful atmosphere. *[$] Average main: C$12 ✉ 340 Yonge St., 2nd fl., Dundas Square Area ☎ 416/593–0333 🌐 www.saladking.com [M] Dundas.*

The Senator
$$ | **DINER** | The Senator diner has the distinction of being the oldest continuously running restaurant in Toronto, and it's a tried-and-true destination for the pretheater crowd, families, gently hungover locals, and everyone in between. Classic diner staples are dressed up with homey touches like house-smoked salmon and fresh-squeezed juices. **Known for:** timeless appeal of 1940s style; live music at upstairs wine bar; comfort-food favorites. *[$] Average main: C$18 ✉ 249 Victoria St., Dundas Square Area ☎ 416/364–7517 🌐 thesenator.com [M] Dundas.*

Uncle Tetsu's Japanese Cheesecake
$ | **JAPANESE** | When this Japanese franchise came to Canada, people lined up to try their take on cheesecake, which is a little eggier, firmer, and less sweet than the typical New York variety of cheesecake. The company was so successful, they launched two sister locations steps from the original: Uncle Tetsu's Japanese Bake serves three flavors of cheese tart (a pastry shell filled with a custardlike cheesecake filling) next door (596 Bay Street), while down the street at Uncle Tetsu To Go (191 Dundas Street West) they sell dome-shape "angel hat" cakes. **Known for:** long lines at peak hours; signature boxed cheesecakes; matcha cheesecakes on Monday and Thursday. *[$] Average main: C$10 ✉ 598 Bay St., Dundas Square Area ☎ 591/591–0555 🌐 uncletetsu-ca.com [M] Dundas.*

🛏 Hotels

Chelsea Hotel
$$ | **HOTEL** | **FAMILY** | Canada's largest hotel has long been popular with families and tour groups, so be prepared for a flurry of activity. **Pros:** extremely family-friendly vibe; adults-only swimming pool; good service. **Cons:** long lines at check-in and check-out; fills up with tour groups; slow elevators. *[$] Rooms from: C$225 ✉ 33 Gerrard St., Dundas Square Area ☎ 416/595–1975, 800/243–5732 🌐 chelseatoronto.com 🛏 1635 rooms 🍴 No meals [M] College or Dundas.*

DoubleTree by Hilton Downtown
$$ | **HOTEL** | This laid-back hotel is a quick walk to the hustle and bustle of Dundas Square and the cultural offerings of the Eaton Centre. **Pros:** a couple of excellent restaurants; reasonable rates for the location; helpful service. **Cons:** decor is a bit dated; parking fills up quickly; some rooms are small. *[$] Rooms from: $250 ✉ 108 Chestnut St., Dundas Square Area ☎ 416/977–5000 🌐 www.doubletree.hilton.com 🛏 486 rooms 🍴 No meals [M] St. Patrick.*

Marriott Eaton Centre
$$$ | **HOTEL** | Shoppers love the Marriott because it's right next door to the Eaton Centre and steps from Dundas Square. **Pros:** knowledgeable employees; superconvenient location; large guest rooms. **Cons:** may be noisy; parking area fills up quickly; free Wi-Fi only for loyalty members. *[$] Rooms from: C$325 ✉ 525 Bay St., Dundas Square Area ☎ 416/597–9200, 800/905–0667 🌐 www.marriotteatoncentre.com 🛏 451 rooms 🍴 No meals [M] Dundas.*

Pantages Hotel
$$ | **HOTEL** | Clean lines, gleaming hardwood flooring, and brushed-steel accents exude contemporary cool at this all-suites hotel. **Pros:** central location close to Eaton Centre and St. Lawrence Market; 24-hour restaurant on-site; great for long stays. **Cons:** some rooms in need

of upgrading; lobby and lower floors can be noisy; no on-site parking. $ *Rooms from: C$212* ✉ *200 Victoria St., Dundas Square Area* ☎ *416/362–1777* ⊕ *www.pantageshotel.com* ⟿ *95 suites* ⦿ *No meals* Ⓜ *Queen.*

Saint James Hotel
$$ | HOTEL | With a facade dotted with bay windows and topped with a wall of glass, this boutique hotel has plenty of clean-cut charm, with modern rooms with handsome hardwood floors and contemporary furniture. **Pros:** breakfast included—a rarity in Toronto; good value for the area; comfortable beds. **Cons:** some rooms can be dark; some street noise; long walk to parking. $ *Rooms from: C$239* ✉ *26 Gerrard St. E, Dundas Square Area* ☎ *416/645–2200* ⊕ *www.thesaintjameshotel.com* ⟿ *36 rooms* ⦿ *Free breakfast* Ⓜ *Dundas.*

Nightlife

With more neon lights than anywhere else in the city, and a big central square used for outdoor concerts and films, Yonge–Dundas Square is almost always busy. There are a number of good bars ideal for a drink before or after a show.

BARS
Jazz Bistro
BARS/PUBS | Finding a quiet place to relax and listen to great music is not so common in Toronto but, luckily, there's the Jazz Bistro. The sound system is state-of-the-art and the beautiful Steinway piano is affectionately referred to by regulars as the Red Pops. Blues, jazz, Latin, and world music acts perform almost every night. There's food, too. ✉ *251 Victoria St., Dundas Square Area* ☎ *416/363–5299* ⊕ *www.jazzbistro.ca* ⊘ *Closed Mon.* Ⓜ *Dundas.*

The Queen and Beaver Public House
BARS/PUBS | Toronto's British heritage thrives at this classy bar with a full restaurant, where the black-and-white photos on the walls reveal its true

passion: soccer. A Manchester United game is never missed, though NHL and other sporting events are also shown. The wine list is admirable for a pub while the beer and cider selection is focused on Ontario brews. Dressed-up British staples—available in the bar or ground-floor dining room—range from Scotch eggs to an excellent hand-chopped beef burger. ✉ *35 Elm St., Dundas Square Area* ☎ *647/347–2712* ⊕ *www.queenandbeaverpub.ca* Ⓜ *Dundas.*

Performing Arts

The Yonge and Dundas area is home to some of the most notable historical theaters in the city, including the Elgin and Winter Garden.

MAJOR VENUES
★ **Elgin and Winter Garden Theatre Centre**
THEATER | This jewel in the crown of the Toronto arts scene consists of two former vaudeville halls, built in 1913, one on top of the other. It's the last operating double-decker theater complex in the world (the Elgin is downstairs and the Winter Garden upstairs) and a Canadian National Historic Site. Until 1928, the theaters hosted silent-film and vaudeville legends like George Burns, Gracie Allen, and Edgar Bergen with Charlie McCarthy. Today's performances are still surrounded by magnificent settings: Elgin's dramatic gold-leaf-and-cherub-adorned interior and the Winter Garden's *A Midsummer Night's Dream*–inspired decor, complete with tree branches overhead. These stages host Broadway-caliber musicals, comedians, jazz concerts, operas, and Toronto International Film Festival screenings. Guided tours (C$12) are offered twice a week. ✉ *189 Yonge St., Dundas Square Area* ☎ *416/314–2871 tours* ⊕ *www.heritagetrust.on.ca/ewg* Ⓜ *Queen.*

★ **Massey Hall**
CONCERTS | Near-perfect acoustics and handsome, U-shape tiers have made Massey Hall a great place to enjoy music

Did You Know?

After being shuttered for decades, the restored Elgin and Winter Garden Theatre Centre is now a dazzling venue for everything from major musical theater productions to Toronto International Film Festival premieres.

since 1894—the year it opened with a performance of Handel's *Messiah*. It's always been a venerable place to catch big-time solo acts like Neil Young and Gilberto Gil, comedians, indie bands, and occasional dance troupes. *Massey Hall is slated to reopen after renovations in 2020.* ✉ *178 Victoria St., at Shuter St., Dundas Square Area* ☎ *416/872–4255* ⊕ *www.masseyhall.com* Ⓜ *Queen.*

THEATER
Ed Mirvish Theatre
THEATER | This 1920 vaudeville theater has had numerous names over the years, including the Pantages, the Imperial, and most recently the Canon. Now named in honor of local businessman and theater impresario Ed Mirvish, it's one of the most architecturally and acoustically exciting live theaters in Toronto. The theater itself is considered one of the most beautiful in the world and was refurbished in 1989. Designed by world-renowned theater architect Thomas Lamb, it has a grand staircase, gold-leaf detailing, and crystal chandeliers. ✉ *244 Victoria St., Dundas Square Area* ☎ *416/872–1212, 800/461–3333* ⊕ *www.mirvish.com* Ⓜ *Dundas.*

Shopping

Dundas Square is the go-to place for chain stores and cheap souvenir shops, which line Yonge Street to the north (though their numbers are beginning to dwindle). The mammoth Eaton Centre shopping mall has more than 230 stores (Coach, Banana Republic, and the Apple Store, to name a few).

BOOKS
The Silver Snail
BOOKS/STATIONERY | Independent bookstores have largely been driven out of this high-rent area, but the Snail is a little patch of geeky paradise at the city's busiest intersection. The long-running comic book shop, which occupies a second-floor space above Yonge Street,

is a prime source for marquee releases and indie graphic novels, along with tons of collectibles. You can people-watch at a window seat in the café with a drink from their specialty menu, like the Black Widow raspberry mocha. ✉ *329 Yonge St., Dundas Square Area* ☎ *416/593–0889* ⊕ *silversnail.com* Ⓜ *Dundas.*

SHOPPING CENTERS
★ Eaton Centre
SHOPPING CENTERS/MALLS | The 1.7-million-square-foot Eaton Centre shopping mall has been both praised and vilified since it was built in the 1970s, but it remains incredibly popular. From the graceful glass roof, arching 127 feet above the lowest of the mall levels with artist Michael Snow's exquisite flock of fiberglass Canada geese floating poetically in open space down to all the shops, there's plenty to appreciate.

There's a huge selection of shops and eateries, but here is a simple guide: the basement level contains the massive Urban Eatery food court. From there, the prices get higher with the altitude, with the top-floor Saks Fifth Avenue being every label-conscious shopper's dream.

✉ *220 Yonge St., Dundas Square Area* ☎ *416/977–6751* ⊕ *www.torontoeatoncentre.com* Ⓜ *Dundas, Queen.*

SPAS
Elmwood Spa
SPA/BEAUTY | This four-floor spa, located a few steps away from Yonge-Dundas Square, is a convenient spot to spend a day unwinding. A wide variety of facials, scrubs, and massages are available; those who spend a certain amount on services get complimentary access to the complex's swimming pool, a whirlpool, and steam rooms. The on-site restaurant serves light fare, with a prix-fixe option available and a patio on-site; there's also a juice bar. ✉ *18 Elm St., Dundas Square Area* ☎ *416/977–6751* ⊕ *elmwoodspa.com* Ⓜ *Dundas.*

Chapter 6

CHINATOWN, KENSINGTON MARKET, AND QUEEN WEST

Updated by
Jesse Ship

⦿ Sights
★★★★★

🍴 Restaurants
★★★★★

🏨 Hotels
★★★☆☆

🛍 Shopping
★★★★★

🍸 Nightlife
★★★★★

NEIGHBORHOOD SNAPSHOT

TOP EXPERIENCES

■ **Hit the Streets:** Kensington Market is overflowing with bohemian spirit, especially on Sunday when the streets fill with buskers, food vendors, street artists.

■ **A Little Bit of This, A Little Bit of That:** Dim sum in Chinatown is the best way to sample a wide selection of everything that's on the menu.

■ **Spend the Afternoon Shopping:** It's changed a lot over the years, but Queen West is still busy, buzzy, and a great place to shop.

■ **Meet the Old Masters:** At the well-regarded Art Gallery of Ontario you can take in works by Rembrandt, Warhol, Monet, and Matisse, to name a few.

■ **Eat Your Head Off:** If you're looking to try something new, the eateries on Queen West serve dishes that span the globe.

GETTING HERE

The Osgoode subway station is ideal for getting to Queen West, as is the 501 streetcar. The 510 Spadina streetcar (which originates at the Spadina subway station) services Chinatown and Kensington Market.

PLANNING YOUR TIME

When on Queen West, the Campbell House merits at least a half hour; the Art Gallery of Ontario an hour or more. Chinatown is at its busiest (and most fun) on weekends, but be prepared for very crowded sidewalks and much jostling. Kensington is great anytime, although it can feel a bit sketchy at night, and it gets mobbed on weekend afternoons. Just strolling around any of these neighborhoods can gobble up an entire afternoon.

QUICK BITES

■ **Blackbird Baking Co.** Hearty sandwiches on mouthwatering sourdough bread, traditional brioche buns, and creative palm-size Viennoiseries like tomato danishes and quirky chocolate corks fly off the shelves at this legendary boulangerie. ⊠ *172 Baldwin St., Kensington Market* ⊕ *blackbirdbakingco.com* Ⓜ *Nassau St.*

■ **Café Pamenar.** There's no better place for a quick espresso or another pick-me-up than at the poured-concrete walls of this uberhip meeting spot, complete with both front and back patios. ⊠ *307 Augusta St., Kensington Market* ⊕ *cafepamenar.com*

■ **King's Cafeé.** King's Café has become a mainstay for diners seeking vegan grub with an Asian accent. Artists, students, and young professionals flock. ⊠ *192 Augusta Ave., Kensington Market* Ⓜ *St. Patrick*

The areas along Dundas and Queen streets typify Toronto's ethnic makeup and vibrant youthfulness. To many locals, the Dundas and Spadina intersection means Chinatown and Kensington Market. While aging hipsters bemoan the fall of Queen West, which is bit by bit becoming an extension of the Eaton Centre, it's still a go-to for stalwart live music venues.

Chinatown and Kensington Market, often explored together, are popular destinations for tourists and locals alike. On a weekend morning, the sidewalks are jam-packed with pedestrians shopping for cheap produce and Chinese trinkets, lining up for a table at one of Chinatown's many restaurants, or heading to "the Market" for a little afternoon shopping. On the last Sunday of each month (May–October), Kensington Market goes car-free for Pedestrian Sundays, as the streets explode with live entertainment, street performances, and vendors selling handicrafts and clothing.

Queen West is busy any time of the year, mostly with teenagers hanging out at the Bell Media HQ (formerly MuchMusic studios) building and young fashionistas-in-training shopping up a storm.

Chinatown

Toronto's largest Chinatown has been going strong since a wave of Chinese immigration in the 1960s, and though rents are rising and hip cafés and streetwear boutiques have been creeping into the area, this stretch of Spadina Avenue is still home to some of the city's best Chinese eateries. Toronto's Chinatown has a population of more than 100,000 and it's packed with restaurants, bakeries, herbalists, and markets selling fresh fish and produce markets. It's busy all the time, especially at its epicenter, the Spadina–Dundas intersection.

Sights

★ Art Gallery of Ontario
MUSEUM | The AGO (as locals refer to it) is hard to miss: the monumental glass and titanium facade designed by Toronto native son Frank Gehry hovering over the main building is a stunning beauty. Near the entrance, you'll find visitors of all ages climbing in and around Henry Moore's *Large Two Forms* sculpture, located in Grange Park, just south of the gallery. Inside, the collection, which had an extremely modest beginning in 1900, is now in the big leagues, especially in terms of its exhibitions of Canadian paintings from the 19th and 20th centuries.

Anthony
Kym & Carole
Anthony & Family

Did You Know?

The Art Gallery of Ontario was architect Frank Gehry's first building in Canada, and the gorgeous Galleria Italia is one of its highlights.

Be sure to take a pause in the light and airy Walker Court, to admire Gehry's spiraling Baroque-inspired spiral staircase.

The Canadian Collection includes major works by the members of the Group of Seven (a group of Canadian landscape painters in the early 20th century, also known as the Algonquin School), as well as artists like Cornelius Krieghoff, David Milne, and Homer Watson. The AGO also has a growing collection of works by such world-famous artists as Rembrandt, Warhol, Monet, Renoir, Rothko, Picasso, Rodin, Degas, Matisse, and many others. The bustling Weston Family Learning Centre offers art courses, camps, lectures, and interactive exhibitions for adults and children alike. Free tours (daily 11 to 3 and Wednesday evening at 7) start at Walker Court. ✉ *317 Dundas St. W, at McCaul St., Chinatown* ☎ *416/979–6648, 416/979–6648* ⊕ *www.ago.net* 💵 *C$25* ⊘ *Closed Mon.* Ⓜ *St. Patrick.*

Spadina Avenue

NEIGHBORHOOD | The part of Spadina Avenue (pronounced "Spa- *dye*-nah") that runs through Chinatown, from Dundas Street to Queen Street, has never been chic. For decades it has housed a collection of inexpensive stores, import–export wholesalers, ethnic food stores, and eateries, including some first-class, plastic-table-cloth Chinese restaurants. Each new wave of immigrants—Jewish, Chinese, Portuguese, East and West Indian, South American—has added its own flavor to the mix. While gentrification is apparent in the form of modern bubble-tea shops and traditional Northern and Southern Chinese cuisine expanding past Cantonese mainstays, the basic bill of fare is still bargains galore: yards of remnants piled high in bins, designer clothes minus the labels, and the occasional rock-and-roll nightspot and late night greasy spoons. A streetcar line runs down the wide avenue to Front Street. ✉ *Spadina St., between Dundas St. and Spadina Ave., Chinatown.*

🍴 Restaurants

While urban sprawl has led to the creation of many mini-Chinatowns in the city, this is the original. University students and chefs from all over the city gather here for bubble tea, cheap eats, and late-night bites. There are various regional Chinese cuisines from spicy Szechuan to exotic Cantonese. Weekend mornings are a perfect for dim sum—it's a great way to sample Chinese staples.

AGO Bistro

$$$ | **BISTRO** | Like the art gallery in which it's located, this bistro was also designed by "starchitect" Frank Lloyd Wright, whose touches are seen in the minimalist decor and geometric ceilings. The dishes themselves, like the Basque-style eggs with chorizo, or grilled cornish hen with dandelion greens on coconut curry, are plated as works of art. **Known for:** prix-fixe meals inspired by gallery exhibits; French meets Western Canadian dishes; handcrafted cocktails. Ⓢ *Average main: C$24* ✉ *317 Dundas St. W, Chinatown* ✛ *Dundas and Beverly* ☎ *416/979–6688* ⊕ *ago.ca/dine/ago-bistro* ⊘ *Closed Mon.* Ⓜ *St. Patrick.*

Pho Pasteur

$ | **VIETNAMESE** | When you're having a late-night craving for Vietnamese food, this is the place for authentic bowls of pho or hearty curries with a side of crusty baguette to sop up the sauces. To drink, savor a slow-drip coffee with sweetened condensed milk or an exotic fruit milkshake in flavors like soursop or avocado. **Known for:** South Vietnamese–style goat curry; open around the clock; no-frills decor. Ⓢ *Average main: C$10* ✉ *525 Dundas St. W, Chinatown* ☎ *416/351–7188* 🚫 *No credit cards* Ⓜ *St. Patrick.*

R&D

$$$ | **ASIAN FUSION** | The idea here is that traditional Asian street food can exist side by side with modern haute cuisine, in a backdrop of fiery open kitchens and cavernous dining rooms. Experimental

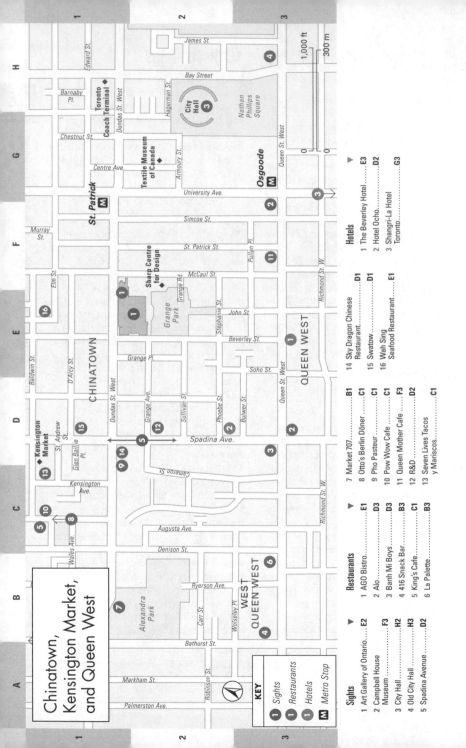

Chinatown, Kensington Market, and Queen West

KEY
- **1** Sights
- **1** Restaurants
- **1** Hotels
- **M** Metro Stop

Sights ▶
1 Art Gallery of Ontario......**E2**
2 Campbell House
Museum......................**F3**
3 City Hall........................**H2**
4 Old City Hall................**H3**
5 Spadina Avenue.........**D2**

Restaurants ▶
1 AGO Bistro..................**E1**
2 Alo.............................**D3**
3 Banh Mi Boys.............**D3**
4 416 Snack Bar............**B3**
5 King's Cafe.................**C1**
6 La Palette...................**B3**

7 Market 707.................**B1**
8 Otto's Berlin Döner.......**C1**
9 Pho Pasteur................**C1**
10 Pow Wow Cafe............**C1**
11 Queen Mother Cafe......**F3**
12 R&D.........................**D2**
13 Seven Lives Tacos
y Mariscos................**C1**

14 Sky Dragon Chinese
Restaurant................**D1**
15 Swatow.....................**D1**
16 Wah Sing
Seafood Restaurant......**E1**

Hotels ▶
1 The Beverley Hotel.......**E3**
2 Hotel Ocho.................**D2**
3 Shangri-La Hotel
Toronto....................**G3**

1,000 ft
300 m

entrées borrow European ingredients like cauliflower couscous, maple syrup, and pan-seared foie gras on brioche. **Known for:** nightly "Lucky 7" cocktail hour; tasty beef cheek banh mi; dim sum-style appetizers. $ *Average main: C$23 ⊠ 241 Spadina Ave., Chinatown ✛ 1 block south of Dundas ⊕ www.rdspadina.com ⊙ No lunch* Ⓜ *Osgoode.*

★ Sky Dragon Chinese Restaurant
$ | **CANTONESE** | Downtown Toronto's quintessential dim sum eatery overlooks all of Chinatown from its secret rooftop perch at the Dragon City Mall. Carts with towers of bamboo steamed baskets containing shrimp dumplings or black bean sauce chicken feet ("phoenix claws" in Chinese), banquet-size platters of noodles, and traditional delicacies like black or yellow curried cuttlefish are pushed around the hall by gregarious servers who tick off boxes from your order list as they are served. **Known for:** surprisingly expansive views through the huge windows; fans love the traditional Cantonese dim sum service; savory chive and shrimp dumplings. $ *Average main: C$8 ⊠ Dragon City Mall, top fl., 280 Spadina Ave., Chinatown ☎ 416/408–4999* Ⓜ *Spadina.*

Swatow
$ | **CHINESE** | If there is an equivalent to a fast-paced, casual Hong Kong–style diner in Chinatown, this would be it: the food is inexpensive and honest, and the setting is bright and spare. Diners enjoy heaping bowls of congee and customized noodle soups, including the best fish ball and shrimp dumpling bowls in town. **Known for:** excellent fried rice; open on holidays; communal tables. $ *Average main: C$10 ⊠ 309 Spadina Ave., Chinatown ☎ 416/977–0601 ⊕ www.swatowtoronto. com ⊟ No credit cards* Ⓜ *St. Patrick.*

Wah Sing Seafood Restaurant
$$ | **CHINESE** | One of a jumble of Asian eateries clustered on a tiny street opposite Kensington Market, this spacious restaurant is beloved for its two-for-one lobster deals. The crustaceans are delicious and tender, served either with black-bean sauce or a ginger-and-green-onion sauce. **Known for:** aquarium filled with a selection of fresh fish; whole braised duck is a favorite; simple and delicious dishes. $ *Average main: C$17 ⊠ 47 Baldwin St., Chinatown ☎ 416/599–8822 ⊕ www.wahsing.ca* Ⓜ *St. Patrick.*

▼ Nightlife

BARS
Cold Tea
BARS/PUBS | This bar in the heart of Kensington Market has a tucked-away entrance and intimate setting that give it an underground thrill. Head through the corridor of an indoor mini-mall, and you'll find a cozy room where rotating DJs play eclectic sets that encompass hip-hop, funk, electro, and garage rock. On Sunday afternoon, up-and-coming local chefs take turns manning the backyard patio BBQ for pop-up lunches. ■ **TIP→ There's no sign, so be sure to ask locals if you're having a hard time finding the place.** ⊠ *60 Kensington Ave., Chinatown* ☎ Ⓜ *Queen's Park.*

⊖ Shopping

ART GALLERIES
Bau-Xi Gallery
ART GALLERIES | Paul Wong, an artist and dealer from Vancouver, started this gallery, which is directly across the street from the Art Gallery of Ontario. The paintings and sculpture are a window into contemporary Canadian art, with both emerging and established artists featured. Just a few steps down at 324 Dundas West is Bau-Xi Photo, which shows Canadian and international fine art photography. ⊠ *340 Dundas St. W, at McCaul St., Chinatown* ☎ *416/977–0600 ⊕ www.bau-xi.com* Ⓜ *St. Patrick.*

Toronto's network of streetcars provides an excellent method of transportation for getting around downtown.

GIFTS AND SOUVENIRS
shopAGO
BOOKS/STATIONERY | Exiting through this gift shop is not mandatory, but you'll want to check out the overwhelming selection of curiosities, from touring exhibit memorabilia to books on maximal architecture, to pop art–inspired toys to prints of celebrated paintings. Adults and kids can shop side by side among the books and fun educational items. ⊠ *317 Dundas St. W, at McCaul St., Chinatown* ☎ *416/979–6610* ⊕ *www.ago.net/shop* Ⓜ *St. Patrick.*

Textile Museum Shop
CRAFTS | Tucked away on the second floor of the already hidden Textile Museum, this shop is one of the city's best-kept secrets and an absolute treasure trove. It overflows with textile-based art from Canadian artisans, as well as works by craftspeople from around the world keeping traditional, and often disappearing, skills alive. There are loads of books, scarves galore, unusual bags and hats, and crafty stuff for kids, too; many items

are accessibly priced. ■ **TIP→ Check out the changing exhibition on the second and third floors while you're here (admission charge) to develop a taste for the shop's featured items; past exhibits have included Finnish designer Marimekko and Afghan war rugs.** ⊠ *55 Centre Ave., at Dundas St. W and University Ave., Chinatown* ☎ *416/599–5321* ⊕ *www.textilemuseum. ca* Ⓜ *St. Patrick.*

HOME DECOR
Tap Phong Trading Co. Inc.
CERAMICS/GLASSWARE | The mops, brooms, and multicolor bins and buckets stacked outside make this kitchenware and restaurant equipment store appear much like all the other Chinese knickknack shops along Spadina. However, once you're inside you'll find endless aisles stacked to the rafters with rice bowls and bamboo steamers, and restaurateurs piling up their shopping trollies with glasses and servingware to feed the masses. ■ **TIP→ A gap halfway along the north wall leads to the industrial-scale equipment.** ⊠ *360 Spadina Ave., south of Baldwin*

St., Chinatown ☎ *416/977–6364* ⊕ *www. tapphong.com* Ⓜ *Spadina.*

Kensington Market

This collection of colorful storefronts, crumbling brick houses, delightful green spaces, and funky street stalls titillates all the senses. On any given day you can find Russian rye breads, Mexican paletas stands, fresh fish, imported cheese, and ripe fruit. And Kensington's collection of vintage-clothing stores is the best in the city.

The neighborhood took root in the early 1900s, when Russian, Polish, and Jewish inhabitants set up stalls in front of their houses. Since then, the area or "Kensington Market"—named after the area's major street, Kensington Street—has become a sort of United Nations of stores. Jewish and Eastern European shops sit side by side with Portuguese and Caribbean ones, as well as with a sprinkling of Vietnamese and Chinese establishments. ■TIP➜ **Weekends are the best days to visit, preferably by public transit; parking is difficult. Also note that the neighborhood is pedestrianized from dawn to dusk on the last Sunday of every month.**

🍴 Restaurants

In true Toronto fashion, Kensington Market's restaurants are a blend of cuisines from Mexican to French. There are plenty of spots to grab a quick bite, but there are also some stand-out places for a leisurely meal.

King's Cafe
$ | **ASIAN FUSION** | In a neighborhood where the bohemian vegetarian lifestyle is the norm, King's Café has become a mainstay for artists, students, and young professionals seeking vegan grub with an Asian accent. The setting is a serene and airy eatery with wide windows looking out onto bustling Augusta Avenue. **Known**

for: vegan takes on dim-sum classics; purple rice in lovely bento boxes; shop sells tea and spices. $ *Average main: C$11* ⊠ *192 Augusta Ave., Kensington Market* ☎ *416/591–1340* ⊕ *kingsvegetarianfood.ca* Ⓜ *St. Patrick.*

Market 707
$ | **INTERNATIONAL** | For a unique take on cheap eats, head east of Bathurst to Market 707, a strip of food stalls built out of repurposed shipping containers. Highlights include poutine and fresh crepes at NomNomNom Crepes; Colombian snacks and desserts (including cricket empanadas) by Cookie Martinez; soul-warming Filipino at Kanto by Tita Flips; and the gooey double cheese burger tater tots at Stuff'd Grilled Cheese. **Known for:** huge variety of cuisines available; street-side eating; innovative urban design. $ *Average main: C$9* ⊠ *707 Dundas St. W, Kensington Market* ✛ *East of Bathurst St.* ☎ *416/392–0335* ⊕ *scaddingcourt.org/market-707* ⊙ *Closed Mon.* ⊟ *No credit cards* Ⓜ *St. Patrick.*

Otto's Berlin Döner
$ | **GERMAN** | Otto's brings a nightlife-worthy spin to street snacks. The owners are former club promoters who fell in love with Berlin's most popular street eats and set about bringing them to Toronto. **Known for:** wide selection of beers on tap; Berlin-style street food; lightning-fast service. $ *Average main: C$10* ⊠ *256 Augusta Ave., Kensington Market* ☎ *647/347–7713* ⊕ *www.ottosdoner.com* Ⓜ *Queen's Park.*

Pow Wow Cafe
$$ | **CANADIAN** | Chef Shawn Adler prepares dinner-plate-covering "tacos" at his rustic 12-seater café and similarly sized front patio. Mains include piles of toppings for fusion brunch-focused dishes that incorporate everything from Indian curries, poached duck eggs, and edible flowers. **Known for:** smoked salmon croquettes are the perfect appetizer; try the beef taco with cumin sour cream; large portions are guaranteed. $ *Average*

main: C$18 ✉ *213 Augusta Ave., Kensington Market* ✣ *Augusta and Baldwin* ☎ *416/551–7717* 💳 *No credit cards.*

★ **Seven Lives Tacos y Mariscos**
$ | MEXICAN | With only 10 seats, this taco joint almost always has long lines, but it's worth the wait. The menu brings the best of SoCal and Tijuana seafood together, featuring taco options like the *gobernador* (smoked marlin and shrimp), and a vegetarian option with corn fungus (trust us, it tastes better than it sounds). **Known for:** delicious shrimp and cheese tacos; range of fiery hot sauces; gluten-free tortillas available. [$] *Average main: C$6.50* ✉ *69 Kensington Ave., Kensington Market* ☎ *416/803–1086* [M] *St. Patrick.*

Shopping

Tucked behind Spadina west to Bathurst Street, between Dundas and College streets to the south and north, is this hippie-meets-hipster collection of inexpensive vintage-clothing stores, cheap ethnic eateries, coffee shops, head shops, and specialty food shops specializing in cheeses, baked goods, fish, dry goods, health food, and more. **■ TIP➔ Be warned—this area can be extraordinarily crowded on weekends; do not drive.** Take the College streetcar to Spadina or Augusta, or the Spadina streetcar to College or Nassau.

CLOTHING

Bungalow
ANTIQUES/COLLECTIBLES | Teak tables, chairs, and cabinets give this vintage shop the feel of a strangely cavernous 1970s bungalow. Organized racks are filled with Hawaiian and second-hand T-shirts, vintage 1970s dresses, and comfortably worn jeans, but you'll also find new styles, too. ✉ *273 Augusta Ave., Kensington Market* ☎ *416/598–0204* 🌐 *www.bungalow.to* [M] *Spadina.*

Courage My Love
CLOTHING | The best and longest-running vintage store in Kensington Market is crammed with the coolest retro stuff, from sunglasses to sundresses, plus an ample supply of cowboy boots, and gently used Birkenstock sandals for guys and gals, all at low prices. Not everything is secondhand here: there's a wall of sparkly Indian-inspired clothing, lots of costume jewelry, Mexican luchador masks, and a selection of unique buttons. ✉ *14 Kensington Ave., Kensington Market* ☎ *416/979–1992* [M] *St. Patrick.*

Tom's Place
CLOTHING | Find bargains aplenty on brand-name suits and shirts from brands like Calvin Klein, Armani, and DKNY at this remnant from the market's old-world textile industry days. The larger-than-life Tom Mihalik, the store's owner, keeps his prices low (and will often go lower, if you ask politely). The sales staff can quickly navigate the selection and help you put together a complete and well-accessorized look. ✉ *190 Baldwin St., at Augusta St., Kensington Market* ☎ *416/596–0297* 🌐 *www.toms-place.com* [M] *St. Patrick.*

GIFTS AND SOUVENIRS

Kid Icarus
BOOKS/STATIONERY | At this old-school printing company, you'll find a range of whimsical illustrations including band posters, mock-retro tourism posters, and other one-of-a-kind creations. You'll also find screen-printed Greetings from Toronto postcards, art supplies, and contemporary indie crafts in the gift shop. ✉ *205 Augusta Ave., Kensington Market* ☎ *416/977–7236* 🌐 *www.kidicarus.ca* [M] *Spadina.*

Queen West

Queen West has become increasingly corporate as the years pass and rents rise, but this mazelike array of back alleys is a homegrown outdoor shrine to street art. The result of a city revitalization project, Graffiti Alley (sometimes referred to as Rush Lane) serves as an ever-changing museum of work by some of the city's foremost street artists, and is a perennially popular setting for music videos and photo shoots.

Sights

Campbell House Museum

MUSEUM | The Georgian mansion of Sir William Campbell, the sixth chief justice of Upper Canada, is now one of Toronto's best house museums. Built in 1822 in another part of town, the Campbell House was moved to this site in 1972. It has been restored with elegant early-19th-century furniture, and knowledgeable guides detail the social life of the upper class. Don't overlook the "Lost & Found" garden exhibit, salvaged from heritage buildings. ✉ 160 Queen St. W, Queen West ☎ 416/597–0227 ⊕ www.campbellhousemuseum.ca ⊠ C$10 ⊗ Closed Jan. and Mon. Ⓜ Osgoode.

City Hall

GOVERNMENT BUILDING | The design for Toronto's modern city hall, just across the way from the Old City Hall building, resulted from a 1956 international competition that received 520 submissions from architects from 42 countries. The winning presentation by Finnish architect Viljo Revell was controversial—two curved towers of differing height—but logical: an aerial view of City Hall shows a circular council chamber sitting like an eye between the two towers that contain office space. Revell died before his masterwork was opened in 1965, but the building has become a symbol of the thriving metropolis. A remarkable mural within the main entrance, Metropolis, was constructed by sculptor David Partridge from 100,000 nails.

Annual events at City Hall include November's Cavalcade of Lights celebration, featuring fireworks and live music amidst the glow of more than 525,000

lights illuminated across both the new and old city halls.

In front of City Hall, the 9-acre **Nathan Phillips Square** (named after the mayor who initiated the City Hall project) has become a gathering place for everything from royal visits to protest rallies, picnic lunches, and concerts. The reflecting pool is a delight in summer, and even more so in winter, when it becomes a skating rink. The park is also home to a Peace Garden for quiet meditation and Henry Moore's striking bronze sculpture The Archer. ✉ 100 Queen St. W, Bay St., Queen West ☎ 416/338–0338 ⊕ www.toronto.ca Ⓜ Queen.

Old City Hall

GOVERNMENT BUILDING | Opened in 1899, and used until 1965 when the "new" City Hall was built across the street, the old municipal building now operates solely as a courthouse. This imposing building was designed by E. J. Lennox, who was also the architect for Casa Loma and the King Edward Hotel. Note the huge stained-glass window as you enter. The fabulous gargoyles above the front steps were apparently the architect's witty way of mocking certain turn-of-the-20th-century politicians; he also carved his name under the eaves on all four faces of the building. The building has appeared in countless domestic and international TV shows and feature films. ✉ 60 Queen St. W, Queen West ⊗ Closed weekends Ⓜ Queen.

Restaurants

Queen West is a boisterous mix of galleries, hip clothing stores, and lots of good, reasonably priced restaurants.

★ Alo

$$$$ | **FRENCH FUSION** | The 10- to 16-course dinners here breathed a new life into the concept of the tasting menu for many Torontonians, thanks to a chef who channels refined French cooking techniques into beautifully composed plates. Past

Did You Know?

In 1973, an album of photographs found in a trash bin was donated to the Campbell House Museum. It included almost 60 interior images of the house from 1885 and formed the basis of the home's renovation that began in the late 1990s.

courses from the ever-changing offerings include striped bass with chanterelles and baby artichokes, Nova Scotia lobster tail paired with romesco and shishito peppers, and rack of pork offset with bing cherries, Swiss chard, and a dusting of pistachios. **Known for:** need to reserve weeks in advance; multicourse tasting menus; stunning presentation. $ *Average main: C$135* ⊠ *163 Spadina Ave., 3rd fl., Queen West* ☎ *416/260–2222* ⊕ *www.alorestaurant.com* ◷ *Closed Sun. and Mon.* Ⓜ *Osgoode.*

Banh Mi Boys

$ | **ASIAN** | Brothers David, Philip, and Peter Chau have banh mi in their blood—their parents opened one of the original Vietnamese sandwich shops in China-town—but they've taken the classic and decked it out with top-notch ingredients such as melt-in-your-mouth pork belly, duck confit, and kalbi beef. Other offerings include Asian-inspired tacos and steamed bao. **Known for:** a modern take on a classic eatery; crunchy kimchi fries; five-spice pork belly. $ *Average main: C$9* ⊠ *392 Queen St. W, Queen West* ☎ *416/363–0588* ⊕ *www.banhmiboys. com* Ⓜ *Osgoode.*

416 Snack Bar

$ | **ECLECTIC** | It takes its name from the city's most popular area code, so it's no surprise that 416—a dim, boisterous bar that echoes the general vibe of West Queen West—draws inspiration from the city around it. The menu of inexpensive small plates, best enjoyed with a cocktail or two, is a fun mishmash of cultures, from Jamaican to Chinese to Peruvian, that serves as a one-stop culinary crash course to this city of immigrants. **Known for:** sometimes controversial no-cutlery policy; fun spot for a first date; buzzy atmosphere. $ *Average main: C$8* ⊠ *181 Bathurst St., Queen West* ☎ *416/364–9320* ⊕ *416snackbar.com* ◷ *No lunch Mon.–Thurs.*

★ La Palette

$$$ | **FRENCH** | Known as one of the city's tried and true French bistros, this brightly decorated spot lives up to expectations with a menu full of excellent standards, including steak frites, duck confit, and mussels in white wine. The long bar at the front of the restaurant is a great spot for drinks or solo dining. **Known for:** short but well-chosen wine list; three-course prix-fixe dinner; great brunch. $ *Average main: C$28* ⊠ *492 Queen St. W, Queen West* ☎ *416/929–4900* ⊕ *www.lapalette. ca* Ⓜ *Osgoode.*

Queen Mother Cafe

$$ | **ASIAN FUSION** | A laid-back neighborhood institution, the Queen Mother has been popular with art students and broadcast-media types since the 1980s. The food is international, leaning toward Southeast Asian with European accents. **Known for:** atmosphere is somewhere between a pub and a pastry shop; try the chicken with a zesty lime coriander sauce; gluten-free salad bowls. $ *Average main: C$16* ⊠ *208 Queen St. W, Queen West* ✛ *At St. Patrick St.* ☎ *416/598–4719* ⊕ *www.queenmother-cafe.ca* Ⓜ *Osgoode.*

🛏 Hotels

In this trendsetting neighborhood, along Queen Street West beyond Bathurst Street, the hotels get more experimental and cutting-edge the farther west you go. Many highlight local art and music, and have noteworthy restaurants that practice sustainability.

The Beverly Hotel

$$ | **HOTEL** | A hip crowd congregates at the slender Beverly Hotel on Queen West, where the rooms feel like hip bachelor pads. **Pros:** feel the breeze on the spacious patio; high-tech concierge service; cutting-edge design. **Cons:** some rooms get street noise, especially in the morning; not all rooms have windows; standard rooms are small. $ *Rooms*

from: C$179 ⊠ 335 Queen St. W, Queen
West ☎ 416/493–2786 ⊕ www.bever-
leyhotels.com ⥁ 18 rooms ⦿ No meals
Ⓜ Osgoode.

Hotel Ocho

$$ | HOTEL | In a turn-of-the-century
warehouse building, this boutique hotel's
exposed brick-and-beam look typifies the
Queen West "cool" factor. **Pros:** close to
dozens of bars and restaurants; full-ser-
vice international restaurant; beautiful
renovation. **Cons:** restaurant often closed
for events; minimal breakfast offerings;
loud air-conditioners. Ⓢ *Rooms from:
C$199 ⊠ 195 Spadina Ave., Queen West
⊹ 1 block north of Queen and Spadina
☎ 416/593–0885 ⊕ www.hotelocho.
com ⥁ 12 rooms ⦿ Free breakfast
Ⓜ Osgoode.*

Shangri-La Hotel Toronto

$$$$ | HOTEL | It's hard to miss the distinc-
tive giant windows of the luxury chain's
Toronto location, where the level of chic-
ness meets the high standard of service.
Pros: luxury pool with private cabanas
and built-in TVs; big-name restaurants
on-site; 42-seat screening room. **Cons:**
pricey dim-sum and lobby tea service;
check-in can be slow; lobby can get very
busy. Ⓢ *Rooms from: C$550 ⊠ 188 Uni-
versity Ave., Queen West ⊹ University
and Richmond ☎ 647/788–8888 ⊕ www.
shangri-la.com/toronto ⥁ 202 rooms
⦿ No meals Ⓜ Osgoode.*

 Nightlife

BARS

BarChef

BARS/PUBS | The dark apothecarian interior
at BarChef features dimly lit chande-
liers and tabletop candles, which set
the stage for the wild and wonderful
concoctions that force patrons to reim-
agine classic cocktails. The bartender's
bag of tricks includes liquid nitrogen, so
cocktails foam over like a foggy mist onto
the table or turn into ice shards for a sen-
sory experience that looks as good as it

tastes. Purists can order a classic French
absinthe fountain while fans of whiskey
should order the signature Vanilla and
Hickory Smoked Manhattan, served in a
smoke-filled jar (but be warned, it clocks
in at a hefty C$50). While not highlight-
ed, a full page of the menu is devoted
to meats, cheeses, and elevated bar
snacks. ⊠ *472 Queen St. W, Queen West
☎ 416/868–4800 ⊕ www.barcheftoronto.
com.*

Bar Hop Brewco

BARS/PUBS | One of the city's most
interesting destinations for beer, Bar Hop
Brewco features an ever-changing lineup
of 40 rare and one-off beers on tap. The
location just off Queen West features an
aging room for beers, a large and sunlit
rooftop patio overlooking the main drag,
and a menu of refined beer-laced eats
like Porter-glazed garlicky mushrooms,
bacon and blue cheese mussels with
baguette, and bone marrow poutine.
⊠ *137 Peter St., Queen West ☎ 647/348–
1137 ⊕ www.barhopbar.com Ⓜ Osgoode.*

★ Drom Taberna

BARS/PUBS | Part rustic Balkan eatery, part
Gypsy cabaret, Drom Taberna is alive
with the spirit of the Romani people.
Every night of the week you'll be able to
experience a wide range of global sounds
from Middle-Eastern influenced Flamen-
co to interactive Balfolk dancing. Menu
must-tries include čevapi (Bosnian grilled
meat staple), goulash, and, of course, no
meal would be complete without a bowl
of Ukrainian-style borscht. Armenian,
Croatian, and Georgian wines dominate
the drinks list, along with a dozen different herbal digestifs, rakijas, and palinkas
(fruit brandies). ⊠ *458 Queen St. W,
Queen West ☎ 647/748–2099 ⊕ www.
dromtaberna.com Ⓜ Osgoode.*

MUSIC VENUES

★ Horseshoe Tavern

MUSIC CLUBS | This legendary, low-
ceilinged rock bar on Queen West has
earned a reputation as the place to play
for local acts and touring bands alike.

Opened in 1947 as a country music venue, the Shoe (as it's often called) hosted greats like Loretta Lynn, Willie Nelson, Hank Williams, and the Carter Family. The venue's scope widened to include the emerging folk, rock, and punk scenes in the 1960s and '70s, giving way to early appearances by the Police, Tom Waits, and the Talking Heads. The Rolling Stones even played a now-legendary surprise set here in 1997. Today, the venue books rock, indie, and punk acts from home and abroad. ⊠ *370 Queen St. W, at Spadina Ave., Queen West* ☎ *416/598–4226* ⊕ *www.horseshoetavern.com* Ⓜ *Osgoode.*

The Rex Hotel Jazz & Blues Bar

MUSIC CLUBS | Legendary on the Toronto jazz circuit since it opened in the 1980s, the Rex has two live shows every night, and multiple acts on weekend afternoons and evenings. Shows range from free (bring some cash for when the band passes the tip jar) to C$10. The kitchen serves diner fare, and there are even affordable hotel rooms available on-site. ⊠ *194 Queen St. W, at St. Patrick St., Queen West* ☎ *416/598–2475* ⊕ *www. therex.ca* Ⓜ *Osgoode.*

Rivoli

MUSIC CLUBS | One of Queen West's oldest venues, the Rivoli showcases indie music, theater, and comedy. Arcade Fire, Adele, and Tori Amos all graced the intimate back room's stage early in their careers, and for a cover charge (usually under C$12), you can catch what might be Toronto's next big thing. The low-lit front dining room offers a cozy atmosphere for snacking on their famous "wookie" balls or pad thai, while the front patio is prime real estate for watching eclectic Torontonians go about their days. Head upstairs to shoot some pool at one of 11 pay-by-the-hour tables. ⊠ *332 Queen St. W, at Spadina Ave., Queen West* ☎ *416/596–1501* ⊕ *www. rivoli.ca* Ⓜ *Osgoode.*

Performing Arts

DANCE
The National Ballet of Canada

DANCE | Canada's internationally recognized classical-ballet company was founded in 1951 and is made up of more than 70 dancers and its own orchestra boasting alumni Karen Kain as Artistic Director. It's the only company in Canada to perform a full range of traditional full-length ballet classics, including frequent stagings of *Swan Lake* and *The Nutcracker.* The company also performs contemporary works and is dedicated to the development of Canadian choreography. The season runs late fall through spring at the Four Seasons Centre for the Performing Arts, Canada's first purpose-built ballet opera house. ⊠ *Four Seasons Centre for the Performing Arts, 145 Queen St. W, Queen West* ☎ *416/345–9595, 866/345–9595 outside Toronto* ⊕ *national. ballet.ca* Ⓜ *Osgoode.*

THEATER
Theatre Passe Muraille

THEATER | Toronto's oldest alternative theater company, established in 1968, focuses on presenting themes of the unique Canadian cultural mosaic through collaborative productions and has launched the careers of many actors and playwrights. ⊠ *16 Ryerson Ave., near Queen and Bathurst Sts., Queen West* ☎ *416/504–7529* ⊕ *www.passemuraille. ca* Ⓜ *Osgoode or Bathurst.*

Shopping

ANTIQUES
Abraham's Trading Inc.

ANTIQUES/COLLECTIBLES | Indicative of a Queen West long gone, the most remarkable thing about Abraham's is that somehow it survives. Handwritten signs snarl "don't even think about it" amid a jumble of haphazardly piled rusty props and dusty "antiques" from doctor's bags and deer trophies to worn church doors, creepy clown shoes, and a sparkling collection of 1950s microphones. Purchasing anything will take some guts—few prices are marked, although everything, they say, is for sale. ✉ *635 Queen St. W, Queen West* ☎ *416/504–6210* Ⓜ *Osgoode or Bathurst.*

ART GALLERIES
401 Richmond

ART GALLERIES | Packed with galleries, a couple of interesting shops, and two cafés, this beautifully refurbished industrial building is an essential component of an exploration of Toronto's contemporary art scene. Check out **YYZ Artists' Outlet,** which holds consistently engaging shows in its two rooms, or **Gallery 44** for contemporary photography. There's also the respected artist collective **Red Head Gallery**. Make sure you don't miss well-stocked **Swipe** for books on all things design and **Spacing** for stylish Toronto-themed T-shirts, prints, and knickknacks that make perfect souvenirs. ✉ *401 Richmond Ave., Queen West* ☎ *416/595–5900* ⊕ *www.401richmond.net* ☾ *Closed Sun.* Ⓜ *Spadina or Osgoode.*

BOOKS
Swipe Design | Books + Objects

BOOKS/STATIONERY | Books on advertising, art, architecture, and urban planning pack the shelves of this aesthetically pleasing store, fittingly located in the arty 401 Richmond heritage building. Part of the store is devoted to modern gifts, including elegant writing tools, modern jewelry, and Pantone-theme everything. ✉ *B–04, 401 Richmond St. W, at Spadina Ave., Queen West* ☎ *416/363–1332, 800/567–9473* ⊕ *www.swipe.com* Ⓜ *Osgoode or Spadina.*

CLOTHING
Black Market

CLOTHING | Determined vintage buffs hunt through the racks of band T-shirts, faded jeans, worn shoes, and biker jackets in this unfinished upstairs warehouse-style location. They're also famous for their signature in-house screen-print tee

designs. ✉ *347 Queen St. W, Queen West* ☎ *416/599–5858* ⊕ *www.blackmarkettoronto.com* Ⓜ *Osgoode.*

Durumi

CLOTHING | Feminine, Korean-inspired styles such as slip dresses, wide-leg trousers, blouse-y tops, and delicate jewelry are sold at Durumi. ✉ *416 Queen St. W, west of Spadina, Queen West* ☎ *647/727–2591* ⊕ *www.thedurumi.com* Ⓜ *Osgoode or Spadina.*

Lululemon Athletica

CLOTHING | While there are several locations across Toronto for this Canadian yoga brand, their massive concept store on Queen West is a must-visit for runners and yogis alike. Along with plenty of staple athletic and loungewear for men and women, there's a juice bar, and a 1,000 square foot yoga and dance community studio upstairs. ✉ *318 Queen W, at Spadina Ave., Queen West* ☎ *416/703–1399* ⊕ *www.lululemon.com* Ⓜ *Osgoode.*

Original

CLOTHING | A blaze of rainbow colors, Original is glamorous, life-affirming, and more than a little outrageous. If you're heading to a gala or you're after a crinoline dress (in fuchsia), you *need* to come here. The endless selection of platforms, pumps, and wedges is outdone only by the dress section, found up a multicolor flight of stairs. ✉ *515 Queen St. W, at Augusta Ave., Queen West* ☎ *416/603–9400* Ⓜ *Osgoode.*

Tribal Rhythm

CLOTHING | A few vintage gems and pretty silk scarves may be found among the army jackets, cub scout uniforms, and 1970s polyester shirts and cowgirl attire, but most of the inventory is simply fun, kitschy, and kooky. Imported Thai and Indian trinkets, rows of body jewelry, tiaras, and wigs are part of the charming and eclectic mix. ✉ *248 Queen St. W, below street level, at John St., Queen West* ☎ *416/595–5817* Ⓜ *Osgoode.*

MUSIC
Duer

CLOTHING | Specially designed in B.C., these jeans and chinos are made for biking, climbing, or... the boardroom. The secret is their highly breathable and stretchy fabrics that feature reinforced stitching in the necessary "pain" points along with trendy cuts and colors. ✉ 491 Queen St. W, Queen West ☎ 647/794–1341 ⊕ www.duer.ca Ⓜ Osgoode.

Sonic Boom

MUSIC STORES | More than 1,500 daily arrivals fill the rows of this bright and cavernous mostly secondhand CD, vinyl, and DVD shop famous for their Broadway stage-caliber window installations. They carry many albums of local indie musicians—if the timing is right, you might catch one of them giving a live in-store performance. ✉ 215 Spadina Ave., at Sullivan, Queen West ☎ 416/532–0334 ⊕ www.sonicboommusic.com Ⓜ Spadina or Osgoode.

SHOES, HANDBAGS, AND LEATHER GOODS
Getoutside

SHOES/LUGGAGE/LEATHER GOODS | There are styles for men and women at this buzzy Queen W. mainstay, including Hunter wellies, Frye boots, Birkenstock sandals, Sperry top-siders, and a great selection of Laurentian Chief and Minnetonka street moccasins and mukluks. There are loads of Converse and Vans sneakers, too. ✉ 437 Queen St. W, at Spadina Ave., Queen West ☎ 416/593–5598 ⊕ www.getoutsideshoes.com Ⓜ Osgoode or Spadina.

SPAS
The Ten Spot

SPA/BEAUTY | With 16 locations around Toronto, this chain of beauty bars specializes in waxing, manicures, and facials and carries a selection of beauty products from independent and luxury brands. ✉ 749 Queen St. W, Queen West ☎ 416/915–1010 ⊕ www.the10spot.com.

SPECIALTY GIFTS
Malabar Ltd

SPECIALTY STORES | If you're in the market for fake blood or eyelashes, a 1950s wig, or a prosthetic nose, than look no further than Malabar. However, the real treasures are found in the costume rental department. Whether you're after a bishop's cassock, caveman's hides, a Bavarian dirndl, or Edwardian frock and parasol, the costume maker upstairs has pieced one together, which you can check out on the racks groaning under decades' worth of designs. Dancewear for adults and children can be found as well, from pointe ballet shoes and tutus to leotards and leg warmers. ✉ 14 McCaul St., Queen West ☎ 416/598–2581 ⊕ www.malabar.net Ⓜ Osgoode.

SPORTING GOODS
MEC

SPORTING GOODS | Mountain Equipment Co-op's flagship store is as busy as basecamp at Mt. Kilimanjaro. It's an excellent spot to pick up emergency winter gear, water purification tablets, or a camping coffee kit. The merino undershirts are highly coveted as they'll keep you toasty on winter nights. ✉ 300 Queen St. W, at Beverly St., Queen West ☎ 416/340–2667 ⊕ www.mec.ca/en/stores/toronto Ⓜ Osgoode.

Chapter 7

WEST QUEEN WEST, OSSINGTON, AND PARKDALE

7

Updated by
Natalia Manzocco

👁 Sights	🍴 Restaurants	🛏 Hotels	👜 Shopping	🍸 Nightlife
★★☆☆☆	★★★★★	★★★★☆	★★★★★	★★★★★

NEIGHBORHOOD SNAPSHOT

TOP EXPERIENCES

■ **Discover Up-and-Coming Designers:** Browse West Queen West's indie boutiques to find the city's coolest clothes.

■ **Take a Stroll in the Park:** Head to leafy Trinity Bellwoods Park for some people-watching in the shade.

■ **Grab a Brew:** Go for a bar crawl along Ossington and West Queen West, stopping at the Bellwoods Brewery patio.

■ **Hang with the Hipsters:** Take in a live performance or an art exhibit at the Gladstone Hotel or the Drake Hotel.

■ **Expand Your Culinary Horizons:** Eat delicious Tibetan food in Parkdale, or a mix of everything in West Queen West.

GETTING HERE

To get to West Queen West, take the 501 Queen streetcar and get off at Gladstone. For Parkdale, take the same streetcar to Landsdown or Roncesvalles Avenue.

To explore Ossington, take the 510 Queen streetcar to Ossington, the 505 Dundas streetcar to Ossington, or take the Line 2 subway to Ossington station and then take the 63 Ossington bus south.

PLANNING YOUR TIME

Afternoons (particularly weekends) are great for strolling and shopping along Queen. West Queen West and Ossington's nightlife scene tends to pull in people throughout the week, but things really get hopping on Friday and Saturday night.

QUICK BITES

■ **Bang Bang.** The lines might be long at this ice-cream shop specializing in artisanal flavors like "Thank You Very Matcha"—but oh is it worth the wait. ⊠ *93A Ossington Ave., Ossington* ⊕ *bangbangicecream.ca.*

■ **Cafe Neon.** Head to this colorful café for locally roasted espresso and reasonably priced brunch. ⊠ *1024 Queen St. W, West Queen West* ⊕ *cafeneon.ca.*

■ **Loga's Corner.** The atmosphere is basic but the Tibetan dumplings are super-tasty at this family-run counter-serve spot. ⊠ *216 Close, Parkdale.*

Originally a residential area for Portuguese immigrants and a home to Vietnamese karaoke bars and restaurants, Ossington and West Queen West are now *the* place for bohemian artists to set up shop, young chefs to take risks, and hipsters to party until the sun comes up. Neighboring Parkdale is also getting in on the scene, too.

Toronto is sprawling, but the city's excellent public transportation system makes it a cinch to get outside the city center to explore these hipper regions of the city's west end. Head out along Queen Street west of Bathurst, dubbed "West Queen West" by locals, and you'll start to see the neighborhood change. While it's still possible to find a run-down hardware store shouldering a high-end hipster bar, more of the latter are moving in these days. Many of the familiar chains that populate Queen West are spreading into the area as the neighbourhood gentrifies, but there's still plenty of indie boutiques, local restaurants, and hip watering holes that capitalize on the area's cool cred.

West Queen West

West Queen West's major landmarks, the Drake Hotel and the Gladstone Hotel, enjoy much success for their creative, eclectic decor and their happening nightlife. Businesses like these, which revolutionized the once-shabby district and gave it its current ubercool image, helped pave the way for a second wave of émigrés. An eclectic smattering of restaurants and more than 300 art galleries vie for real estate with fair-trade coffee shops and boutiques featuring Canada's hottest new designers. Trinity Bellwoods Park punctuates the neighborhood at the center and provides a beautiful setting for a picnic or a bench break. The area is served by the 301 and 501 trams, but the Metro does not go out here.

◉ Sights

Trinity Bellwoods Park
CITY PARK | FAMILY | Bellwoods (as the locals call it) is the top destination for west-enders to kick back on a sunny day. The tree-lined park runs between Dundas West and Queen West, which makes for a scenic stroll if you're heading between neighborhoods. It's a great spot for picnicking and people-watching—or dog-watching, if you take a bench next to the dog bowl. It's especially attractive in mid-May, when the cherry trees bloom pink, or when the leaves turn in the fall. ✉ *790 Queen St. W, West Queen West.*

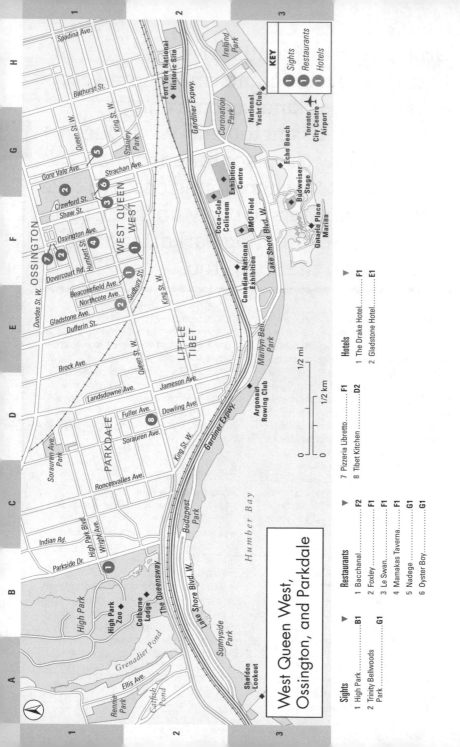

West Queen West, Ossington, and Parkdale

KEY

- ❶ Sights
- ❶ Restaurants
- ❶ Hotels

1/2 mi

1/2 km

🍴 Restaurants

West Queen West is home to some of the city's best restaurants in a range of cuisines from classic French to Asian fusion and all manner of other options.

Bacchanal

$$$ | FRENCH | Just off the main West Queen West drag, this modern French spot is swathed in blue velvet and brass, with an atmosphere that feels intimate despite the restaurant's considerable size. The food is classic French, with a twist and an artistic eye for plating; options range from hors d'ouevres to mains like steak frites and sea bream. **Known for:** beautifully made cocktails; wallpaper featuring local landmarks; tasty desserts. [$] *Average main: C$27* ✉ *60 Sudbury St., West Queen West* ☎ *416/586–1188* 🌐 *bacchanal.ca* 🕒 *No lunch.*

Le Swan

$$ | FRENCH | Once a classic Toronto diner, this intimate spot from local restaurateur Jen Agg pays homage to its greasy-spoon roots but with a French twist. The frequently evolving menu balances steak frites and Nicoise salads with tuna melts, onion rings, and grilled cheeses. **Known for:** vintage diner setting; excellent cocktails; late-night fondue. [$] *Average main: C$20* ✉ *892 Queen St. W, West Queen West* ☎ *416/536–4440* 🌐 *leswan.ca* 🕒 *No lunch Mon.–Thurs.*

Nadège

$ | BAKERY | This hot-pink patisserie is a top destination for Torontonians with a sweet tooth. Inside, long glass cases are filled with petits fours and fanciful pastries, as well as savory options like croissant sandwiches and salads, while the walls are lined with a candy shop's worth of sweets (all made in-house). **Known for:** on the corner of Trinity Bellwoods Park; chocolates in cute packaging; rainbow color macarons. [$] *Average main: C$10* ✉ *780 Queen St. W, West Queen West* ☎ *416/203–2009* 🌐 *nadege-patisserie.com.*

Oyster Boy

$$$ | SEAFOOD | Whether you order them baked, fried, or raw, oysters are the thing at this casual neighborhood spot. A chalkboard spells out what's fresh and available, along with sizing and prices for each, and there is an excellent selection of house-made condiments. **Known for:** extensive selection of oysters from Prince Edward Island; oyster shucking class on weekends; sustainably sourced seafood. [$] *Average main: C$25* ✉ *872 Queen St. W, West Queen West* ☎ *416/534–3432* 🌐 *oysterboy.ca* 🕒 *No lunch weekdays.*

🛏 Hotels

★ The Drake Hotel

$$$ | HOTEL | More than just a hotel, the Drake is also a bar, a club, and an art gallery that has been a focal point for the local media for well over a decade. **Pros:** locally made snacks and drinks in the minibar; stylish rooms packed with quirky touches; design-forward atmosphere. **Cons:** glass-doored bathrooms offer little privacy; party crowd takes over on weekends; smallish rooms. [$] *Rooms from: C$289* ✉ *1150 Queen St. W, West Queen West* ☎ *416/531–5042* 🌐 *www.thedrake.ca* 🔑 *19 rooms* 🍽 *No meals.*

Gladstone Hotel

$$ | HOTEL | Some boutique hotels pop art on their walls and call it a day, but at this Victorian-era beauty (complete with an antique elevator), the guest rooms are used as a canvas by a rotating cast of local artists. **Pros:** gallery-like atmosphere; very comfortable beds; on-site art installations. **Cons:** some noise from nearby trains (earplugs are provided); lacks niceties like room service; building shows signs of wear. [$] *Rooms from: C$249* ✉ *1214 Queen St. W, West Queen West* ☎ *416/531–4635* 🌐 *www.gladstonehotel.com* 🔑 *37 rooms* 🍽 *No meals.*

West Queen West is home to an increasing number of trendy boutiques and cutting-edge galleries.

Nightlife

BARS

★ The Drake Underground

BARS/PUBS | Locals know the Drake as a hub for art, culture, food, and perhaps above all—nightlife, with multiple spaces hosting parties, shows, and events on any given night. The basement is home to the Drake Underground, a venue that hosts live music and DJ nights, while the rooftop Sky Yard patio serves drinks surrounded by eye-popping art installations. The main floor restaurant has seasonally driven lunch, dinner, and brunch. ⊠ *1150 Queen St. W, West Queen West* ☎ *416/531–5042* ⊕ *www.thedrakehotel.ca.*

★ Gladstone Ballroom & Melody Bar

BARS/PUBS | The Gladstone draws an artsy Toronto crowd that appreciates a multitude of creative endeavors like music performances, poetry slams, burlesque shows, and more. The Ballroom is the main event space, with soaring ceilings, exposed brick walls, and a long, dark-wood bar. The Melody Bar serves cocktails until late most nights. There are also art galleries on the second, third, and fourth floors of the hotel. ⊠ *1214 Queen St. W, Queen West* ☎ *416/531–4635* ⊕ *www.gladstonehotel.com.*

✖ Performing Arts

THEATERS

The Great Hall

MUSIC | This sweeping Queen Anne Revival–style building, built in 1889, is one of the city's grandest concert venues, with four event spaces packed over three stories. The biggest is the Main Hall, a cavernous auditorium with a second-floor gallery overlooking the main floor below, though events are also often held in the basement-level Longboat Hall, which was once a gymnasium in the building's former life as a YMCA. The space hosts everything from touring bands to theater events to craft shows. Stop in to Otto's Bierhalle, which occupies the ground floor, for craft beer and great German-style snacks.

✉ *1087 Queen St. W, West Queen West* ☎ *416/792–1268* ⊕ *thegreathall.ca.*

The Theatre Centre

THEATER | Built in 1909 as a library and funded by industrialist Andrew Carnegie (of Carnegie Hall fame), this heritage property underwent extensive renovations and reopened as a theater space in 2016. There's a café and bar as well. ✉ *1115 Queen St. W, West Queen West* ☎ *416/538–0988* ⊕ *theatrecentre.org.*

Shopping

West of Bathurst, Queen Street is the place to go for cool shops and slick home goods stores. The cool quotient steps up a notch as the street extends farther west, beyond Trinity Bellwoods Park, with mid-century modern antique shops, cutting-edge galleries, and a flurry of big name designers.

ART GALLERIES
★ Craft Ontario Shop

CRAFTS | This shop, run by the Ontario Crafts Council, stocks an excellent selection of Canadian crafts, including blown glass, fine woodwork, textiles, jewelry, and pottery—from earthy stoneware to contemporary ceramics. There's also a gallery featuring work by artists and craftspeople from around Ontario. Upstairs is The Devil's Workshop, which sells jewelry by local makers and hosts a popular DIY wedding band workshop. ✉ *1106 Queen St. W, West Queen West* ☎ *416/921–1721* ⊕ *www.craftontario. com.*

BOOKS
★ Type Books

BOOKS/STATIONERY | The selection of carefully selected fiction and nonfiction at Type Books includes many hard-to-find authors, as well as fun cards and gifts. The art and architecture section has pride of place at the front of the shop and the extensive children's area is in a bright spot up a few steps at the back.

✉ *883 Queen St. W, West Queen West* ☎ *416/366–8973* ⊕ *www.typebooks.ca.*

CLOTHING
★ Gravitypope

CLOTHING | This Canadian chain, frequented by fashionistas in the know, has an impressive selection that includes Paul Smith, Commme des Garçons, and Marni. The collections include menswear and womenswear, but shoes are the specialty, with designers including Church's, Camper, Hunter, Rag & Bone, Doc Martens,and many more. ✉ *1010 Queen St. W, West Queen West* ☎ *647/748–5155* ⊕ *www.gravitypope.com.*

Horses Atelier

CLOTHING | This homegrown womenswear label counts some of Toronto's coolest artists, musicians, and actors among its fans. The tiny flagship shop stocks the latest in Horses' limited-run pieces, all hand-sewn in Toronto. The chic, albeit pricey, modern staples include peasant-sleeve dresses, quirky coveralls, and workwear-inspired jackets. ✉ *198 Walnut Ave., West Queen West* ☎ *416/504–9555* ⊕ *horsesatelier.com* ☉ *Closed Mon.*

Town Moto

SPECIALTY STORES | Hard-core bikers and Sunday riders alike will love this shop that's jam-packed with all types of motorcycle gear. On top of stylish biker jackets, there's an impressive selection of helmets, goggles, and natty biker boots, as well as motorcycle-theme posters by local artists and a slew of T-shirts. ✉ *132 Ossington Ave., West Queen West* ☎ *416/856–8011* ⊕ *www.townmoto.com.*

HOME DECOR
Quasi Modo

HOUSEHOLD ITEMS/FURNITURE | Design classics such as Herman Miller lounge chairs and Noguchi lamps are just a sampling of the high-end design pieces you'll find here—there's not a knock-off in sight. There's also sleek modern homewares for the kitchen and bathroom as well. ✉ *1079 Queen St. W, West Queen West*

🕾 *416/703–8300* ⊕ *www.quasimodo-modern.com* ⊘ *Closed Sat.–Mon.*

Urban Mode

HOUSEHOLD ITEMS/FURNITURE | Modern and trend-oriented furniture and home decor at this West Queen West spot include the playful furniture designs of Blu Dot, along with space-age sofas from Softline and bold Scandinavian creations from Muuto. ✉ *145 Tecumseth St., West Queen West* 🕾 *416/591–8834* ⊕ *www.urbanmode.com* ⊘ *Closed Sun.*

GIFTS

Drake General Store

GIFTS/SOUVENIRS | Only-in-Canada gifts like Mountie paraphernalia, patterned thermal onesies, super-soft Toronto-made Shared tees, and log-shaped pillows are tucked into every nook and cranny of this offbeat shop, an offshoot of the Drake Hotel across the street. The selection is a mix of fun, beautiful, and inexplicable, running the gamut from the Drake's exclusive designs to hip brands from across Canada and around the world. ✉ *1151 Queen St. W, West Queen West* 🕾 *416/538–2222* ⊕ *www.drakegeneral-store.ca.*

SHOES, HANDBAGS, AND LEATHER GOODS

Heel Boy

SHOES/LUGGAGE/LEATHER GOODS | A tried-and-true spot for cool and cute footwear for both sexes, Heel Boy stocks the unique styles by well-known brands like Hunter, Ted Baker, Sam Edelman, and Superga, as well as on-trend bags and accessories. ✉ *773 Queen St. W, West Queen West* 🕾 *416/362–4335* ⊕ *www.heelboy.com.*

Zane

JEWELRY/ACCESSORIES | This sleek accessory boutique is the place to visit for trendy offbeat like handbags by Rebecca Mink-off and local designer Opelle; Le Specs sunglasses; and stunning handmade jewelry from Canadian indie designers like Jenny Bird, Biko, and Captve.

✉ *753 Queen St. W, West Queen West* 🕾 *647/352–9263* ⊕ *www.visitzane.com.*

Ossington

If your Toronto travel plans include a bar crawl, odds are you'll end up on the Ossington strip, which has become one of the city's hottest nightlife destinations in recent years.

Restaurants

★ Foxley

$$ | ASIAN FUSION | Like the appealingly bare-bones aesthetic of its space (exposed brick, hardwoods, candlelight), this creative Asian-Spanish bistro offers unadorned dishes that are jammed with flavor. After traveling for a year, chef-owner Tom Thai returned to Toronto with inspiration from places like Asia, Latin America, and the Mediterranean and the menu features a couple dozen tapas-style offerings, including spicy blue crab and avocado salad, lamb and duck prosciutto dumplings, and grilled side ribs with sticky shallot glaze. **Known for:** well-priced wine list; daily ceviche specials; seasonal back patio. Ⓢ *Average main: C$20* ✉ *207 Ossington St., Ossington* 🕾 *416/534–8520* ⊘ *No lunch. Closed Sun.*

★ Mamakas Taverna

$$$ | GREEK | The Danforth might be the epicenter of Greek food in Toronto, but across town on trendy Ossington, Mamakas is doing some of the city's best Greek cooking. Diners snack on classics mezes like rich, creamy tzatziki and roasted eggplant before diving into more unusual dishes like lamb carpaccio or tea-brined chicken. **Known for:** Athenian market-inspired decor; seafood flown in from Greece; delicious desserts. Ⓢ *Average main: C$28* ✉ *80 Ossington Ave., Ossington* 🕾 *416/519–5996* ⊕ *mamakas.ca* ⊘ *No lunch.*

Pizzeria Libretto

$$ | PIZZA | Authentic thin-crust pizzas are fired in an imported wood-burning oven at this pizza joint that adheres to the rules set by Naples's pizza authority. Go classic with the Margherita D.O.P.—with San Marzano tomatoes, fresh basil, and *fior di latte* mozzarella—or branch out with *nduja* (spicy salami) or duck confit pies. **Known for:** casual atmosphere; vegan and gluten-free options; prix-fixe weekday lunch deal. $ *Average main: C$16* ✉ *221 Ossington Ave., Ossington* ☎ *416/532–8000* ⊕ *www.pizzerialibretto. com.*

Nightlife

BARS

Bellwoods Brewery

BREWPUBS/BEER GARDENS | This restaurant, bar, and on-site brewery has been a smash hit since it opened in 2012. If the sun is shining, expect a line for the spacious patio, a great spot to sample the always evolving craft beer selection. Sour beer fans should try their seasonal fruit-infused Jelly King, which has beer drinkers queueing up at the bottle shop on release day. The hearty snacks run the gamut from Canadian cheeses and terrine to a crispy Newfoundland cod sandwich. ✉ *126 Ossington Ave., Ossington* ⊕ *bellwoodsbrewery.com.*

★ The Lockhart

BARS/PUBS | Don't go in expecting wizarding robes and animatronic owls at this Harry Potter–theme bar. Instead, think of the laid-back, neon-lit little watering hole as the cocktail bar J. K. Rowling's Diagon Alley never had. Grab a seat next to the wall of Potions and Elixirs and spot the references hidden around the bar while sipping fantastical cocktails like the Befuddlement Draft served on fire in a glass cauldron. ✉ *1479 Dundas St. W, Little Portugal* ☎ *647/748–4434* ⊕ *www. thelockhart.ca* ☞ *Closed Mon.*

Reposado

BARS/PUBS | The Toronto bar buzz is largely centered on Ossington Avenue, where bars, shops, and galleries have sprung up like wildflowers over the past few years. One of the first (it opened in 2007) and still going strong is this classy tequila bar. The dark wood, large windows, big back patio, and mix of DJs and live jazz set the tone for a serious list of tequilas meant to be sipped, not slammed, and Mexican nibbles like tequila-cured salmon with crostini. ✉ *136 Ossington Ave., Ossington* ☎ *416/532–6474.*

DANCE CLUBS

Lula Lounge

DANCE CLUBS | Latin-music lovers of all ages dress up to get down to live Afro-Cuban, Brazilian, and salsa music at this old-school hot spot. Pop and rock musicians also perform occasionally. Fridays and Saturday salsa nights include a dinner prix-fixe (C$59), a salsa lesson, and a live band performance. Lula is also an arts center, with dance and drumming lessons and a multitude of festivals and cultural events. ✉ *1585 Dundas St. W, Little Portugal* ☎ *416/588–0307* ⊕ *www. lula.ca.*

Shopping

ART GALLERIES

Stephen Bulger Gallery

ART GALLERIES | The collection of roughly 30,000 photos focuses on historical and contemporary Canadian photography, with ongoing exhibitions. ✉ *1356 Dundas St. W, Little Portugal* ☎ *416/504–0575* ⊕ *www.bulgergallery.com* ۞ *Closed Sun. and Mon.* Ⓜ *Dundas.*

CLOTHING

Annie Aime

CLOTHING | Bright comfy threads with a European aesthetic and a focus on sustainable production are the focus here. Expect items like chunky knits from Icelandic brand Matthildur, breezy dresses by France's Cotelac, and

Turkish-made deconstructed sweaters from Crea Concept. The eye-catching graffiti painting inside makes for a perfect fashion backdrop. ⊠ *42 Ossington Ave., Ossington* ☎ *416/840–5227* ⊕ *www. annieaime.com.*

I Miss You Vintage

CLOTHING | The immaculately restored picks in this upscale consignment shop include familiar names such as Pucci, Hermès, Dior, and Yves Saint Laurent. Gentlemen can head next door to I Miss You Man for vintage Versace button-downs, gently used Acne jackets, and Dior shades—all in near-mint condition. ⊠ *63 Ossington Ave., Ossington* ☎ *416/916–7021* ⊕ *imissyouvintage.com.*

Victoire

CLOTHING | This Ottawa-based boutique has its finger firmly on the pulse of home-grown fashion, stocking edgy cocktail dresses from Montréal designer Eve Gravel, cute sundresses from Canadian label Birds of North America, and a treasure trove of jewelry and fun gifts. ⊠ *129A Ossington Ave., Ossington* ☎ *416/588–6978* ⊕ *www.victoireboutique.com.*

VSP Consignment

CLOTHING | Want to score a designer label on a dime? Head to this beautifully laid out consignment store. The staff curate a selection of gently-worn pieces from Prada, Marni, Theory, Celine, and other top-shelf brands. ⊠ *1410 Dundas St. W, Little Portugal* ☎ *416/588–9821* ⊕ *www. vspconsignment.com.*

MUSIC

★ Rotate This

MUSIC STORES | Music lovers in the know come here for underground and independent music from Canada, the United States, and beyond. ⊠ *186 Ossington Ave., Ossington* ☎ *416/504–8447* ⊕ *www.rotate.com.*

Parkdale

Farther west than even West Queen West is Parkdale, a fairly gritty neighborhood that's become home to North America's largest Tibetan community. Shops offering everything from beef *momos* (dumplings) to singing bowls infuse the area with a unique local character. In neighboring Roncesvalles is High Park, a sprawling green space with a beautiful pond.

 Sights

★ High Park

CITY PARK | **FAMILY** | One of North America's loveliest parks, High Park (at one time the privately owned countryside "farm" of John George Howard, Toronto's first city architect) is especially worth visiting in summer, when the many special events include professionally staged Shakespeare productions. Hundreds of Torontonians and guests arrive at dinnertime and picnic on blankets before the show. Admission is by donation. Grenadier Pond in the southwest corner of the park is named after the British soldiers who, it's said, crashed through the soft ice while rushing to defend the town against invading American forces in 1813. In summer there are concerts on Sunday afternoon, and there is skating in winter. At the south end of High Park, near Colborne Lodge, is the **High Park Zoo,** which is open daily from dawn to dusk. It's more modest than the Toronto Zoo but a lot closer to downtown and free. Kids love walking among the deer, Barbary sheep, emus, yaks, llamas, peacocks, and bison. **Colborne Lodge** was built more than 150 years ago by Howard on a hill overlooking Lake Ontario. This Regency-style "cottage" contains its original fireplace, bake oven, and kitchen, as well as many of Howard's drawings and paintings. Other highlights of the 399-acre park are a large swimming pool, tennis courts, fitness trails, and hillside

Did You Know?

Toronto's largest public park is popular with hikers, who enjoy its many trails. There's also a modest zoo and Colborne Lodge, the home of John Howard, who once owned this land and gave it to the city under the condition that it remain a park. In the yard of Colborne House you can find a cannon that once stood on the lakefront as a deterrent to U.S. forces, who considered invading Toronto during the War of 1812.

gardens with roses and sculpted hedges. There's limited parking along Bloor Street north of the park, and along the side streets on the eastern side. **■ TIP→ June through August, on the first and third Sunday, free 1½-hour walking tours depart across the street from Grenadier Restaurant at 10:30 am.** ✉ *Bordered by Bloor St. W, Gardiner Expressway, Parkside Dr., and Ellis Park Rd. Main entrance off Bloor St. W at High Park Ave., Bloor West Village* ☎ *416/392–1748* 🌐 *www.highpark.org* [M] *High Park.*

🍴 Restaurants

Tibet Kitchen

$ | NEPALESE | Parkdale has a number of great *momo* (Tibetan dumplings) places, but Tibet Kitchen stands out with a cozy sit-down atmosphere and a menu that takes just enough liberties with classic recipes. Chicken, beef, and veggie dumplings are all great, but you can also get them doused in mild curry broth or a sweet, tangy tamarind sauce. **Known for:** the chili chicken gets rave reviews; traditional drinks like butter tea; good portion sizes. [$] *Average main: C$12* ✉ *1544 Queen St. W, West Queen West* ☎ *416/913–8726* 🌐 *tibetkitchen.ca* 🕒 *Closed Tues.*

🛍 Shopping

CLOTHING

In Vintage We Trust

CLOTHING | Looking for a vintage jacket bearing the logo of your favorite sports team? You'll probably find it at this Parkdale boutique, which stocks hip retro clothing at reasonable prices. Vintage denim, broken-in concert tees, and even vinyl records are on the shelves. ✉ *1580 Queen St. W, West Queen West* ☎ *416/781–0395* 🌐 *invintagewetrust.com.*

JEWELRY AND ACCESSORIES

Studio Brillantine

GIFTS/SOUVENIRS | While most of the shops in Parkdale are down-to-earth and practical, Studio Brillantine skews trendy with Comme des Garcons wallets, Issey Miyake foldable bags, Vivienne Westwood jewelry, Alessi kitchenware, and collectible vinyl toys. ✉ *1518 Queen St. W, West Queen West* ☎ *416/536–6521* 🌐 *studiobrillantine.com.*

Chapter 8

LESLIEVILLE, GREEKTOWN, LITTLE INDIA, AND THE BEACHES

8

Updated by
Natalia Manzocco

Sights ★★☆☆☆ **Restaurants** ★★★★☆ **Hotels** ★★☆☆☆ **Shopping** ★★★★☆ **Nightlife** ★★★☆☆

NEIGHBORHOOD SNAPSHOT

TOP EXPERIENCES

■ **Discover Interesting Eateries:** Dig into a gyro in Greektown, or eat a dosa that's larger than your head in Little India.

■ **Head Back to the Beach:** Toronto has some pretty stretches of sand, many of them in a neighborhood helpfully called The Beaches.

■ **Music All Night Long:** Take in some of the best local bands at the Danforth Music Hall or the Opera House.

■ **Find a Bargain:** Browse the hip boutiques and vintage stores along the main drag in Leslieville.

■ **Look for the Lighthouse:** Tommy Thompson Park is the place for sailing, biking, or bird-watching.

GETTING HERE

To explore Leslieville, take the 501 Queen streetcar east from downtown to Coxwell Avenue and walk west along Queen Street East. To get to Little India, take the same streetcar east to Coxwell Avenue.

To get to Greektown, take the Line 2 Bloor-Danforth subway to Pape station and walk west along Danforth Avenue.

PLANNING YOUR TIME

With its array of small boutiques, Leslieville is a good place to stroll around in during the day. Stick around for dinner or grab a nightcap—the low-key bar scene tends to attract locals throughout the week. By contrast, The Beaches are great to explore on a sunny day, tough the area tends to be pretty dead after dark. Little India and Greektown both tend to come alive during the day on weekends, when locals and families are out in full force, and both are busy destinations for dinner on Friday and weekends.

QUICK BITES

■ **Ed's Real Scoop.** There are two locations of this ice-cream parlor along Queen East, serving unique and delicious flavors (try the toasted marshmallow) and fresh waffle cones. ✉ 920 Queen St. E, Leslieville; 2224 Queen St. E., The Beaches ⊕ edsrealscoop.com

■ **Leslieville Pumps.** A 24-hour gas station serves some of the best barbecue in the area? Yes; the poutine is good, too. ✉ 929 Queen St. E, Leslieville ⊕ leslievillepumps.com

■ **Messini.** This reliable spot for gyros offers both dine-in and quick-service takeout. ✉ 445 Danforth Ave., The Danforth ⊕ messini.ca Ⓜ Chester

Toronto's East End may be removed from the big tourist draws, but the area is home to charming neighborhoods, beaches, and some of the city's best international restaurants.

Along Queen Street East, the thoroughfare that passes through many of the city's most interesting neighborhoods, Leslieville is home to an increasingly hip mix of bars, shops, and restaurants. The offerings here lean toward local designer boutiques, chic eateries, and a number of indie coffee shops. To the north is the Danforth, better known to locals as Greektown. Late-night tavernas and authentic eateries keep this neighborhood busy at all hours. Every August the Taste of the Danforth (⊕ www.tasteofthedanforth.com) shows off the area's best.

Running along Gerrard Street north of Leslieville is the area known as Little India. The neighborhood hosts the largest collection of South Asian businesses in North America, and includes everything from crystal sellers to sari shops. The area comes alive in the evening and on weekends, when families head out for a meal or street snacks.

Pass through Leslieville along Queen East and you'll get to The Beaches, a laid-back area lined with heritage homes. The beaches that give the area its name are a popular destination for swimmers and sunbathers in the summertime. Businesses here cater to well-to-do local families, with funky womenswear, relaxed dining, and cute home goods shops. An annual jazz festival in July (⊕ beachesjazz.com) attracts thousands of listeners.

Leslieville

This low-key neighborhood has tons of hidden-gem restaurants, stores, and cafés, but it's also become an epicenter of the city's recent brewery boom.

Sights

Tommy Thompson Park
CITY PARK | This park comprises a peninsula that juts 5 km (3 miles) into Lake Ontario. It was created from bricks and rubble from construction sites around the city and sand dredged for a new port. It has quickly become one of the best areas in the city for cycling, jogging, walking, sailing, photography, and especially bird-watching. The strange, artificial peninsula is home (or a stopover) to the largest breeding colony of double-crusted cormorants in North America, as well as dozens of species of terns, ducks, geese, and great egrets. At the end of the spit of land, you'll find a red-and-white lighthouse, in addition to amazing views of downtown and an awesome sense of isolation in nature. Bird-watching is best from May to mid-October. To get here, head east along Queen Street to Leslie Street, then south to the lake. No private vehicles are permitted in the park. ⊠ Entrance at foot of Leslie St., south of Lakeshore Blvd. E, Leslieville ☎ 416/661–6600 ⊕ www.tommythompsonpark.ca.

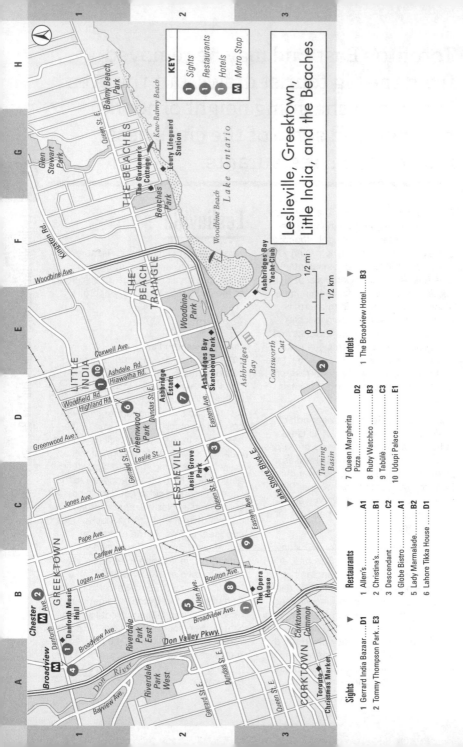

Leslieville, Greektown, Little India, and the Beaches

KEY
- **1** Sights
- **1** Restaurants
- **1** Hotels
- **M** Metro Stop

0	1/2 mi
0	1/2 km

Sights ▶

1 Gerrard India Bazaar	D1
2 Tommy Thompson Park	E3

Restaurants ▶

1 Allen's	A1
2 Christina's	B1
3 Descendant	C2
4 Globe Bistro	A1
5 Lady Marmalade	B2
6 Lahore Tikka House	D1
7 Queen Margherita Pizza	D2
8 Ruby Watchco	B3
9 Tabülé	C3
10 Udupi Palace	E1

Hotels ▶

1 The Broadview Hotel	B3

🍴 Restaurants

Descendant
$$$ | **ITALIAN** | Toronto has its fair share of delicate, thin-crust Neapolitan pizza, but this is where the locals go to indulge their carb cravings with thick Detroit-style pies cooked in rectangular pans. Go simple with the classic pepperoni, or try an international twist with the Jaffna (a twist on Sri Lankan *kothu roti*) or a jerk chicken version with pineapple. **Known for:** hip industrial setting; good selection of local beers; long waits at peak times. [$] *Average main: C$21* ✉ *1168 Queen St. E, Leslieville* ☎ *647/347–1168* 🌐 *descendantdsp.com* ⏲ *Closed Mon.*

★ Lady Marmalade
$$ | **ECLECTIC** | A Leslieville staple for more than a decade, this restaurant occupies an airy two-floor space with huge windows in a gorgeous old home just north of the main Queen East drag. It's a lovely spot for hearty, homey brunch dishes like cheddar jalapeño waffles, washed down with coffee in vintage Corningware mugs. **Known for:** classy, modern dining room; great variations on eggs Benedict; long waits at peak times. [$] *Average main: C$16* ✉ *265 Broadview Ave., Leslieville* ☎ *647/351–7645* 🌐 *ladymarmalade.ca* ⏲ *No dinner.*

Queen Margherita Pizza
$$ | **PIZZA** | One of the best pizza places east of town, this industrial-chic space with dark wooden floors and tables is all about authenticity when it comes to the Neapolitan pizza oven. Favorites include the classic Margherita, topped with tomato sauce, mozzarella, and basil, as well as the Dominator, with rapini, fennel sausage, and smoked mozzarella. **Known for:** Neapolitan-style pies with gently charred crusts; don't pass up the appetizers; scrumptious desserts. [$] *Average main: C$18* ✉ *1402 Queen St. E, Unit 8, Leslieville* ☎ *416/466–6555* 🌐 *www.qmpizza.com* ⏲ *No lunch Fri.* [M] *Pape.*

Ruby Watchco
$$$$ | **CANADIAN** | Chef Lynn Crawford, a household name in Canada, runs this industrial-chic restaurant, where hyper-local sourcing dictates the one starter, main, cheese course, and dessert available per evening (though vegetarian options are available). If you decide to place your trust in Crawford's hands, you can count on your meal to be farm-fresh and bursting with flavor. **Known for:** run by a celebrity chef; four-course tasting menu; intimate atmosphere. [$] *Average main: C$58* ✉ *730 Queen St. E, Leslieville* ☎ *416/465–0100* 🌐 *rubywatchco.ca* ⏲ *No lunch. Closed Sun. and Mon.*

★ Tabülè
$$ | **MIDDLE EASTERN** | Bold Middle Eastern flavors and spices are showcased at Tabülè, where traditional appetizers include baba ghanoush and hummus served with warm flatbread, and standout falafel fried to a deep golden brown and served with thick, rich tahini sauce. Grilled meats and seafood are also excellent. **Known for:** Moroccan-chic decor; varied drinks list; colorful back patio. [$] *Average main: C$19* ✉ *810 Queen St. E, Leslieville* ☎ *416/465–2500* 🌐 *www.tabule.ca* [M] *Broadview.*

🛏 Hotels

The Broadview Hotel
$$$ | **HOTEL** | This dramatic historic building is the setting for one of the hippest hotels in town, with quirky rooms, stylish restaurants, and a sprawling rooftop deck. **Pros:** fun and funky decor is a hipster paradise; also a hopping nightlife destination; best bet in this part of town. **Cons:** party vibe not everyone's cup of tea; some rooms get street noise; no spa or workout area. [$] *Rooms from: C$350* ✉ *106 Broadview Ave., Leslieville* ☎ *416/362–8439* 🌐 *thebroadviewhotel.ca* 🔑 *58 rooms* 🍴 *No meals.*

Nightlife

BARS

The Rooftop at the Broadview Hotel
BARS/PUBS | This hotel's sceney rooftop bar has become the East End's number-one party spot. The lounge space is encased in a glass pyramid that allows for stunning views of the surrounding city, with a wraparound open-air deck. If the top floor isn't your scene, there's also a neon-bathed terrace a few doors down, plus a chill downstairs bar space perfect for a glass of wine and a few oysters from their daily selection. ⌧ *Broadview Hotel, 106 Broadview Ave., Leslieville* ☎ *416/362–8439* ⊕ *thebroadviewhotel.ca.*

WAYLA
BARS/PUBS | An east-end stronghold for the city's queer scene, WAYLA (an acronym for "what are you looking at?") welcomes a varied crowd to its warren-like space, which includes a dance floor. Live music, comedy, karaoke, dance parties, and DJ residencies are all on the calendar. ⌧ *996 Queen St. E, Leslieville* ☎ *416/901–5570* ⊕ *waylabar.ca.*

MUSIC VENUES

Opera House
MUSIC CLUBS | This late 19th-century vaudeville theater retains some of its original charm, most notably in its proscenium arch over the stage. The 850-capacity venue hosts internationally touring acts of all genres. Locals like to reminisce about seeing such diverse acts as Nirvana, Lucinda Williams, Kings of Leon, LCD Soundsystem, M.I.A., and the Black Keys, here. ⌧ *735 Queen St. E, Leslieville* ☎ *416/466–0313* ⊕ *www.theoperahousetoronto.com.*

🅢 Shopping

Head east to Leslieville, a slice of Queen East stretched between Carlaw and Greenwood. Once noted mostly for antiques and junk shops, Leslieville has become the place for hip clothing boutiques and brunch spots.

ANTIQUES

★ Gadabout
ANTIQUES/COLLECTIBLES | This antique shop is a rummager's paradise. The shelves groan with 1950s salt and pepper shakers, snake skin handbags, costume jewelry, and Hudson's Bay blankets, and there are racks of vintage clothing that range from the 1800s to the 1970s. There's even an extensive section of vintage menswear. You can rifle through the scores of carefully labeled drawers to find magicians' business cards, Nana Mouskouri specs, and creepy vintage curling irons. Display cases burst with curios—medicinal bottles, a collection of eggshell-faced Japanese dolls, and a feng shui compass. ⌧ *1300 Queen St. E, Leslieville* ☎ *416/463–1254* ⊕ *www.gadabout.ca.*

ART GALLERIES

Arts Market
ANTIQUES/COLLECTIBLES | More than 50 artisans and purveyors display their wares in tiny spaces where vintage collections rub shoulders with mixed-media paintings, artisanal soaps, and rhubarb jam. ⌧ *1114 Queen St. E, Leslieville* ☎ *416/546–8464* ⊕ *www.artsmarket.ca.*

CLOTHING

Any Direct Flight
CLOTHING | At the eastern edge of Leslieville, Any Direct Flight offers retro-inspired yet contemporary designs for women. The spacious, exposed-brick rooms have comfy couches encouraging leisurely browsing of the feminine yet edgy collection of slouchy pants, sweater dresses, and asymmetric tops. You can even mull over your clothing options at the in-store café. ⌧ *1382 Queen St. E, Leslieville* ☎ *416/504–0017.*

Bergström Originals
CLOTHING | Christina Bergström's bold, bright designs are created with an eye for quality and wearability. Slip on an

ankle-length dress in multicolor stripes, or a punchy printed blouse, and you'll see what we mean. There's also a great selection of chunky heels and colorful flats from brands like Fly London. ✉ *781 Queen St. E, Leslieville* ☎ *416/595–7320* 🌐 *www.bergstromoriginals.com.*

Doll Factory by Damzels

CLOTHING | The Doll Factory carries 1950s gingham and sailor-inspired pin-up looks from Toronto designers Damzels in this Dress, and other rock 'n' roll retro designs from across the continent. Chunky heels and polka-dot wedges are on the shelves, as are high-waisted bikinis perfect for flattering those curves. Another branch can be found in Roncesvalles at 394 Roncesvalles Avenue. ✉ *1122 Queen St. E, Leslieville* ☎ *416/598–0509* 🌐 *www.damzels.com.*

Good Neighbour

CLOTHING | This hip boutique, which occupies two floors of a Victorian home, is a one-stop shop for the whole fashion-forward family. The women's section features cute dresses from indie brands, denim from Citizens of Humanity, and lingerie by Fortnight and Mary Young. Head up the steep stairs to the men's section, which features Filson bags and upscale toiletries. ✉ *935 Queen St. E, Leslieville* ☎ *647/350–0663* 🌐 *goodnbr.com.*

Greektown

This area along Danforth Avenue named after Asa Danforth, an American contractor who cut a road into the area in 1799, has a dynamic ethnic mix, although it's primarily a Greek community. In the heart of the neighborhood, east of Chester subway station is the area referred to as "Greektown," with its bakeries turning out mouthwatering baklava, tyropita (cheese pie), and touloumbes (fried cinnamon-flavored cakes soaked in honey), and a number of late-night taverns. Summer is the best season to visit, as most eateries have patios open and are busy until the wee hours of morning.

🍴 Restaurants

Historically known as Greektown, the Danforth has gotten an infusion of international restaurants, which makes for more varied dining options.

Allen's

$$$ | **IRISH** | Slide into a well-worn wood booth or sit at a checkered table at this low-key steak house, complete with oak bar and pressed-tin ceiling. The steaks and Guinness-braised lamb shanks get rave reviews, but the hamburgers, ground in-house, might be Allen's secret weapon. **Known for:** willow-shaded patio in summer; 380 types of whiskey; decadent desserts. [$] *Average main: C$25* ✉ *143 Danforth Ave., Danforth* ☎ *416/463–3086* 🌐 *www.allens.to* [M] *Broadview.*

Christina's

$$ | **GREEK** | **FAMILY** | Who doesn't have a foodie love affair with Greek appetizers? At Christina's, you can order them individually or as a large platter combination that comes with warm pita. **Known for:** ample portions of Greek classics; heated patio open year-round; live music on weekends. [$] *Average main: C$20* ✉ *492 Danforth Ave., Danforth* ☎ *416/463–4418* 🌐 *www.christinas.ca* [M] *Chester.*

Globe Bistro

$$$ | **CANADIAN** | The motto here is "think global. eat local," and the Globe does justice to this by letting locally raised main ingredients like elk and rainbow trout shine in Canadian-inspired dishes. The interior is classy, if a tad dated; weather permitting, you may want to try the swanky rooftop patio. **Known for:** sample everything at the dinnertime tasting menu; eclectic wine list with a Canadian focus; popular brunch. [$] *Average main: C$27* ✉ *124 Danforth Ave., Danforth* ☎ *416/466–2000* 🌐 *www.globebistro.*

Greektown serves some of the best Greek food in North America.

com 🕑 *Closed Mon. and Tues. No lunch Wed. and Thurs.* Ⓜ *Broadview.*

Nightlife

BARS
Dora Keogh
BARS/PUBS | Crossing the threshold into this Danforth pub, decked out with cozy wooden booths (or "snugs") is like time-warping to the Emerald Isle. Folk, rock, and traditional Irish musicians perform here regularly, and the Guinness is always flowing. ✉ *141 Danforth Ave., Danforth* 📞 *416/778–1804* 🌐 *dorakeogh. to* Ⓜ *Broadview.*

The Only Cafe
BARS/PUBS | The delightfully divey Only, on a relatively quiet stretch of the Danforth, is known as one of the city's best beer bars, with 25 taps plus more than 200 bottles and cans. The atmosphere is dim and raucous, with 1990s alt-rock blasting on the stereo. During the day, half of the bar is a coffee shop. ✉ *972 Danforth Ave., Danforth* 📞 *416/463–7843* 🌐 *www. theonlycafe.com* Ⓜ *Donlands.*

MUSIC VENUES
★ Danforth Music Hall
MUSIC CLUBS | Built as a cinema in 1919, this stately theater is now a live music venue that attracts popular touring acts the run the gamut of punk, rock, rap, folk, and electronic music, and even stand-up comedy. Notable performers here have included Rihanna, Blue Rodeo, St. Vincent, and Dave Chappelle. ✉ *147 Danforth Ave., Danforth* 📞 *416/778–8163* 🌐 *www.thedanforth.com* Ⓜ *Broadview.*

Shopping

Greektown is best known as a place to eat, and appropriately there's a fair amount of culinary retail to go along with the grazing. Carrot Common, just east of Chester subway, houses New Age businesses like the Big Carrot and its juice bar, yoga and massage studios, along with a few independent boutiques.

FOOD

The Big Carrot

FOOD/CANDY | This popular health-food supermarket carries good selections of organic produce, health and beauty aids, and vitamins. There's a vegetarian café and juice bar on-site and freshly prepared foods for takeout. ✉ *348 Danforth Ave., Danforth* ☎ *416/466–2129* 🌐 *www.thebigcarrot.ca* [M] *Chester.*

HOME DECOR

IQ Living

HOUSEHOLD ITEMS/FURNITURE | If you like kitchen gadgets, you might lose a few hours here. Check out the rainbow array of Emile Henry ceramic cookware, Le Creuset enamelware, and bright nesting bowls and utensils by the innovative Joseph Joseph. There's also a vast selection of insulated lunch boxes and bags, including take-along bento boxes can be found, along with funky Popsicle molds, barware, and any other obscure gadget your kitchen may be lacking. ✉ *542 Danforth Ave., Danforth* ☎ *416/466–2727* 🌐 *www.iqliving.com* [M] *Pape or Chester.*

Little India

Follow your nose through the sweets shops, food stalls, and curry restaurants, and allow your eyes to be dazzled by storefront displays of jewelry, Hindu deities, and swaths of sensuous fabrics ablaze with sequins. The area really comes alive in the evening, when those with hungry bellies stroll in search of a fiery madras, creamy korma, or hearty masala curry. Many of the restaurants offer inexpensive but delicious buffet lunches and dinners, and they get especially busy on weekends.

The area is home to a diverse group of people, and there are many festivals throughout the year. During the biggest event, the three-day Festival of South Asia in July (🌐 *www.festivalofsouthasia.com*), stages are set for colorful music and dance performances, and the streets fill with the tantalizing scents of snack stalls and the calls of vendors peddling everything from henna tattoos to spicy corn on the cob. In late autumn, the Hindu Festival of Lights (Diwali) is celebrated with a fun and fiery street fete.

👁 Sights

Gerrard India Bazaar

NEIGHBORHOOD | The Gerrard India Bazaar isn't a place, exactly. It's a strip of Gerrard Street that's home to more than 100 shops and restaurants with a South Asia flavor. One of the city's top cultural landmarks, it's the place to find colorful saris, ceramic incense burners, and *barfi* (a milk-based dessert) and other handmade sweets. It's also home of the Festival of South Asia. ✉ *Gerrard St., between Greenwood Ave. and Coxwell Ave., Toronto.*

🍴 Restaurants

Lahore Tikka House

$$ | **NORTH INDIAN** | A trip to Little India isn't complete without hitting up this raucous Pakistani-North Indian spot, popular with locals and families. You might have a bit of a long wait at peak times (generally Friday and weekend nights), but standout biryani, kebabs, tandoori chicken, and sizzling plates of tikka will be your reward. **Known for:** colorful tuk-tuks and rickshaws as decor; huge covered side patio; house-made kulfi for dessert. [$] *Average main: C$16* ✉ *1365 Gerrard St. E, Little India* ☎ *416/406–1668* 🌐 *lahoretikkahouse.com.*

Udupi Palace

$$ | **INDIAN** | The fluorescent lights and metal chairs lend this basement restaurant a rather basic atmosphere but all is forgiven when you taste the *dosas* (pancakes made with fermented rice batter) at this meat-free Indian restaurant, beloved by herbivores and omnivores alike. They also do excellent renditions

of classic snacks like *pakoras* and *bhaji*, as well as curries like *aloo gobi* or *saag paneer*. **Known for:** wide range of vegetarian and vegan dishes; sunny dining room; sharable dishes. [$] *Average main: C$15* ✉ *1460 Gerrard St. E, Little India* ☎ *416/405–8189* 🌐 *udupipalace.ca.*

The Beaches

This neighborhood's official name has been a source of controversy since the 1980s: The Beach versus The Beaches. It boils down to whether you view the four separate beaches—Woodbine, Balmy, Kew, and Scarboro—as one collective entity. When the area decided to welcome tourists with fancy, emblematic street signs, the long-running debate surfaced. While officially "The Beach" won, most Torontonians still call the neighborhood The Beaches.

Beaches

Kew-Balmy Beach

BEACH—SIGHT | Just a 10-minute walk east on the boardwalk from Woodbine Beach, the officially merged stretch of Kew Beach, Scarboro Beach, and Balmy Beach is a bit pebbly and slightly more secluded, making it ideal for those seeking a quieter stroll or a dip in the lake. Look for the historic Leuty Lifeguard Station, which was built in the 1920s. Kayak and stand-up paddleboard rental shops sit along the shore. **Amenities:** food and drink; lifeguards; parking (paid); showers; toilets. **Best for:** walking; sunrise; swimming. ✉ *1 Beech Ave., The Beach* 🌐 *toronto.ca/parks.*

Woodbine Beach

BEACH—SIGHT | The largest, and probably best-known, of all the area beaches spans 37.5 acres along the coast of Lake Ontario. You'll find beachgoers of all ages swimming, sunbathing, picnicking, strolling the boardwalk, and playing volleyball on one of the numerous outdoor courts. There are a few takeout restaurants here, as well as the upscale Neruda restaurant. **Amenities:** food and drink; lifeguards; parking (paid); showers; toilets. **Best for:** partiers; sunrise; swimming; walking. ✉ *1675 Lake Shore Blvd. E, The Beach* 🌐 *toronto.ca/parks.*

Activities

WATER SPORTS

Kayak and canoe rentals are fairly easy to come by at The Beaches, but stand-up paddleboarding has become an increasingly popular activity on the Lake Ontario shores.

Surf The Greats

SURFING | This Leslieville surf shop offers introductory courses in lake surfing and stand-up paddleboarding. Surfing classes are scheduled a few days in advance to ensure you'll have good weather conditions. You can also join tours of hidden locations around the waterfront. ✉ *250 Carlaw Ave., Unit 101, Leslieville* ☎ *647/479–8969* 🌐 *surfthegreats.org.*

Shopping

The Beaches is known for casual-clothing stores, gift and antiques shops, and bars and restaurants.

FOOD

Nutty Chocolatier

FOOD/CANDY | A Beaches institution, the Nutty Chocolatier serves ice cream in house-made waffle cones, as well as handmade molded chocolates and truffles from Port Perry, just northeast of Toronto. The old-school candy—Charleston Chew and Tootsie Rolls—and British imports like Irn Bru, Walker's Crisps, Flakies, and Yorkshire Tea are equally popular. ✉ *2179 Queen St. E, The Beach* ☎ *416/698–5548* 🌐 *thenuttychocolatier.com.*

HOME DECOR
Seagull Classics Ltd.
HOUSEHOLD ITEMS/FURNITURE | Cottage-chic is the name of the game at this popular home decor shop that's all about cute, woodsy decor items like rugs, retro deck chairs, and Tiffany-style lamps. There's a nice selection of furniture, and they also do custom orders. ⊠ *1974 Queen St. E, The Beach* ☎ *416/690–5224* ⊕ *www. seagullclassics.com.*

SHOES, HANDBAGS, AND LEATHER GOODS
Nature's Footwear
SHOES/LUGGAGE/LEATHER GOODS | Established in 1978, this tiny, family-run shoe shop specializes in comfortable walking shoes. They carry an impressive selection of styles, sizes, and widths by Birkenstock, Crocs, Keds, and Sperry Topsiders, as well as moccasins and Sorel and Kamik boots for winter. ⊠ *1971a Queen St. E, The Beach* ☎ *416/691–6706.*

Chapter 9

QUEEN'S PARK, THE ANNEX, AND LITTLE ITALY

Updated by
Natalia Manzocco

👁 Sights	🍴 Restaurants	🛏 Hotels	🛍 Shopping	🍸 Nightlife
★★★★☆	★★★★★	★☆☆☆☆	★★☆☆☆	★★★☆☆

NEIGHBORHOOD SNAPSHOT

TOP EXPERIENCES

■ **Feel Like Royalty at Casa Loma:** This grand display of extravagance has 98 rooms, two towers, creepy passageways, and lots of secret panels.

■ **Take a Culinary Trip:** Grab some great eats—Italian or otherwise—in Little Italy, which has gone from take-out pizza to dining destination.

■ **Stroll Around Stunning Queen's Park:** Visit the handsome parliamentary buildings around the perimeter of one of the city's prettiest parks.

■ **Show Your School Spirit:** Explore the University of Toronto's historic campus, starting with the splendor of Hart House.

■ **Go Out on the Town in The Annex:** Linger over a coffee or a pint in one of the city's most happening neighborhoods.

GETTING HERE

Use the subway to reach the University of Toronto (St. George and Queen's Park stations), Casa Loma (Dupont station), The Annex (Spadina and Bathurst stations), and Queen's Park (Queen's Park station). Little Italy can be reached by streetcar 506 along College Street (since College Street turns into Carlton Street at Yonge, this streetcar's often also called the "Carlton Car").

PLANNING YOUR TIME

The Queen's Park and Annex areas are nice places to take a stroll any time of year because many of the attractions bring you indoors. A visit to the legislature and one or two of the museums or libraries would make a nice half-day (or more) program. Give yourself at least a few hours for a full tour of Casa Loma and about an hour for the Bata Shoe Museum. Make an evening of dinner and drinks in Little Italy.

QUICK BITES

■ **Flock.** This quick-service chain tops delicious salads with fresh rotisserie chicken. ⊠ *661 University Ave., Queen's Park* ⊕ *eatflock.com* Ⓜ *Queen's Park*

■ **One Love Vegetarian.** This Caribbean veggie joint is beloved for its corn soup and roti. ⊠ *854 Bathurst St., The Annex* ⊕ *oneloveveg.tel* Ⓜ *Bathurst*

■ **P.G. Cluck's.** Folks come from all over for this take-out counter's fried chicken sandwiches. ⊠ *610 College St., Little Italy* ⊕ *pgclucks. com*

This vast area that encompasses a huge chunk of Toronto's downtown core holds several important attractions, but it couldn't feel further from a tourist trap if it tried, bringing together Toronto's upper crust, Ontario's provincial politicians, Canada's intellectual set, and a former Italian neighborhood turned entertainment district.

Take a break in one of The Annex's many casual spots and you could be rubbing shoulders with a student cramming for an exam, a blocked author looking for inspiration, or a busy civil servant picking up a jolt of caffeine to go.

The large, oval Queen's Park circles the Ontario Provincial Legislature and is straddled by the sprawling, 160-acre downtown campus of the University of Toronto. Wandering this neighborhood will take you past century-old colleges, Gothic cathedrals, and plenty of quiet benches overlooking leafy courtyards and student-filled parks.

The University of Toronto's campus overflows west into The Annex, where students and scholarly types while away the hours after class. This frantic section of Bloor Street West abounds with ethnic restaurants and plenty of student-friendly cafés and bars, plus two of the city's must-see attractions: the Bata Shoe Museum and Casa Loma.

Similarly energetic is Little Italy, where music spills out of lively eateries and patios are packed in the summertime. The myriad wine bars and boutique clubs in this neighborhood attract a mix of locals and tourists.

Queen's Park

To locals, Queen's Park refers to not only the neighborhood, but the historic Ontario Legislative Building that serves as the seat of the provincial government. Built in 1893, the pink sandstone building takes its cues from British architecture, with a hefty collection of artwork from Canada and abroad. Just a few blocks west, you'll hit the edge of the University of Toronto's sprawling campus, which is packed with stately buildings, including the neo-Gothic Hart House. Bibliophiles won't want to miss the Thomas Fisher Rare Book Library, which is home to a Babylonian cuneiform tablet and one of the few surviving copies of Shakespeare's First Folio.

 Sights

Hart House
COLLEGE | Looking for all the world like a setting from one of the Harry Potter novels, this neo-Gothic student center

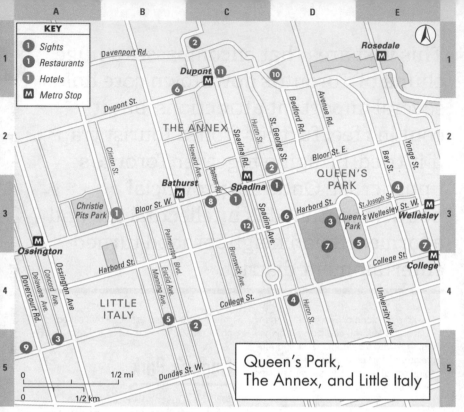

Queen's Park, The Annex, and Little Italy

opened its door in 1919. Originally restricted to male students, Hart House has been open to women since 1972. Keep your eyes peeled for artwork scattered throughout the building, including a revolving collection of works by famed Canadians like Emily Carr and evocative landscape paintings by the Group of Seven. As many as 200 works are on display throughout the building, most of which can be viewed by anyone willing to wander in and out of the rooms. Each year new pieces are carefully chosen by a committee made up of mainly students, and today the collection is reported to be worth several million dollars. Part of a federation with University of Toronto Art Centre, the **Justina M. Barnicke Gallery** comprises two rooms of mixed-media art showcasing homegrown talent. The stained-glass windows and vaulted ceiling in the Great Hall are impressive, but so is chef Suzanne Baby's cuisine at the resident **Gallery Grill.** Try one of the grilled fish dishes, house-made pasta, or a creative vegetarian option while enjoying the elegant surroundings. ⊠ *University of Toronto, 7 Hart House Circle, Queen's Park* ☎ *416/978-2452* ⊕ *www.harthouse. ca* Ⓜ *Museum.*

Lillian H. Smith Branch of the Toronto Public Library

LIBRARY | FAMILY | Honoring the memory of the city's first children's librarian, this branch houses the Osborne Collection of Early Children's Books, which contains nearly 80,000 items ranging from the 14th century to the present. In addition, the Merril Collection of Science Fiction, Speculation, and Fantasy includes another 80,000 items, on everything from parapsychology to UFOs. ⊠ *239 College St., Queen's Park* ☎ *416/393-7746* ⊕ *www. torontopubliclibrary.ca* ⊠ *Free* Ⓜ *Queen's Park.*

Ontario Legislative Building

GOVERNMENT BUILDING | This 1893 Romanesque Revival building, made of pink Ontario sandstone, has a wealth of exterior detail; inside, the huge, lovely halls echo half a millennium of English architecture. The long hallways are hung with hundreds of oils by Canadian artists, many of which capture scenes of the province's natural beauty. Take one of the frequent, 30-minute-long tours from the lobby to see the chamber where the 124 MPPs (members of provincial parliament) meet. The many statues dotting the lawn in front of the building, facing College Street, include one of Queen Victoria and one of Canada's first prime ministers, Sir John A. Macdonald. The lawn is also the site of Canada Day celebrations and the occasional political protest. These buildings are often referred to simply as Queen's Park, after the park surrounding them. ⊠ *1 Queen's Park, Queen's Park* ☎ *416/325-0061* ⊠ *Free* ⊘ *No guided tours weekends early Sept.–mid-May* Ⓜ *Queen's Park.*

Thomas Fisher Rare Book Library

LIBRARY | Early writing artifacts such as a Babylonian cuneiform tablet, a 2,000-year-old Egyptian papyrus, and books dating to the beginning of European printing in the 15th century are shown here in exhibits changing three times annually. Subjects of these shows might include William Shakespeare, Galileo Galilei, Italian opera, or contemporary typesetting. Registration is required to use the collections, so bring some form of identification with you, but there's no admission fee to view the exhibition area. ⊠ *University of Toronto, 120 St. George St., Queen's Park* ☎ *416/978-5285* ⊕ *fisher.library.utoronto.ca* ⊠ *Free* ⊘ *Closed weekends* Ⓜ *St. George.*

University of Toronto

COLLEGE | Almost a city unto itself, the University of Toronto's student and staff population numbers about 100,000. The institution dates to 1827, when King George IV signed a charter for a "King's College in the Town of York, Capital of Upper Canada." The Church of England had control then, but by 1850 the college was proclaimed nondenominational, renamed the University of Toronto, and put under the control of the province. Then, in a spirit of Christian competition, the Anglicans started Trinity College, the Methodists began Victoria, and the Roman Catholics began St. Michael's; by the time the Presbyterians founded Knox College, the University was changing at a great rate. Now the 12 schools and faculties are united and accept students from all over the world. The architecture is interesting, if uneven, as one might expect on a campus that's been built in bits and pieces over 150 years. ✉ *Visitors Centre, 25 King's College Circle, Queen's Park* ☎ *416/978–5000* 🌐 *www.utoronto.ca* [M] *St. George, Queen's Park.*

🍴 Restaurants

Crown Princess

$$$ | CHINESE | There's luxury—and then there's the ostentatious dining room at Crown Princess, where every possible surface is done up in marble, velvet, or rococo scrollwork. Lunches here are devoted to dim sum, and the har gow and siu mai are among some of the finest in the city. **Known for:** well-heeled clientele; beautifully presented dishes; attentive service. [$] *Average main: C$25* ✉ *1033 Bay St., Queen's Park* ☎ *416/923–8784* 🌐 *crown-princess.ca* [M] *Wellesley.*

Fran's

$$ | DINER | For generations, hungry Torontonians have ended up at this reliable round-the-clock diner for classic breakfasts and greasy-spoon dishes. Burgers and Benedicts are staples, but they also branch out with pastas, bar snacks, and mains like steak and roasted chicken. **Known for:** retro diner atmosphere; 24-hour service; year-round upstairs patio. [$] *Average main: C$16* ✉ *20 College St., Queen's Park* ☎ *416/923–9867* 🌐 *fransrestaurant.com* [M] *College.*

🎫 Performing Arts

CLASSICAL MUSIC

MacMillan Theatre

MUSIC | Performances by professors and students of the University of Toronto Faculty of Music and visiting artists, ranging from symphony to jazz to full-scale operas, take place September through May at the 815-seat MacMillan Theatre. Smaller-scale performances fill the 496-seat **Walter Hall.** ✉ *University of Toronto Faculty of Music, Edward Johnson Bldg., 80 Queen's Park Crescent, Queen's Park* ☎ *416/408–0208* 🌐 *www.music.utoronto.ca* [M] *Museum.*

THEATER

Hart House Theatre

THEATER | The main theater space of the University of Toronto since 1919, Hart House mounts four emerging-artist and student productions from September to March. At least one musical and one Shakespeare play are always part of the program. ✉ *7 Hart House Circle, Queen's Park* ☎ *416/978–2452* 🌐 *www.harthousetheatre.ca* [M] *Museum, St. George, Queen's Park.*

The Annex

Born in 1887, when the burgeoning town of Toronto engulfed the area between Bathurst Street and Avenue Road north from Bloor Street to the Canadian Pacific Railway tracks at what is now Dupont Street, the countrified Annex soon became an enclave for the well-to-do; today it attracts an intellectual set. Timothy Eaton of department-store fame built a handsome structure at 182 Lowther Avenue (since demolished). The prominent Gooderham family, owners of a distillery, erected a lovely red castle at the corner of St. George Street and Bloor Street, now the home of the exclusive York Club.

Did You Know?

A statue of Sir John A. Macdonald, Canada's first prime minister, presides over the grounds of the Ontario Legislative Building. You can take tours of the pink sandstone building and observe the provincial parliament in session.

As Queen Victoria gave way to King Edward, old money gave way to new money and ethnic groups came and went. Upon the arrival of developers, many Edwardian mansions were demolished to make room for bland 1960s-era apartment buildings.

Still, The Annex, with its hundreds of attractive old homes, can be cited as a prime example of Toronto's success in preserving lovely, safe streets within the downtown area. Examples of late-19th-century architecture can be spotted on Admiral Road, Lowther Avenue, and Bloor Street, west of Spadina Avenue. Round turrets, pyramid-shape roofs, and conical spires are among the pleasures shared by some 15,000 Torontonians who live in this vibrant community, including professors, students, writers, lawyers, and other professional and artsy types. Bloor Street between Spadina and Palmerston keeps them fed and entertained with its bohemian collection of used-record stores, whole-foods shops, juice bars, and restaurants from elegant Italian to aromatic Indian.

Sights

Bata Shoe Museum

MUSEUM | Created by Sonja Bata, wife of the founder of the Bata Shoe Company, this shoe museum holds a permanent collection of more than 13,000 foot coverings and, through the changing fashions, highlights the craft and sociology of making shoes. Some items date back more than 4,000 years. Delicate 16th-century velvet platforms, iron-spiked shoes used for crushing chestnuts, and smugglers' clogs are among the items on display. Elton John's boots have proved wildly popular, but Elvis Presley's blue (patent leather, not suede) shoes give them a run for their money. ✉ *327 Bloor St. W, The Annex* ☎ *416/979–7799* 🌐 *www.batashoemuseum.ca* 🎟 *C$14* [M] *St. George.*

Casa Loma

HOUSE | FAMILY | A European-style castle, Casa Loma was commissioned by Sir Henry Pellatt, a soldier and financier. Pellatt spent more than C$3.5 million to construct his dream (that's in 1913 dollars; it would cost about C$20 million today), only to lose his house to the tax man a decade later. Some impressive details are the giant pipe organ, the 60-foot-high ceiling of the Great Hall, and the extensive, 5-acre estate gardens. The rooms are copies of those in English, Spanish, Scottish, and Austrian castles, including Windsor Castle's Peacock Alley. This has been the location for many a horror movie and period drama, an episode of the BBC's *Antiques Roadshow*, and several Hollywood blockbusters, including *Chicago* and *X-Men*. Included in the admission price is a self-guided audio tour (available in eight languages). **■ TIP→ A tour of Casa Loma is a good 1½-km (1-mile) walk, so wear sensible shoes.** ✉ *1 Austin Terr., The Annex* ☎ *416/923–1171* 🌐 *www.casaloma.org* 🎟 *C$30* ⏲ *Gardens closed Oct.–Apr.* [M] *Dupont.*

Restaurants

Annex Food Hall

$ | INTERNATIONAL | Groups divided over what to eat for lunch should make a beeline for this hip food court, which packs in some of Toronto's favorite quick-service restaurants. Among your options in this industrial-style building: Chinese buns from Mean Bao, fried chicken sandwiches from P.G. Clucks, and hearty vegan fare from Urban Herbivore. **Known for:** variety of takeout stalls; relaxed atmosphere; ever-changing pop-ups. [$] *Average main: C$12* ✉ *384 Bloor St. W, The Annex* 🌐 *theannexfoodhall.com* [M] *Spadina.*

Fat Pasha

$$$ | MIDDLE EASTERN | A hit with locals, this cozy spot from the family that launched other popular neighborhood eateries like Rose & Sons and Big Crow

is Middle Eastern food at its finest. The menu is a love letter to classics like hummus and pita, falafel with tahini, with a few novel creations thrown in for good measure, like the date grilled cheese on the brunch menu. **Known for:** belly up to the bar for a Middle Eastern beer; specialties like halloumi-stuffed cauliflower; hang out on the hidden back patio. $ Average main: C$28 ✉ 414 Dupont St., The Annex ☎ 647/340–6142 ⊕ fatpasha.com ☻ No lunch Mon. and Tues. Ⓜ Dupont.

Future Bistro
$ | **CAFÉ** | Aside from European-style baked goods, this spot also serves old-world recipes like borscht, buckwheat cabbage rolls, and potato-cheese pierogi slathered with thick sour cream. It's a place beloved by the pastry-and-coffee crowd, students wanting generous portions, and people-watchers, from early morning until late at night. **Known for:** sunny patio draws a local crowd; huge selection of house-made desserts; all you can eat pierogi on Wednesday. $ Average main: C$12 ✉ 483 Bloor St. W, The Annex ☎ 416/922–5875 ⊕ futurebistro.ca Ⓜ Spadina.

Le Paradis
$$ | **FRENCH** | This bistro-on-a-budget is the kind of neighborhood place you hope to find in Paris—checkerboard floors, walls covered with black-and-white photographs, and waiters rushing around in starched aprons. Almost everything on the menu of seasonal offerings is under C$20, with options including boeuf bourguignonne, duck leg confit with a cherry gastrique, and classic dessert options like flourless chocolate cake and crème caramel. **Known for:** cheerful atmosphere; well-priced wine list; inventive daily specials. $ Average main: C$17 ✉ 166 Bedford Rd., The Annex ☎ 416/921–0995 ⊕ www.leparadis.com ☻ No lunch Ⓜ Dupont.

Live Organic Food Bar
$$ | **VEGETARIAN** | The sunny decor will charm you, but the real appeal here lies with the amazing raw foods menu. A manicotti made with cashew-dill ricotta, cherry tomatoes, pumpkin Parmesan, and zucchini noodles is a crowd favorite. **Known for:** house-made juices and smoothies; industrial-chic patio; weekend brunch menu. $ Average main: C$16 ✉ 264 Dupont St., The Annex ☎ 416/515–2002 ⊕ www.livefoodbar.com Ⓜ Dupont.

Piano Piano
$$$ | **ITALIAN** | On a quiet stretch of Harbord home to some of the city's most understatedly delicious restaurants lies this romantic trattoria that's popular with couples and families alike. The menu spans from antipasti and fresh pastas to excellent blistered-crust pizzas, seafood (like grilled octopus and whole roasted seabass) and cute desserts. **Known for:** broad menu of Italian classics; family-friendly downstairs dining room; signature rose-patterned wallpaper. $ Average main: C$24 ✉ 88 Harbord St., The Annex ☎ 416/929–7788 ⊕ pianopianotherestaurant.com.

Hotels

While most of the hotel action happens to the east in Yorkville, boutique hotel properties are making inroads into the Annex. The long residential streets running north hide quiet B&Bs that lend a small-town feel to the middle of the city.

Clinton and Bloor B&B
$$ | **B&B/INN** | At the western end of the Annex, this elegant B&B has a trio of homey suites that will make you feel like you're guest in someone's home. **Pros:** a short stroll from Christie Pits Park; owner is a wealth of information; good value. **Cons:** some noise from street and subway; books up quickly; dated decor. $ Rooms from: C$209 ✉ 390 Clinton St., The Annex ☎ 416/898–8461

🌐 *clintonandbloor.com* 🛏 *3 rooms* 🍴 *Free breakfast* [M] *Christie.*

★ Kimpton Saint George

$$$ | HOTEL | A splashy C$40 million renovation gave this historic hotel the full boutique treatment while emphasizing its eye-grabbing architectural details. **Pros:** beautifully designed rooms and public spaces; great proximity to both Yorkville and the Annex; cloud-soft custom mattresses. **Cons:** few bathrooms have tubs; small portions at restaurant; some street noise. [$] *Rooms from: C$325* ✉ *280 Bloor St. W, The Annex* ☎ *416/968–0010* 🌐 *kimptonsaintgeorge.com* 🛏 *188 rooms* 🍴 *No meals* [M] *Spadina.*

Nightlife

Along Bloor between Spadina and Bathurst, the Annex is an established neighborhood of leafy side streets with large Victorian houses that attracts university students and young professionals to its mix of true-blue pubs and well-loved lounges.

BARS

Kinka Izakaya Bloor

BARS/PUBS | Wowing local audiences with its rowdy atmosphere—every guest is greeted with a cheerful hello in Japanese by both kitchen and serving staff when you walk through the door—Kinka has gained a cultlike following. A few shots of sake are a must-try, but don't miss the imported plum wine or Japanese vodka-infused cocktails. The food is delicious and perfect for sharing. ✉ *559 Bloor St. W, The Annex* ☎ *647/343–1101* 🌐 *www.kinkaizakaya.com* [M] *Bathurst.*

Playa Cabana Hacienda

BARS/PUBS | The Hacienda, as it's fondly known, offers a small patio tucked away on the second floor as well as a massive one to the rear. The interior wows with a wild and wonderful assortment of glowing bar signs, industrial lamps, leather horse saddles, and endless bottles of booze. Another plus: great tacos. ✉ *14 Dupont St., The Annex* ☎ *647/352–6030* 🌐 *www.playacabana.ca/hacienda* [M] *Dupont.*

MUSIC VENUES

Lee's Palace

MUSIC CLUBS | Some of the most exciting young bands in rock, indie, and punk play at this club with a psychedelic graffiti facade on the edge of the University of Toronto campus. Grab an Indian-style roti from the service window between sets. Upstairs is the Dance Cave, a no-frills dance club popular with students. ✉ *529 Bloor St. W, The Annex* ☎ *416/532–1598* 🌐 *www.leespalace.com* [M] *Bathurst.*

Performing Arts

CLASSICAL MUSIC

Tafelmusik

MUSIC | Internationally renowned as one of the world's finest period ensembles, Tafelmusik presents baroque and classical music on original instruments. Most performances are held in Trinity–St. Paul's Centre, a stunningly revitalized church hall. Tafelmusik's Sing-Along *Messiah* at Massey Hall is a rollicking Christmas season highlight where the audience is invited to join in. ✉ *Trinity–St. Paul's Centre, Jeanne Lamon Hall, 427 Bloor St. W, The Annex* ☎ *416/964–6337* 🌐 *www.tafelmusik.org* [M] *Spadina.*

FILM

Hot Docs Ted Rogers Cinema

FILM | If you like your films factual, informative, and inspiring, then the Hot Docs Cinema is for you. Come here for documentaries on political movements, such as *Under the Sun,* or perhaps something more esoteric like *Mussels in Love*. The theater is the permanent home of the annual Hot Docs festival. ✉ *506 Bloor St. W, The Annex* ☎ *416/637–3123* 🌐 *www.hotdocscinema.ca* [M] *Bathurst.*

THEATER

Tarragon Theatre

THEATER | This converted warehouse presents plays by new and established Canadian playwrights. Maverick companies often rent the smaller of the Tarragon's theaters or one of the studio spaces upstairs for interesting experimental works. ⊠ 30 Bridgman Ave., The Annex ☎ 416/531–1827 ⊕ www.tarragontheatre. com Ⓜ Dupont.

🛍 Shopping

In a neighborhood near the University of Toronto campus populated by academics, students, and '60s hippies, a mix of restored and run-down Victorians and brick low-rises house cafés and bistros, used-book and music stores, and the occasional fashion boutique.

BOOKS

Bakka Phoenix

BOOKS/STATIONERY | Canada's oldest science fiction and fantasy bookstore, Bakka Phoenix has several thousand new and used titles for adults, young adults, and children, as well as some graphic novels. The knowledgeable staff is always on hand to give advice. ⊠ 84 Harbord St., The Annex ☎ 416/963–9993 ⊕ www. bakkaphoenixbooks.com.

BMV

BOOKS/STATIONERY | An impressive selection of new and used books is shelved side by side over two floors at BMV (which stands for "Books Magazines Video"). The staff is knowledgeable and helpful. ⊠ 471 Bloor St. W, The Annex ☎ 416/967–5757 ⊕ www.bmvbooks.com Ⓜ Spadina.

CLOTHING

Common Sort

CLOTHING | The best-dressed Torontonians clear out their closets at this consignment store, which always has something cheap and cheerful on the racks. Brands range from fast-fashion to vintage to designer; the eagle-eyed might even spot some Marni or Max Mara. ⊠ 444 Bloor St. W, The Annex ☎ 416/532–5990 ⊕ commonsort.com Ⓜ Bathurst.

Risqué

CLOTHING | Trendy dresses, blouses, jumpers, and jeans from independent brands, including plenty of Canadian designers, fill this boutique. The colorful, of-the-moment selections change weekly. ⊠ 404 Bloor St. W, The Annex ☎ 416/960–3325 ⊕ risqueclothing.ca Ⓜ Spadina.

Secrets From Your Sister

CLOTHING | The art of the brassiere is taken seriously at this bra-fitting boutique. Knowledgeable (but pretension-free) staffers are on hand for advice. A fitting session can be booked online or in-person, and usually lasts from 30 minutes to an hour. Or you can simply peruse the massive selection of prêt-à-porter undergarments, including sports, fashion, strapless, seamless, and nursing bras in wide-ranging sizes and fits. ⊠ 560 Bloor St. W, The Annex ☎ 416/538–1234 ⊕ www.secretsfromyoursister.com Ⓜ Bathurst.

HOME DECOR

Nella Cucina

HOUSEHOLD ITEMS/FURNITURE | Shop alongside Toronto chefs for quality kitchen supplies—cheese knives, seafood shears, or unique showpieces like locally made salvaged-wood platters—at this shop that also hosts cooking classes upstairs. ⊠ 876 Bathurst St., The Annex ☎ 416/922–9055 ⊕ nellacucina.ca ⊙ Closed Sun. Ⓜ Bathurst.

Little Italy

Little Italy has had its share of identities—first a stronghold for Portuguese and Italian families, then a burgeoning nightclub district—and now, finally, seems to have found a way to balance the two. Unsurprisingly, a good meal is very far away here. There are plenty of classic dining destinations like Cafe

Diplomatico, a low-key Italian spot known for its popular side patio. But a new guard of Italian restaurants like the imaginative, fine dining-influenced Il Covo and sleekly modern Giulietta have also settled in. The area is also home to a buzzy bar scene that comes alive on weekends.

 Restaurants

Some of the city's best pastas and pizzas are served up in Little Italy, a place where chefs still strive to reproduce the taste of Nonna's cooking. Specialties like charcuterie and ceviche have local followings, as do the quaint patios and neighborhood bakeries.

★ Bar Raval
$$ | SPANISH | Inside a breathtaking room swathed in undulating waves of wood, you'll find Bar Raval, a tapas restaurant known for some marvelous food and drink. Stop by during the day and pick a *pintxo* (a single-serving snack served on a skewer) or two off the bar, feast on house-smoked tins of seafood and miniature blood sausage and egg toasts for a full meal, or stop in late for a nightcap. **Known for:** covered patio is always popular; standing-room-only setting; sherry and vermouth. ⓢ *Average main: C$20* ✉ *505 College St., Little Italy* ☎ *647/344–8001* ⊕ *www.thisisbarraval.com.*

Chiado
$$$$ | PORTUGUESE | It's all relaxed elegance at this Portuguese spot, where the dining room looks spiffy with polished wood floors and plum velvet armchairs. The exquisite fish, which form the menu's base, are flown in from the Azores and Madeira. **Known for:** excellent grilled seafood; classic Portuguese dishes; top-notch service. ⓢ *Average main: C$45* ✉ *864 College St. W, Little Italy* ☎ *416/538–1910* ⊕ *www.chiadorestaurant.com* ⊗ *No lunch weekends.*

Duff's Famous Wings
$$ | AMERICAN | FAMILY | At this classic Toronto chicken joint, crispy wings and drumettes are served with pristine celery sticks and creamy dill or blue-cheese dressing. Beware: the "medium" option is very spicy, and the sauces only get hotter from there. **Known for:** short menu focuses on pub grub; loud, lively atmosphere; great for families. ⓢ *Average main: C$13* ✉ *558 College St. W, Little Italy* ☎ *416/963–4446* ⊕ *www.duffsfamouswings.ca.*

Giulietta
$$$$ | ITALIAN | Traditional Italian food gets a modern twist at this intimate eatery focused largely on fresh fish and seafood. The sharing-oriented menu features delightful fresh pastas and wood-fired pizzas, but seafood lovers should go straight for dishes like tender grilled octopus with white beans and salsa verde or cioppino made with crab and Newfoundland cod. **Known for:** ultramodern interior design; sizeable list of mostly Italian wines; after-dinner liqueur cart. ⓢ *Average main: C$35* ✉ *972 College St., Little Italy* ☎ *416/964–0606* ⊕ *giu.ca* ⊗ *No lunch. Closed Sun.*

Nightlife

College Street between Bathurst and Ossington isn't so much an old-school Italian neighborhood these days as it is a prime destination for bars and restaurants of all cuisines. Student-friendly pubs and rowdy clubs mix with candlelit martini bars. The party often spills out onto the streets on weekends.

BARS
Birreria Volo
BARS/PUBS | The family that runs this narrow beer bar has a side business importing rare brews from all over the world, so you know whatever's on tap—whether it's brewed in Ontario or Belgium—is going to be stellar. The setting feels decidedly old-world, complete with weathered brick walls and a hidden patio space that feels like a walled-off

Did You Know?

In the summer, the sidewalk patio of Café Diplomatico is one of the neighborhood's most popular spots, with umbrellas offering plenty of shade for the outdoor tables.

courtyard. ✉ *612 College St., Little Italy* ☎ *416/531–7373* ⊕ *birreriavolo.com.*

Café Diplomatico

BARS/PUBS | Holding court over a central Little Italy corner since 1968, Diplomatico is popular for its big sidewalk patio with umbrella-shaded tables, one of the best places in the city for people-watching. "The Dip," as it's locally known, serves up middle-of-the-road Italian fare until midnight or later. ✉ *594 College St., Little Italy* ☎ *416/534–4637* ⊕ *www.cafediplomatico.ca.*

The Caledonian

BARS/PUBS | This pub is dedicated to all things Scottish. If the massive mural of the St. Andrew's Cross decorating the cozy back patio doesn't give it away, the enormous whiskey selection certainly will. There are more than 400 single malts, with selections dating all the way back to the 1950s and '60s. The pub also hosts frequent tasting events featuring various distillers, and serves hearty Highland eats (haggis—real and vegan—included). ✉ *856 College St., Little Italy* ☎ *416/577–7472* ⊕ *thecaledonian.ca.*

La Carnita

BARS/PUBS | Originally started as a pop-up taco stand, La Carnita became a permanent fixture when lines started forming well into the late evening. The tacos, hand-crafted cocktails, and sweet churros are well worth the wait. The space is filled with funky graffiti and the sounds of vintage beats, hip-hop, and DJ mixes. ✉ *501 College St., Little Italy* ☎ *416/964–1555* ⊕ *www.lacarnita.com.*

MUSIC VENUES

Free Times Cafe

MUSIC CLUBS | There's live acoustic and folk music every night of the week on this casual eatery's backroom stage, plus a highly popular traditional Jewish brunch buffet called "Bella! Did Ya Eat?" complete with live klezmer music every Sunday. ✉ *320 College St., Queen's Park* ☎ *416/967–1078* ⊕ *www.freetimescafe.com.*

Mod Club Theatre

MUSIC CLUBS | This sexy black-on-black space has great sight lines, killer acoustics, and amazing lighting. Past shows have included Lana Del Rey and Digitalism, but upstart Canadian indie rockers are frequent guests. The Mod Club is also a popular venue for DJs and dance nights, and it's not uncommon for the venue to host an early live show, then clear the venue out for the dance crowd. ✉ *722 College St., Little Italy* ☎ *416/588–4663* ⊕ *www.themodclub.com.*

 # Shopping

BOOKS

Balfour Books

BOOKS/STATIONERY | This hushed second-hand bookshop has a tempting selection of coffee table–size art and photography books. There's also more "luggage-friendly" fiction, too. ✉ *468 College St., Little Italy* ☎ *416/531–9911* ⊕ *balfourbooks.squarespace.com.*

JEWELRY AND ACCESSORIES

Lilliput Hats

CLOTHING | Wide-brimmed hats decorated with silk orchids, extravagant fascinators, close-fitting cloches, and practical straw hats that pack flat in your carry-on—all these can be found at Lilliput Hats. For men there are trilbies, wide-brimmed fedoras, and pork pies. Karyn Ruiz, who has a huge following, works away with her team of milliners in the back half of the shop. ✉ *462 College St., Little Italy* ☎ *416/536–5933* ⊕ *www.lilliputhats.com* ☉ *Closed Sun.*

MUSIC

★ Soundscapes

MUSIC STORES | Crammed with pop, rock, jazz, blues, folk, ambient, psychedelic, garage, avant-garde, and electronic titles, this shop satisfies hipsters of all stripes. It's also a great place to pick up tickets for local concerts. ✉ *572 College St., Little Italy* ☎ *416/537–1620* ⊕ *www.soundscapesmusic.com.*

Chapter 10

YORKVILLE, CHURCH AND WELLESLEY, ROSEDALE, AND CABBAGETOWN

Updated by
Natalia Manzocco

👁 **Sights**
★★★★☆

🍴 **Restaurants**
★★★★☆

🛏 **Hotels**
★★★★★

🛍 **Shopping**
★★★★★

🍸 **Nightlife**
★★★★☆

TORONTO'S FILM SCENE

So many films are shot in Toronto (the city has posed as everywhere from Paris to Moscow) that it's earned the nickname "Hollywood North." The highlight of the cinematic year is the world-renowned Toronto International Film Festival.

North America's third-largest film production center after L.A. and New York, Toronto keeps cameras rolling with its excellent local crews and production facilities, and plenty of filmmaker tax credits. It helps, too, that Toronto's chameleonic streets easily impersonate other cities and time periods. Credits include: the Distillery District as Prohibition-era Chicago (*Chicago*), Casa Loma as the school for young mutants (*X-Men*), and the U of T campus as Harvard (*Good Will Hunting*). Spotting Toronto "tells" in films is fun, but locals get even more jazzed when the city represents itself for a change, as in 2010's *Scott Pilgrim vs. the World*.

MORE FESTIVALS

Hot Docs. North America's largest documentary film festival. April. ✉ *The Annex* ⊕ *www.hotdocs.ca.*

Inside Out Toronto LGBT Film Festival. This major event features films made by and about lesbian, gay, bi, and transgender people. Late May. ✉ *Toronto* ⊕ *www.insideout.ca/torontofestival.*

Toronto After Dark. Dedicated to horror, sci-fi, and thriller films. Late October. ✉ *Toronto* ⊕ *www.torontoafterdark.com.*

TORONTO INTERNATIONAL FILM FESTIVAL

Widely considered the most important film festival in the world after Cannes and Sundance, TIFF is open to the public and even the star-studded galas are accessible to the average joe. More than 300 of the latest works by great international directors and lesser-known independent-film directors from around the world are shown. Movies that premiere at TIFF have gone on to win Academy Awards and launch the careers of emerging actors and directors. In recent years, TIFF audiences have been among the first in the world to see *La La Land*, *Slumdog Millionaire*, and *Juno*, to mention just a few. The red carpet is rolled out and paparazzi get ready for big-budget, star-studded premieres, for which actors and directors may be on hand afterward for Q&As. Along with the serious documentaries, foreign films, and Oscar contenders, TIFF has fun with its Midnight Madness program, screening campy horror films, comedies, and action movies into the wee hours. ⊠ *TIFF Bell Lightbox, 350 King St. West, at John St., Harbourfront* ☎ *416/599–2033, 888/258–8433* ⊕ *www.tiff.net.*

DOING THE FESTIVAL

When: The 11-day festival begins in early September.

Where: Screenings are at movie theaters and concert halls throughout the city, as are ticket booths, but the festival HQ is the TIFF Bell Lightbox building, at *350 King St. W (at John St.).*

Tickets: If you plan to see 10 or more films, consider a festival ticket package (these go on sale in July); you can choose screenings on the website. Individual tickets go on sale four days before the start of the festival. Advance ticket prices start at C$19 per regular film and C$29 for premium screenings. If you have your heart set on something specific and you don't get a ticket, keep checking each morning at 8.

WHERE TO WATCH

Oddball series and theme nights: Revue, Royal

Documentaries: Bloor HotDocs Cinema

Pure cinephilia: TIFF Bell Lightbox

IMAX: Ontario Science Centre's Shoppers Drug Mart OMNIMAX Theatre (Toronto's only 70mm celluloid IMAX); Cineplex Cinemas Yonge-Dundas; Scotiabank Theatre, Cinesphere

3-D: Scotiabank Theatre; TIFF Bell Lightbox; Varsity and Varsity VIP; Cineplex Cinemas Yonge-Dundas (which also offers select films in 4DX, featuring motion seats and environmental effects like water and wind)

Summer films alfresco: Harbourfront Centre (Wednesday, free); TIFF in the Park (Wednesday, free); Kew Gardens (Wednesday, free), Yonge-Dundas Square (Tuesday, free). Most screenings start at sunset (usually around 8:30 or 9 pm) and run through July and August.

NEIGHBORHOOD SNAPSHOT

TOP EXPERIENCES

■ **Get Cultured:** Take in the Gardiner Museum or the Royal Ontario Museum, two of the city's finest.

■ **Discover The Village:** Experience LGBTQ culture in Church and Wellesley, better known to locals as The Village.

■ **Alternative Shopping:** Browse a wide range of interesting indie boutiques in Church and Wellesley and Rosedale.

■ **Get Out the Credit Card:** Discover Canada's homegrown fashion houses along Yorkville's upscale "Mink Mile."

■ **Walking Tour:** Take a stroll through Cabbagetown, known for its beautiful cottages.

GETTING HERE

Church and Wellesley is located along Church Street, which runs parallel to Yonge Street a few blocks east. To get to the heart of the action, take the subway to Wellesley and walk east. You could also take the subway to College and walk north along Church Street, or take the subway to Bloor-Yonge and head south.

Yorkville runs along Bloor Street between the Yonge-Bloor (to the east) and St. George (to the west) subway stations.

For Rosedale, take the subway to Summerhill and walk south along Yonge Street, or take the subway to Rosedale and head north.

PLANNING YOUR TIME

Church and Wellesley tends to come alive on weekends, particularly in the summertime. Yorkville, thanks to its location near the center of the city at Yonge and Bloor, is perpetually buzzing. Rosedale is quieter and more residential.

QUICK BITES

■ **The Black Camel.** This tiny café, just outside the Rosedale subway station, serves some of the city's favorite sandwiches. ⊠ 4 *Crescent, Rosedale* ⊕ *www. blackcamel.ca* Ⓜ *Rosedale*

■ **North of Brooklyn.** This local pizza chain with locations around the city serves great thin-crust slices and garlic knots. ⊠ *469 Church, Church-Wellesley Village* ⊕ *www.northofbrooklyn. com* Ⓜ *Wellesley*

■ **Palm Lane.** Inside the Yorkville Village shopping center, this spot offers flavorful salads and grain bowls. ⊠ *55 Ave., Yorkville* ⊕ *www.palmlane.ca* Ⓜ *Bay*

Located a stone's throw from where Toronto's two main drags (Yonge and Bloor) intersect, Yorkville and Church and Wellesley are close together, but their personalities are a study in contrasts.

Yorkville is one of the ritziest neighborhoods in town, where you'll often see luxury cars pulled up outside the Holt Renfrew department store, or slow-rolling past packed bistro patios. By contrast, Church and Wellesley is a casual, out-and-proud LGBTQ community where locals party late into the night (and then roll out of bed for brunch the next day). To the northeast, tony residential Rosedale is a place to window-shop for fantasy Victorian houses, and around cute clothing and home decor boutiques.

Yorkville

Toronto's equivalent of Fifth Avenue or Rodeo Drive, Yorkville—and Bloor Street in particular, cheekily called "mink mile"—is a dazzling spread of posh shops stocked with designer clothes, furs, and jewels, along with restaurants, galleries, and specialty boutiques. It's also where much of the excitement takes place in September during the annual Toronto International Film Festival, the world's largest and most people-friendly film festival, where the public actually gets to see premieres and hidden gems and attend industry seminars. Klieg lights shine over skyscrapers, cafés teem with the well-heeled, and everyone practices air kisses. Yorkville is also home to a unique park on Cumberland Street, designed as a series of gardens along old property lines and reflecting both the history of the Village of Yorkville and the diversity of the Canadian landscape.

 Sights

Gardiner Museum

MUSEUM | Dedicated to the art of clay and ceramics, this museum has more than 4,000 pieces in its permanent collection, from 17th-century English delftware and 18th-century European porcelain to Japanese Kakiemon-style pottery and Chinese white-and-blue porcelain. If your visit coincides with lunchtime, hit on-site bistro Clay for creative, locally oriented cuisine (and one of the best hidden patios in town). Free guided tours of the museum take place at 2 pm daily and there are drop-in sessions in the clay studio (Wednesday and Friday 6–8 pm; Sunday 1–3 pm; C$15). **■TIP→ Admission is half price on Wednesday after 4 (kids under 18 are always free).** ✉ *111 Queen's Park Crescent, Yorkville* ☎ *416/586–8080* ⊕ *www.gardinermuseum.on.ca* ⊠ *C$12* Ⓜ *Museum.*

★ **Royal Ontario Museum**

MUSEUM | **FAMILY** | The ROM (as the Royal Ontario Museum is known to locals), opened in 1914, is Canada's largest museum and it has a reputation for making its science, art, and archaeology exhibits accessible and appealing. The architecture of the gigantic complex, which includes the ultramodern **Michael**

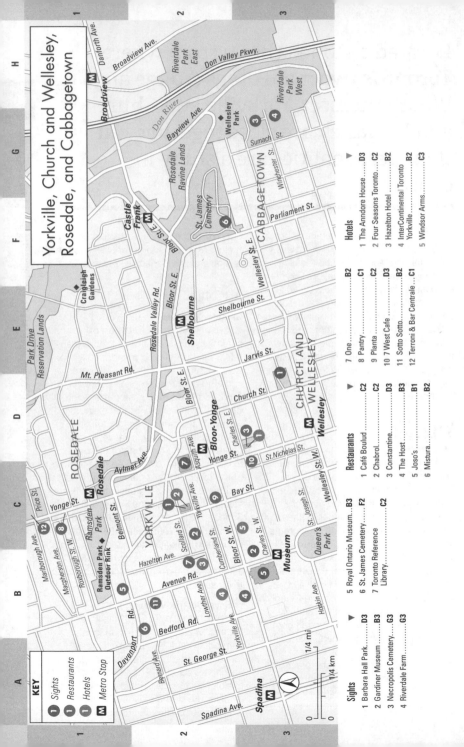

Yorkville, Church and Wellesley, Rosedale, and Cabbagetown

KEY
- ① Sights
- ① Restaurants
- ① Hotels
- Ⓜ Metro Stop

Sights ▶
1 Barbara Hall Park.............D3
2 Gardiner Museum.............B3
3 Necropolis Cemetery.......G3
4 Riverdale Farm.................G3
5 Royal Ontario Museum.....B3
6 St. James Cemetery.........F2
7 Toronto Reference
  Library..............................C2

Restaurants ▶
1 Café Boulud....................C2
2 Chabrol............................C2
3 Constantine......................D3
4 The Host...........................B3
5 Joso's...............................B1
6 Mistura.............................B2
7 One...................................B2
8 Planta...............................C1
9 Planta...............................C2
10 7 West Cafe....................D3
11 Sotto Sotto......................B2
12 Terroni & Bar Centrale....B2

Hotels ▶
1 The Anndore House........D3
2 Four Seasons Toronto.....C2
3 Hazelton Hotel.................B2
4 InterContinental Toronto
  Yorkville.........................B2
5 Windsor Arms..................C3

Lee-Chin Crystal gallery—a series of interlocking prismatic shapes spilling out onto Bloor Street—helps exemplify this.

Other highlights include the **Hyacinth Gloria Chen Crystal Court**, a four-story atrium with aluminum bridges connecting the old and new wings, and an angular pendant skylight through which light pours into the open space. A look through the windows reveals parts of the treasures inside, such as the daunting creatures from the **Age of Dinosaurs** exhibit standing guard. **The Patricia Harris Gallery of Textiles and Costume** angles out 80 feet over Bloor Street from its fourth-floor perch.

The **Daphne Cockwell Gallery of Canada** exhibits an impressive range of First Peoples historical objects and artifacts, from precontact time to the present. The **Chinese Sculpture Gallery** in the Matthews Family Court displays monumental Buddhist sculpture dating from 200 BC through 1900; the **Gallery of Korea** is North America's largest permanent gallery devoted to Korean art and culture. The **Sir Christopher Ondaatje South Asian Gallery** houses the best objects of a 7,000-piece collection that spans 5,000 years, and includes items from Bangladesh, Bhutan, India, the Maldives, Nepal, Pakistan, Sri Lanka, and Tibet. **■ TIP→ The museum stays open late (till 8:30 pm) on the third Monday of every month, during which time admission is free.** ✉ *100 Queen's Park, Yorkville* ☎ *416/586–8000* 🌐 *www.rom.on.ca* 🎟 *C$23* [M] *Museum.*

Toronto Reference Library

LIBRARY | Designed by one of Canada's most admired architects, Raymond Moriyama, who also created the Ontario Science Centre, this five-story library is arranged around a large atrium, which gives a wonderful sense of open space. One-third of the more than 5.5 million items—spread across 82 km (51 miles) of shelves—are open to the public. Audio carrels are available for listening to nearly 40,000 music and spoken-word recordings. The largest Performing Arts Centre in a public library in Canada is on the fifth floor—as is the **Arthur Conan Doyle Room**, which is of special interest to Baker Street fans. It houses the world's finest public collection of Holmesiana, including records, films, photos, books, manuscripts, letters, and even cartoon books starring Sherlock Hemlock of *Sesame Street.* ✉ *789 Yonge St., Yorkville* ☎ *416/395–5577* 🌐 *www.torontopubliclibrary.ca* [M] *Bloor-Yonge.*

🍴 Restaurants

Home to the rich and fabulous, Yorkville is the prime spot for celebrity sightings, especially during the Toronto International Film Festival. Posh bars and lively patios all provide a chance to do a little people-watching, and to sample some of the city's best high-end cuisine.

★ Café Boulud

$$$$ | **FRENCH** | Spearheaded by world-renowned restaurateur Daniel Boulud, Café Boulud occupies the coveted dining room of the Four Seasons Toronto and presents itself as a serene, airy French brasserie decked out with sage-green banquettes and gilded accents. Boulud does simple French fare, executed perfectly, like steak tartare tossed tableside, duck confit, and mouthwatering roast chicken on a bed of crisp-skinned potatoes. **Known for:** classic French food; celebrity chef connection; inventive desserts. [$] *Average main: C$36* ✉ *60 Yorkville Ave., Yorkville* ☎ *416/963–6005* 🌐 *www.cafeboulud.com/toronto* [M] *Bay.*

★ Chabrol

$$$$ | **FRENCH** | Sequestered down a pedestrian walkway in the heart of Yorkville, this petite spot oozes romance. Diners are seated right next to the minuscule, wide-open kitchen and can watch the action as the kitchen turns out gratins, parchment-wrapped whitefish, and seafood stew ("ttoro") in a saffron broth that's poured tableside with choreographed grace. The apple tart, baked to order and smothered in apple-brandy cream, is a must. **Known for:** ultracozy, intimate vibe; modern spin on French food; luxurious desserts. $ *Average main: C$36* ✉ *90 Yorkville Ave., Yorkville* ☎ *416/428–6641* ⊕ *www.chabrolrestaurant.com* Ⓜ *Bay.*

The Host

$$ | **INDIAN** | Waiters bustle around the handsome dining room at this popular spot, carrying baskets of hot naan, an indication of the restaurant's attention to details. The selection of tandoor-cooked entrées, spanning from fish and shrimp to chicken coated in green chili paste, is particularly noteworthy. **Known for:** fine-dining atmosphere; excellent desserts, like gulab jamun (small cakes soaked in rosewater-scented honey); Friday lunch buffet. $ *Average main: C$19* ✉ *14 Prince Arthur Ave., Yorkville* ☎ *416/962–4678* ⊕ *www.welcometohost.com* ☾ *No lunch Mon.* Ⓜ *Bay.*

Joso's

$$$$ | **SEAFOOD** | Sensuous paintings of nudes and the sea and signed celebrity photos line the walls at this two-story seafood institution. The kitchen prepares dishes from the Dalmatian side of the Adriatic Sea, and members of the international artistic community who frequent the place adore the unusual and healthy array of seafood and fish. The black risotto with squid, served in a shareable portion size, is a must, as are the grilled prawns with lemon garlic butter. **Known for:** eccentric, artistic decor; seafood-focused menu; the restaurant has a cameo on Drake's "Take Care" album cover. $ *Average main: C$36* ✉ *202 Davenport Rd., Yorkville* ☎ *416/925–1903* ⊕ *www.josos.com* ☾ *Closed Sun. No lunch Sat.* Ⓜ *Dupont.*

Mistura

$$$ | **ITALIAN** | The combination of comfort and casual luxury here has made Mistura a Yorkville staple. The menu is mostly refined Italian classics, like beef carpaccio with arugula and pasta with wild boar

ragu, and the whole fish is a carefully thought-out triumph. Vegetarians are given their due with signature dishes like beet risotto. **Known for:** luxe versions of Italian dishes; knowledgeable serving staff; sizeable wine list. $ *Average main: C$30* ✉ *265 Davenport Rd., Yorkville* ☎ *416/515–0009* ⊕ *www.mistura.ca* ☾ *Closed Sun. No lunch* Ⓜ *Dupont.*

★ **One**

$$$$ | **INTERNATIONAL** | The modern dining room at One, inside the Hazelton Hotel, is all rich woods, smoked glass, cowhide, and onyx—and thankfully the food lives up to all the razzle-dazzle. "Lobster spoons" with vermouth butter and miso-glazed black cod share space on a broad, varied menu with fresh pastas and exceptional house-aged steaks sourced from Prince Edward Island and Alberta. **Known for:** buzzy streetside patio; excellent seafood and steak; top-notch service. $ *Average main: C$40* ✉ *The Hazelton Hotel Toronto, 118 Yorkville Ave., Yorkville* ☎ *416/961–9600* ⊕ *mcewangroup.ca/one* Ⓜ *Bay.*

Planta

$$$ | **VEGETARIAN** | The upscale-yet-whimsical take on vegan food at Planta caused quite a stir when it opened in 2016, and the restaurant is still a favorite of the Yorkville lunch crowd. Menu standouts include satisfying thin-crust pizzas with vegan ricotta, an excellent veggie burger, and a queso dip that will fool even the pickiest cheese lover. **Known for:** bold, trendy decor; fun cocktails with cold-pressed juices; Sunday brunch. $ *Average main: C$22* ✉ *1221 Bay St., Yorkville* ☎ *647/812–1221* ⊕ *plantarestaurants.com* Ⓜ *Bay.*

★ **Sotto Sotto**

$$$ | **ITALIAN** | This Southern Italian hideaway has been a magnet for visiting celebrities and well-heeled Yorkville locals since the early 1990s, and it's still one of the city's most popular posh restaurants. The dozen or so pastas, including freshly made gnocchi, are reliably excellent, but

the grilled seafood options, spanning Dover sole to scallops to calamari, are stellar. **Known for:** low-lit, intimate setting; refined Italian dishes; wall of celebrity photos. [$] *Average main: C$30* ✉ *120 Avenue Rd., Yorkville* ☎ *416/962–0011* 🌐 *www.sottosotto.ca* 🕒 *No lunch Sun.* [M] *Bay.*

Hotels

★ Four Seasons Toronto

$$$$ | **HOTEL** | Luxury is the name of the game at this gleaming 55-story hotel, where the rooms are done in neutral tones and outfitted with soaking tubs, rain showers, and heated bathroom floors. **Pros:** on-site dining and night-life hot spots; excellent on-site spa; top-notch service. **Cons:** hefty price tag; some rooms look onto residential building next door; modern decor can feel a bit austere. [$] *Rooms from: C$525* ✉ *60 Yorkville Ave., Yorkville* ☎ *416/964–0411* 🌐 *www.fourseasons.com/toronto* 🛏 *259 rooms* 🍴 *No meals* [M] *Bay.*

★ Hazelton Hotel

$$$$ | **HOTEL** | **FAMILY** | The Hazelton is a popular destination for visiting celebrities—and it looks the part, with clubby, modern furnishings, floor-to-ceiling windows, balconies, and bathrooms wrapped in forest-green granite. **Pros:** outstanding service; favorite of Hollywood celebs; great on-site spa. **Cons:** high-quality with the price tag to match; no hope of getting a room during TIFF; low-rise building means underwhelming views. [$] *Rooms from: C$525* ✉ *118 Yorkville, Yorkville* ☎ *647/696–8720* 🌐 *www.thehazeltonhotel.com* 🛏 *77 rooms* 🍴 *No meals* [M] *Bay.*

InterContinental Toronto Yorkville

$$$ | **HOTEL** | This comfortable, refined outpost of the global InterContinental chain is a two-minute walk from the Yorkville shopping area and just across the street from the Royal Ontario Museum. **Pros:** great proximity to shopping and museums; rooftop lap pool and sauna; good value for the area. **Cons:** not as luxe as some other local hotels; bathrooms only have showers; rooms close to street level can be noisy. [$] *Rooms from: C$299* ✉ *200 Bloor St. W, Yorkville* ☎ *416/960–5200* 🌐 *www.toronto.intercontinental.com* 🛏 *212 rooms* 🍴 *No meals* [M] *Bay.*

Windsor Arms

$$$$ | **HOTEL** | Nestled on a side street near some of Yorkville's toniest shops, the Windsor Arms caters to a luxury clientele and personalized service is a priority: there's a high guest-to-staff ratio and 24-hour butlers are on duty. **Pros:** high repeat business due to privacy and personalized service; luxurious, quiet atmosphere; good dining options, including afternoon tea service. **Cons:** high standards mean high prices; some fourth-floor rooms can be noisy if events are being hosted downstairs; rooms book up fast at peak times. [$] *Rooms from: C$398* ✉ *18 St. Thomas St., Yorkville* ☎ *416/971–9666* 🌐 *www.windsorarmshotel.com* 🛏 *28 rooms* 🍴 *No meals* [M] *Bay.*

Nightlife

The trendy bars of Yorkville tend to draw a well-heeled clientele for excellent drinks, food, and views.

BARS

dBar

BARS/PUBS | This high-end lounge in the flagship Four Seasons Toronto is modern and low-key, with top-notch cocktails, including the rose-and-elderflower-infused Yorkville Affair. The food is spearheaded by French chef Daniel Boulud, so the menu goes far above and beyond simple bar bites—the charcuterie is house-made, and larger options include lobster rolls and steak frites. ✉ *21 Avenue Rd., Yorkville* ☎ *416/963–6010* 🌐 *www.fourseasons.com* [M] *Bay.*

Hemingways

BARS/PUBS | One of the few Toronto pubs that isn't overtaken by rowdy sports fans or students, Hemingways is a homey bastion in a sea of Yorkville swank. The three-story complex, with indoor and outdoor spaces (including a heated rooftop patio), is a mishmash of booths, tables, several bars, mirrors, artsy posters, and books. The pub grub menu, which covers everything from brunch to late night, is a big draw, too. About three-quarters of the over-30 professionals who frequent this place are regulars. ⊠ *142 Cumberland St., Yorkville* ☎ *416/968-2828* ⊕ *www. hemingways.to* Ⓜ *Bay.*

 **Performing Arts**

CLASSICAL MUSIC
★ Koerner Hall

MUSIC | This handsome 1,135-seat concert hall pleases performers and audiences with rich acoustics and undulating wood "strings" floating overhead. Acts have included such greats as Yo-Yo Ma, Chick Corea, Ravi Shankar, Midori, Taj Mahal, and Savion Glover. It's part of the TELUS Centre for Performance and Learning. ⊠ *273 Bloor St. W, Yorkville* ☎ *416/408-0208* ⊕ *rcmusic.com* Ⓜ *St. George.*

Shopping

Back in the 1960s, Yorkville was Canada's hippie headquarters. Today it's a well-heeled shopping and dining destination: the place to find high-end everything. The pedestrian-friendly streets in the heart of Yorkville—North of Bloor, west of Bay—are full of designer stores that are fun to browse even if you're not buying, while Bloor Street, from Yonge Street to Avenue Road, is a virtual runway of world-renowned designer shops like Bulgari, Prada, Chanel, and quality chains.

ANTIQUES
Wagman Antiques

ANTIQUES/COLLECTIBLES | Wagman carries a large selection of art deco pieces and lighting, along with Italian (and a few French) pieces from the '40s, '50s, and '60s. This is the place to find a show-stopping glass-veneered sideboard or a Murano glass lamp. Depending on the piece, Wagman can ship to the United States and beyond. ⊠ *224 Davenport Rd., at Avenue Rd., Yorkville* ☎ *416/964-1047* ⊕ *wagmanantiques.com* ☾ *Closed weekends* Ⓜ *Dupont, St George.*

ART GALLERIES
Loch Gallery

ART GALLERIES | This intimate gallery in an old Victorian house almost exclusively exhibits representational historic and contemporary Canadian painting and sculpture, and specializes in 19th- and 20th-century Canadian artists. ⊠ *16 Hazelton Ave., Yorkville* ☎ *416/964-9050* ⊕ *www.lochgallery.com* Ⓜ *Bay.*

BOOKS
Indigo

BOOKS/STATIONERY | This Canadian megachain bookstore has stores all over the country but it's headquartered in Toronto. It has a huge selection of books, magazines, and gift items as well as a Starbucks and occasional live entertainment. ⊠ *55 Bloor St. W, Yorkville* ☎ *416/925-3536* ⊕ *www.chapters.indigo. ca* Ⓜ *Bay.*

CLOTHING
Chanel

CLOTHING | Coco herself would have loved this boutique, one of the company's largest in North America, inside a historical building. Most of the brand's latest offerings, including classic and seasonal bags and accessories are here, and the staff is welcoming, knowledgeable, and helpful, just what you'd expect from a store of this caliber. ⊠ *98 Yorkville Ave., Yorkville* ☎ *416/925-2577* ⊕ *www.chanel. com* Ⓜ *Bay.*

Club Monaco

CLOTHING | This megachain has shops around the world but few know that the brand got its start right here in Toronto. The bright and airy flagship stocks design basics, sleek mid-price sportswear, and career clothes. It's now owned by Ralph Lauren. ✉ *157 Bloor St. W, at Avenue Rd., Yorkville* ☎ *416/591–8837* ⊕ *www. clubmonaco.com* Ⓜ *Museum or Bay.*

★ George C

CLOTHING | If you're put off by the anonymous uniformity of the big designers along Bloor but you have some money to spend and want a touch of originality, head to this three-story Victorian refurb for an inspired selection of bold, sophisticated shoes, bags, and clothes for men and women from French, Italian, American, and Australian designers that you won't find anywhere else. ✉ *21 Hazelton Ave., Yorkville* ☎ *416/962–1991* ⊕ *georgec.ca* Ⓜ *Bay.*

★ Harry Rosen

CLOTHING | This five-floor department store is dedicated to the finest men's fashions, stocked to the gills with suits, shirts, outerwear, shoes, and accessories from designers such as Hugo Boss, Armani, and Zegna. There's also plenty of preppy classics available for those who favor a more relaxed look. ✉ *82 Bloor St. W, Yorkville* ☎ *416/972–0556* ⊕ *www. harryrosen.com* Ⓜ *Bloor-Yonge.*

Hermès

CLOTHING | The Parisian design house caters to the upscale horse- and hound-loving set, with classic sportswear, handbags, and accessories. ✉ *100 Bloor St. W, Yorkville* ☎ *416/968–8626* ⊕ *www.hermes.com* Ⓜ *Bay.*

Hugo Nicholson

CLOTHING | This boutique's selection of evening wear is vast and exclusive: along with gowns by Alaïa, Carolina Herrera, and more, there's also a selection of never-worn vintage pieces, as well as an adjoining Vera Wang bridal boutique. The service is old-school, with exacting alterations, a selection of accessories, and home delivery. ✉ *43 Hazelton Ave., Yorkville* ☎ *416/927–7714* ⊕ *www.hugonicholson.com* Ⓜ *Bay.*

Jacadi

CLOTHING | FAMILY | The city's prettiest and priciest children's clothes are stocked here, in vibrant colors and fine fabrics mostly from Paris. Stylish toys, linens, and baby gear round out the offerings. ✉ *87 Avenue Rd., in Yorkville Village, Yorkville* ☎ *416/923–1717* ⊕ *www.jacadi.com* Ⓜ *Bay.*

Kit and Ace

CLOTHING | "Technical cashmere" is the specialty of this Canadian brand and the shop's copper-and-wood racks are stocked with refined basics for men and women: tees, trousers, button downs, and workout gear, all in neutral hues and sleek fabrics. It's pricier than your average fast-fashion basic, but Kit and Ace's pieces are designed to withstand all kinds of abuse and still look flawless. The store does free alterations in-house, and if you're in need of a caffeine boost, head around back to Sorry Coffee Co. for a latte or an espresso. ✉ *102 Bloor St. W, Yorkville* ☎ *416/640–0287* ⊕ *kitandace.com* Ⓜ *Bay.*

Motion

CLOTHING | This Toronto-based boutique features unique, comfortable clothing in cottons, linens, and wools. Many pieces are designed and made in-house, but outside designers such as Flax and Oska are also featured. Bold, chunky accessories complement the earthy, arty look perfectly. ✉ *106 Cumberland St., Yorkville* ☎ *416/968–0090* ⊕ *www.motionclothing.com* Ⓜ *Bay.*

Neighbour

CLOTHING | Spare and sleek, this white-walled offshoot of a popular Vancouver boutique specializes in fresh, slightly whimsical menswear from cutting-edge brands: tropical shirts from Bode, slick staples from Acne, and updated work-wear pieces by Margaret Howell. This is the place to snag extremely limited-run pieces from big fashion houses like Calvin Klein all the way down to small indie brands. ✉ *126A Davenport Rd., Yorkville* ☎ *416/551–1085* ⊕ *shopneighbour.com* Ⓜ *Bay.*

119 Corbò

CLOTHING | Both legendary and of-the-moment designers—Balenciaga, The Row, Jacquemus, and Stella McCartney, to name a few—are gathered here under one roof, along with some of the finest footwear and accessories in town. ✉ *119 Yorkville Ave., Yorkville* ☎ *416/928–0954* ⊕ *www.119corbo.com* Ⓜ *Bay.*

Over the Rainbow

CLOTHING | This boutique for all things denim has been around since the 1970s and carries every variety of cut and flare: the trendy, the classic, and the questionable from lines like Fidelity and Naked & Famous fill the shelves. ✉ *55 Bloor St. W, inside Manulife Centre, Yorkville* ☎ *416/967–7448* ⊕ *www.rainbowjeans. com* Ⓜ *Bay.*

★ Pink Tartan

CLOTHING | Ontario-born designer Kimberly Newport-Mimran opened this, her flagship store, in 2011 after selling her sophisticated sportswear in high-end shops around the globe. Expect tailored Oxford shirts, classic little black dresses, and crisp, snug-fitting trousers in expensive fabrics, as well as objets d'art, shoes, and accessories hand-picked by the designer. Snap a photo in front of the Instagram-famous pink door before you go. ✉ *77 Yorkville Ave., (entrance on Bellair St.), Yorkville* ☎ *416/967–7700* ⊕ *www.pinktartan.com* Ⓜ *Bay.*

Prada

CLOTHING | The avant-garde designs of this luxury Italian fashion house are overshadowed only by the gleaming interior of the store and the traffic-stopping window displays. ✉ *131 Bloor St. W., Yorkville* ☎ *416/975–4300* ⊕ *www.prada.com* Ⓜ *Bay.*

★ Roots

CLOTHING | The longtime favorite brand for leather jackets, varsity jackets, bags, and basics are crafted from tumbled leather and stamped with the country's national icon (the beaver) at Roots. The homegrown company's impressive flagship store showcases the more modern styling possibilities of their laid-back offerings. ✉ *80 Bloor St. W, Yorkville* ☎ *416/323–3289* ⊕ *www.roots. com* Ⓜ *Bay.*

Second Time Around

CLOTHING | If you're after a designer handbag but can't bear to pay retail, head to this consignment shop tucked inside a low-rise building. The selection is extensive without being overwhelming, and you might find that perfect, lightly used Fendi, Dior, or Celine at an accessible price. High-fashion preowned clothes, including Chanel, Gucci, Vuitton, and Vivienne Westwood, and loads of shoes are here, too. ✉ *70 Yorkville Ave., Unit 9, Yorkville* ☎ *416/916–7669* ⊕ *secondtimea-roundtoronto.com* Ⓜ *Bay.*

Shan

CLOTHING | Montréal designer Chantal Levesque founded this label in 1985, and now stocks locations in more than 25 countries with her creative couture swimwear, swimwear accessories, and wraps. There's a separate collection for men. ✉ *38 Avenue Rd., Yorkville* ☎ *416/961–7426* ⊕ *www.shan.ca* Ⓜ *Bay or St. George.*

DEPARTMENT STORES AND SHOPPING CENTERS

★ Holt Renfrew

DEPARTMENT STORES | This multilevel national retail specialty store is the style leader in Canada. On the ground floor are handbags, watches, cosmetics, and fragrances from London, New York, Paris, and Rome. Head to the upper floors for footwear and clothing from boldface designers (including Fendi, Burberry, and Gucci) as well as items from contemporary designers. Gents can head a few steps west to 100 Bloor Street West to browse Holt's menswear collection at the two-floor Holt Renfrew Men. ■ TIP→ **Concierge service and personal shoppers are available, but just browsing makes for a rich experience.** ⊠ *50 Bloor St. W, Yorkville* ☎ *416/922–2333* ⊕ *www. holtrenfrew.com* Ⓜ *Bay.*

Hudson's Bay

DEPARTMENT STORES | The modern descendant of the Hudson's Bay Company, which was chartered in 1670 to explore and trade in furs, the Bay (as it's known among Canadians) carries mid-price clothing, furnishings, housewares, and cosmetics, including designer names and in-house lines. Another Bay, which shares its sprawling space with a Saks Fifth Avenue location, is located on Yonge Street, connected to Eaton Centre by a covered skywalk over Queen Street. ⊠ *44 Bloor St. E, Yorkville* ☎ *416/972–3333* ⊕ *www.thebay.com* Ⓜ *Bloor-Yonge.*

Yorkville Village

SHOPPING CENTERS/MALLS | Formerly known as Hazelton Lanes, this small upscale shopping mall is home to fashion-forward TNT (short for The Next Trend); structured womenswear by Judith & Charles; Jacadi's Parisian kidswear; and downtown Toronto's only Whole Foods Market. ⊠ *55 Avenue Rd., Yorkville* ☎ *416/968–8600* ⊕ *www.yorkvillevillage.com* Ⓜ *Bay.*

FOOD

McEwan

FOOD/CANDY | In a basement below Yonge and Bloor, this homegrown gourmet grocery store (a spinoff by the restaurant family that includes One and Bymark) caters to the well-to-do and the on-the-go. In the morning there are breakfast burritos, fresh pastries, and cold-pressed juices; at lunch, rows of Le Creuset

Dutch ovens simmer with curries. There's also a carving station with grass-fed beef and porchetta, a beautiful salad bar and prepared food station, and a huge selection of packaged foods that ranges from gourmet potato chips to luxurious splatter-painted chocolate eggs. ⊠ *1 Bloor St. E, Yorkville* ☎ *416/975–0808* Ⓜ *Yonge-Bloor.*

Pusateri's

FOOD/CANDY | From humble beginnings as a Little Italy produce stand, Pusateri's has grown into Toronto's favorite high-end supermarket, with in-house prepared foods, local and imported delicacies, and desserts and breads from the city's best bakers, among many other treats. ⊠ *57 Yorkville Ave., Yorkville* ☎ *416/925–0583* ⊕ *www.pusateris.com* Ⓜ *Bay.*

HOME DECOR

Hollace Cluny

HOUSEHOLD ITEMS/FURNITURE | Though it's off the main shopping drag, Hollace Cluny is a must-visit for modern design aficionados looking for that special piece. Along with classics from brands like Knoll, they carry a huge array of pieces from contemporary designers, with everything from ceramics to eye-popping statement lighting fixtures. ⊠ *245 Davenport Rd., Yorkville* ☎ *416/960–7094* ⊕ *www.hollacecluny.ca* ۞ *Closed weekends* Ⓜ *Bay.*

William Ashley

HOUSEHOLD ITEMS/FURNITURE | The gleaming 12,000-square-foot flagship of this decades-old Toronto chinaware business carries an extensive collection of dishware patterns and crystal glasses that range from Wedgwood to Kate Spade to Waterford. They're happy to pack and ship all over North America. Stop by the Teuscher of Switzerland chocolate boutique on the way out. ⊠ *131 Bloor St. W, Yorkville* ☎ *416/964–2900* ⊕ *www. williamashley.com* Ⓜ *Bay.*

JEWELRY AND ACCESSORIES

Cartier

JEWELRY/ACCESSORIES | The Toronto location of this internationally renowned luxury jeweler caters to the city's elite. The glass cases feature a good selection of the jewelry designer's classic creations, including the triple-gold-band Trinity Ring, the striking nail-shape Juste Un Clou collection, and the diamond-studded Tortue Watch. ⊠ *131 Bloor St. W, Yorkville* ☎ *416/413–4929* ⊕ *www.cartier.com* Ⓜ *Bay.*

Royal De Versailles

JEWELRY/ACCESSORIES | With a reputation as one of Toronto's most luxurious jewelers, Royal De Versailles stocks some of the most striking and elegant pieces in town. Watch aficionados will be particularly impressed by their huge collection of high-end timepieces (they have one of the largest Rolex selections in Canada). ⊠ *101 Bloor St. W, Yorkville* ☎ *416/967–7201* ⊕ *www.royaldeversailles.com* Ⓜ *Bay.*

Tiffany & Co.

JEWELRY/ACCESSORIES | Good things come in little blue boxes, and this two-floor Tiffany location is filled with them—namely, rows and rows of classic, wearable fine jewelry designs. As at other Tiffany locations, the sales staff has a reputation for being patient, helpful, and friendly. ⊠ *150 Bloor St. W, Yorkville* ☎ *416/921–3900* ⊕ *www.tiffany.ca* Ⓜ *Bay.*

SHOES, HANDBAGS, AND LEATHER GOODS

Browns Shoes

SHOES/LUGGAGE/LEATHER GOODS | This Canadian chain of shoe stores carries a grab-bag of mid-tier and upmarket brands in a wide variety of styles. Along with familiar names like Badgley Mishka, Birkenstocks, Dr. Marten, and Jeffrey Campbell, you'll find homegrown brands like La Canadienne (whose waterproof boots are the most stylish way to beat the Toronto slush) and Manitobah Mukluks. ⊠ *110 Bloor St. W, Yorkville* ☎ *416/920–1032* ⊕ *brownsshoes.com* Ⓜ *Bay.*

SPAS

Novo Spa

SPA/BEAUTY | A perennial favorite among Toronto's day-spa enthusiasts, this Yorkville hideaway offers massages (couples, prenatal), facials, manicures, pedicures, and various waxing treatments. The calming staff members always have soothing refreshments on hand. ⊠ *66 Avenue Rd., Yorkville* ☎ *416/926–9303* ⊕ *www.novospa.ca* Ⓜ *Bay.*

Church and Wellesley

Colorful rainbow flags fly high and proud in this vibrant neighborhood, just east of downtown. The area is energetic and boisterous any time of year, but absolutely frenetic during the annual Pride festival and parade in June. Given its long history, the area has evolved into a tight-knit, well-established community, with pharmacies, grocery stores, and dry cleaners rubbing shoulders with a mix of new and decades-old gay- and lesbian-centric nightspots. Glad Day, the world's oldest LGBTQ bookstore, is a must-visit.

Sights

Barbara Hall Park

CITY PARK | **FAMILY** | This pocket-size park is pleasant enough during the day, but at night it comes alive with strings of rainbow-color lights that symbolize the LGBTQ community. There's a mural of gay history on an adjacent building, and tucked away in one corner is the Toronto AIDS Memorial. ⊠ *519 Church St., Church–Wellesley.*

 Restaurants

Constantine

$$$ | **MEDITERRANEAN** | On the ground floor of the recently renovated Anndore House hotel, this sprawling spot's

Toronto Comedians

Toronto has long been a hub for emerging comedic talent. Gilda Radner, John Candy, Dan Aykroyd, Dave Thomas, Martin Short, Eugene Levy, Catherine O'Hara, and Rick Moranis all cut their teeth at Second City or on SCTV, a TV offshoot of the theater and precursor to *Saturday Night Live.* Of course, they all went on to even greater fame in movies and television. Toronto native Lorne Michaels created *SNL*, which itself laid the groundwork for countless comedy careers. A second golden age of Toronto comedy rose in the 1990s with Mike Myers and the *Kids In The Hall*'s Dave Foley, Bruce McCulloch, and Mark McKinney, all of whom got their start at the Bad Dog Theatre. Canadian comedians Jim Carrey and Howie Mandel, on the other hand, debuted at Yuk Yuk's comedy club. Most recently, Samantha Bee frequented the Rivoli before becoming the host of *Full Frontal.* Just to name-drop a few.

open kitchen turns out varied fare like Middle Eastern mezes, pastas, and gorgeously plated desserts. Grilled meats are great here—especially the lamb burger—but vegetarian options abound. The weekend brunch menu lures in locals and hotel guests alike with shakshuka and lemon-ricotta pancakes. **Known for:** buzzy, loungelike atmosphere; grilled Mediterranean specialties; great weekend brunch. [$] *Average main: C$28* ✉ *15 Charles St. E, Church–Wellesley* ☎ *647/475–4436* 🌐 *www.constantineto.com* [M] *Yonge-Bloor.*

7 West Cafe

$$ | **ECLECTIC** | No late-night craving goes unsatisfied at this 24-hour eatery specializing in lighter fare. Soups like Moroccan or vegetarian chili and sandwiches like herbed chicken with honey mustard are comforting and filling. There are also simple wine, beer, and cocktail choices. **Known for:** socializing on the hidden rooftop patio; cozy atmosphere with lots of candles; home-style fare. [$] *Average main: C$15* ✉ *7 Charles St. W, Church–Wellesley* ☎ *416/928–9041* 🌐 *www.7westcafe.com* [M] *Bloor-Yonge.*

Hotels

The Anndore House

$$$ | **HOTEL** | This hip boutique hotel above the popular restaurant Constantine caters to a young, plugged-in clientele with amenities like app-activated temperature control, an on-site barbershop, and record players in every room. **Pros:** great location between Yorkville and Church Street; good value for the area; beautiful common spaces. **Cons:** room design could feel more luxurious; walls are thin; in-room a/c units can be loud. [$] *Rooms from: C$280* ✉ *15 Charles St. E, Church–Wellesley* ☎ *416/924–1222* 🌐 *www.theanndorehouse.com* 🛏 *113 rooms* 🍴 *No meals* [M] *Yonge-Bloor.*

Nightlife

The "Gay Village," the "gayborhood," or just plain old "Church and Wellesley"—whatever you call it, this strip of bars, restaurants, shops, and clubs is a fun, always-hopping hangout for the LGBTQ-plus crowd and their friends.

BARS

Boutique Bar

BARS/PUBS | In comparison to the raucous, glittering scene you'll find nearby, Boutique Bar is a (relatively) low-key spot for a cocktail, whether you're feeling like a classic negroni, a martini, or one of the house creations. If you can, grab a spot on the tiny front patio and watch the comings and goings along Church Street. DJs bring the party on weekends. ⊠ *506 Church St., Church–Wellesley* ☎ *647/705–0006* ⊕ *boutiquebar.ca* Ⓜ *Wellesley.*

Woody's

BARS/PUBS | A predominantly upscale crowd of men, mostly in their twenties to forties, frequents this cavernous pub where DJs mix every night. Weekly events include the Best Chest and Best Butt contests, which are hosted by some of the city's most beloved drag queens. The exterior of Woody's was used on the television show *Queer as Folk.* ⊠ *467 Church St., Church–Wellesley* ☎ *416/972–0887* ⊕ *www.woodystoronto. com* Ⓜ *Wellesley.*

DANCE CLUBS

Crews & Tangos

BARS/PUBS | Downstairs is Crews, a gay and lesbian bar with a stage for karaoke or drag shows (depending on the night), a dance floor in back with a DJ spinning house beats, and a sizable back patio. Upstairs, Tangos has a bar and a small dance floor that gets packed with twenty- to thirtysomething guys and gals kicking it to old-school hip-hop and 1980s beats. The male–female ratio is surprisingly balanced and the drag shows are lots of fun. ⊠ *508 Church St., Church–Wellesley* ☎ *647/349–7469* ⊕ *crewsandtangos.com* Ⓜ *Wellesley.*

 Performing Arts

THEATER

Buddies in Bad Times Theatre

THEATER | Canada's largest queer theater company presents edgy plays and festivals, as well as specialty events like burlesque and stand-up. Pay What You Can tickets are available for select performances—if you want one, head to the box office at midday. ⊠ *12 Alexander St., Church–Wellesley* ☎ *416/975–8555* ⊕ *www.buddiesinbadtimes.com* Ⓜ *Wellesley.*

Shopping

BOOKS

Glad Day Bookshop

BOOKS/STATIONERY | Glad Day is the world's oldest LGBTQ bookstore—no mean feat, especially in high-rent Toronto. Recently relocated to new digs on Church Street, the store is packed with shelves featuring the latest and greatest in queer voices from across Canada and beyond; those shelves are frequently rolled aside to host readings, events, and even dance parties. The bar serves both coffee and alcohol, and the kitchen turns out homey diner-style eats (which are particularly appreciated during weekend drag brunches). ⊠ *499 Church St., Church–Wellesley* ☎ *416/901–6600* ⊕ *gladdaybookshop.com* Ⓜ *Wellesley.*

Rosedale

This posh residential neighborhood northeast of Yorkville has tree-lined curving roads (it's one of the few neighborhoods to have escaped the city's grid pattern), many small parks, and a jumble of oversized late-19th-century and early-20th-century houses in Edwardian, Victorian, Georgian, and Tudor styles. An intricate ravine system weaves through this picturesque corner of downtown, its woodsy contours lined with old-money and old-world majesty. The neighborhood is bounded by Yonge Street, the Don Valley Parkway, St. Clair Avenue East, and the Rosedale Ravine.

 Restaurants

Pantry

$$ | ECLECTIC | This fast-casual takeout spot is an offshoot of one of the city's top catering companies—and though the salads and proteins here are produced in massive quantities, everything is handled with a deft, flavorful touch. Pick a combo size, then choose from the daily mix of multicultural offerings in the display case. Favorites include moist grilled salmon and marinated chicken, andouille sausage, mac and cheese, and tahini-cauliflower salad. **Known for:** quick service; rotating menu of takeout dishes; plenty of vegetarian-friendly options. $ *Average main: C$13* ✉ *1094 Yonge St., Rosedale* ☎ *647/748–1094* ⊕ *orderpantry. com* Ⓜ *Rosedale.*

Terroni & Bar Centrale

$$ | ITALIAN | FAMILY | Local Italian mini-chain Terroni has several locations around the city but this one, with the ground floor Bar Centrale wine bar inspired by Italian train stations, is especially popular. Head upstairs to the bi-level Terroni, where you order locally beloved thin-crust pizzas, seafood spaghetti, and beef carpaccio, along with stunning views of the downtown skyline. **Known for:** excellent thin-crust pizzas; lively atmosphere; fun bar scene. $ *Average main: C$19* ✉ *1095 Yonge St., Rosedale* ☎ *416/925–4020* ⊕ *terroni.com* Ⓜ *Summerhill.*

Performing Arts

CLASSICAL MUSIC

Toronto Mendelssohn Choir

MUSIC | This group of more than 120 choristers was formed in 1894 and performs major classical choral works at various venues, including the lovely Koerner Hall and Yorkminster Park Baptist Church

at Yonge and St. Clair. The choir often performs with the Toronto Symphony Orchestra, including at its annual Christmas performance of Handel's *Messiah.* ✉ *Yorkminster Park Baptist Church, 1585 Yonge St., Rosedale* ☎ *416/598–0422* ⊕ *www.tmchoir.org* Ⓜ *Spadina.*

Activities

Rosedale Ravine

HIKING/WALKING | FAMILY | Though you might not expect it from one of the toniest areas in downtown Toronto, Rosedale is home to a lovely nature trail. It runs in a giant U shape, beginning on Heath Street East near Yonge and St. Clair (on the northern edge of Rosedale), swooping down to just east of Bloor and Sherbourne, then ending at picturesque Mount Pleasant Cemetery. It's an easy stroll, also popular with runners and cyclists. ✉ *Heath St. E, at Yonge, Rosedale* ⊕ *toronto.ca/trails* Ⓜ *St. Clair.*

Shopping

One of Toronto's most exclusive neighborhoods, Rosedale has a strip of upscale antiques and home decor shops, as well as some other specialty shops.

ANTIQUES

Absolutely Inc

ANTIQUES/COLLECTIBLES | Curios, from glass fishing floats to hand-beaded animal sculptures, are sold at this fascinating interiors shop. You'll also find an array of vintage jewelry, antique boxes made of materials ranging from marble to abalone, English campaign furniture, and French architects' drafting tables. ✉ *1236 Yonge St., Rosedale* ☎ *416/922–6784* ⊕ *www.absolutelyinc.com* Ⓜ *Rosedale.*

Putti

ANTIQUES/COLLECTIBLES | This home decor shop is very romantic, and very turn-of-the-century. Everywhere you look, you'll see antiques, reproduction furniture, and home accessories piled so high that they scrape the chandeliers. There's an impressive array of French toiletries, as well as frilly frocks and fairy wings for children's flights of fancy. ⊠ *1104 Yonge St., Rosedale* ☎ *416/972–7652* ⊕ *www.putti.ca* Ⓜ *Rosedale.*

CLOTHING
Tuck Shop Trading Co.
CLOTHING | "Refined Canadiana" is the motto at this shop, which pairs cute, cheery clothing for men and women with home goods worthy of a hip Muskoka cottage. Tees, patterned swim trunks, and statement earrings sit alongside luxe scented candles and embroidered woven baskets. If any of Toronto's neighborhoods have particularly captured your heart, grab one of the winter hats (or, as the locals call 'em, toques) from their house-made City of Neighbourhoods line. ⊠ *1225 Yonge St., Rosedale* ☎ *416/859–3566* ⊕ *tuckshopco.com* Ⓜ *Summerhill.*

SHOES, HANDBAGS, AND LEATHER GOODS
Mephisto
SHOES/LUGGAGE/LEATHER GOODS | These French-made walking shoes have been around since the 1960s and are constructed entirely from natural materials. Passionate walkers swear by them and claim they never, ever wear out—even on cross-Europe treks. Styles, which include options for men and women, run the gamut from smart ankle boots to minimalist slides. ⊠ *1177 Yonge St., Rosedale* ☎ *416/968–7026* ⊕ *ca.mephisto.com* Ⓜ *Summerhill.*

WINE
Summerhill LCBO
FOOD/CANDY | Once a stately railway station, this location of Ontario's provincially owned chain of liquor stores is where vinophiles, scotch lovers, and other locals with a taste for the finer things go hunting for rare bottles. The store also frequently hosts tastings. ■TIP→ **Keep customs limits on alcohol purchases, and whether you'll be checking a bag, in mind before you stock up.** ⊠ *10 Scrivener Sq.,*

Rosedale ☎ *416/922–0403* ⊕ *lcbo.com* Ⓜ *Summerhill.*

Cabbagetown

Mockingly named by outsiders for the cabbages that grew on tiny lawns and were cooked in nearly every house by early Irish settlers in the 1840s, the term is used with a combination of inverse pride and almost wistful irony today (as gentrification has increased real estate value here exponentially). It's fun to stroll around and enjoy the architectural diversity of this funky residential area, and there are a few attractions of interest, too. The enclave extends roughly from Parliament Street on the west—about 1½ km (1 mile) due east of Yonge Street—to the Don River on the east, and from Bloor Street on the north to Shuter Street on the south.

Sights

Necropolis Cemetery
CEMETERY | This nonsectarian burial ground, established in 1850, is the final resting place for many of Toronto's pioneers, including prominent turn-of-the-century black Canadian doctors, businessmen, and politicians. The cemetery's chapel, gate, and gatehouse date from 1872; the buildings constitute one of the most attractive groupings of small Victorian-era structures in Toronto. ⊠ *200 Winchester St., Cabbagetown* ⊹ *10-minute walk from Gerrard and Sumach bus stop* ☎ *416/923–7911.*

Riverdale Farm
FARM/RANCH | This spot once hosted the city's main zoo, but it's now home to a rural community representative of a late 19th-century farm. Permanent residents include horses, cows, sheep, goats, pigs, donkeys, ducks, geese, and chickens. While it's not a petting zoo per se, kids get a real kick out of watching farmers go about their daily chores, which

In addition to producing numerous works by Canadian artists, the Toronto Dance Theatre collaborates with choreographers from throughout the United States and Europe.

include feeding and bathing the animals. The adjacent playground has a wading pool. On Tuesday from mid-May to late October, there's a great farmers' market nearby in Riverdale Park. ⊠ *201 Winchester St., Cabbagetown* ☎ *416/392–6794* 💲 *Free*.

St. James Cemetery

CEMETERY | At the northeast corner of Parliament and Wellesley streets, this cemetery contains interesting burial monuments of many prominent politicians, business leaders, and families in Toronto. The small yellow-brick Gothic Chapel of St. James-the-Less has a handsome spire rising from the church nave and was built in 1861. This National Historical Site is one of the most beautiful churches in the country. ⊠ *635 Parliament St., Cabbagetown* ⊕ *www. stjamescemetery.ca*.

 Performing Arts

★ Toronto Dance Theatre

DANCE | The oldest contemporary dance company in the city, TDT has created more than 100 original works since its beginnings in the 1960s, often using original scores by Canadian composers. Two or three pieces are performed each year in its home theater in Cabbagetown. ⊠ *80 Winchester St., 1 block east of Parliament St., Cabbagetown* ☎ *416/967–1365* ⊕ *www.tdt.org* Ⓜ *Castle Frank*.

Chapter 11

GREATER TORONTO

Updated by
Jesse Ship

Sights	🍴 Restaurants	🛏 Hotels	🛍 Shopping	🍸 Nightlife
★★★★☆	★★★☆☆	★★☆☆☆	★★★☆☆	★★☆☆☆

NEIGHBORHOOD SNAPSHOT

TOP EXPERIENCES

■ **You Make Me Feel So Yonge:** Starting at Eglinton Station, take a stroll along Yonge Street to experience one of the city's most popular shopping and dining districts.

■ **A Must for Animal Lovers:** See more than 5,000 creatures in natural-looking habitats at the Toronto Zoo, one of the city's most popular attractions.

■ **Discover Japan Where You Least Expected It:** From martial arts and traditional dance, you never know what you're going to encounter at the Japanese Canadian Cultural Centre, filled with traditional gardens where you can see sakura blossoms in full bloom.

■ **For the Love of Green Spaces:** Head north or east of the city center and it won't take long to reach the rolling hills and valleys of Don Mills or sylvan reserves at the Kortright Centre.

■ **Take a Trip Back in Time:** The Middle Eastern and Persian artifacts at the spectacular Aga Khan Museum transport you to another era.

GETTING HERE

Buses run from various downtown subway stations to Edwards Gardens, the Ontario Science Centre, the Toronto Zoo, and Black Creek Pioneer Village. You'll need a car to visit the Kortright Centre for Conservation and the McMichael Canadian Art Collection. Canada's Wonderland is most easily reached by car but is also accessible by TTC.

PLANNING YOUR TIME

You can explore each Greater Toronto sight independently or combine a couple of sights in one trip. The Ontario Science Centre and Edwards Gardens are very close together, for example, and would make a manageable day trip; and, if you're driving from the city, you could visit Black Creek Pioneer Village and the Kortright Centre for Conservation on the way to the McMichael Canadian Art Collection. Reserve a full day to get the most bang for your buck at Canada's Wonderland.

QUICK BITES

■ **Milkcow.** Asian desserts are all the rage in Toronto, so find out what everyone's talking about at this Korean favorite that dishes up soft-serve ice cream layered with toppings like cotton candy, honeycomb, and jellybeans. ⊠ *2651 Yonge St., Yonge and Eglinton ⊕ milkcowcafe.ca* Ⓜ *Eglinton*

■ **Pancer's Original Deli.** The legendary deli has been serving kosher-style kishkas, knishes, and oversize smoked-meat-on-rye sandwiches for four generations. ⊠ *3856 Bathurst St. North York ⊕ www.pancersoriginaldeli.com*

■ **Robo Sushi.** Experience the future of food service at this all-you-can-eat Japanese joint where most items are brought to your table by real robots with storage compartments for bellies. ⊠ *865 York Mills Rd., Don Mills* Ⓜ *Don Mills*

You won't get a full Toronto experience if you don't tread far from the Harbourfront or the main drags like Queen and Bloor.

The Greater Toronto Area is what has helped the city earn its unofficial title of the "most multicultural city in the world." To the north and particularly the east is where you'll find the ethnic enclaves, sprawling parks, fascinating museums, and one-of-a-kind attractions that make the region even more intriguing. Most of these must-sees are accessible by public transportation, although a car would make the journey to some of the more far-flung destinations more convenient.

North Toronto

North Toronto encompasses Yonge Street between Eglinton Avenue—the neighborhood's southern, more bold and youthful end, which has garnered the playful nickname "Yonge and Eligible"—and north to Lawrence Avenue, with its more refined restaurants and upscale boutiques. The streets to the east and west of Yonge Street are mainly residential, and at the eastern edge are major tourist attractions: the Ontario Science Centre, a never-ending source of entertainment for the young and young-at-heart; the regal Aga Khan Museum of Islamic Art; and Toronto Botanical Garden and Edwards Gardens, a phenomenal display of flowers and plants.

Sights

★ Aga Khan Museum
MUSEUM | More than 1,000 pieces of Ismaili Muslim art from the collection of renowned philanthropist and religious leader Aga Khan are the focus of this museum. Here you'll find Middle Eastern and Persian artifacts and inscriptions, many so ancient that they are only displayed for a few months at a time to preserve their lifespan. It's worth making the trip for the stunning architecture, which includes a massive main building topped by a silver hexagonal dome and a park distinguished by a glass pyramid more intricate than the one at the Louvre. The museum's mandate is strictly secular, but it's hard not to have a spiritual moment staring into the central courtyard pond. Guided tours are available for C$10. ☒ 77 Wynford Dr., North York ☏ 416/646–4677 ⊕ agakhanmuseum.org ⊠ C$20, free Wed. 4–8. Parking C$10. ⊙ Closed Mon.

★ Japanese Canadian Cultural Centre
COLLEGE | FAMILY | Serving as a community center for Toronto's Japanese community, as well as thousands of lovers of Japanese culture, this space sits amid beautiful traditional gardens. It has literally dozens of different classes in martial arts like Kendo and Aikido, visual arts like Bunka Shishu embroidery, dance classes, and cooking courses. Visiting art shows are frequently in rotation, as well as artist talks, film screenings, or full-fledged film festivals. ☒ 6 Garamond Ct., North York ☏ 416/441–2345 ⊕ jccc.on.ca.

Ontario Science Centre
MUSEUM | FAMILY | It has been called a museum of the 21st century, but it's much more than that. Where else can you stand at the edge of a black hole or get creative with the physics of flight? Even the building itself is extraordinary:

three linked pavilions float gracefully down the side of a ravine and overflow with exhibits that make space, technology, and communications fascinating. The 25,000-square-foot Weston Family Innovation Centre, rife with hands-on activities, is all about experience and problem solving. Younger visitors learn through play in KidSpark, a space specially designed for children eight and under to enjoy and explore. The Planetarium, Toronto's only public planetarium, uses state-of-the-art technology to take participants on a trip around the galaxy. Demonstrations of papermaking, electricity, and more take place daily; check the schedule when you arrive. ✉ *770 Don Mills Rd., at Eglinton Ave. E, North Toronto* ☎ *416/696–1000* 🌐 *www.ontariosciencecentre.ca* 🎟 *C$22, parking C$10.*

Toronto Botanical Garden and Edwards Gardens
GARDEN | FAMILY | The beautiful 17 contemporary botanical garden areas and adjacent estate garden (once owned by industrialist Rupert Edwards) flow into one of the city's most visited ravines. Paths wind along colorful floral displays and exquisite rock gardens. There's also a signposted "teaching garden" for kids to touch and learn about nature. Free general tours between May and early September depart at 2 on Tuesday, 6 on Thursday, and throughout the day on weekends. Refreshments are available from the Garden Café in the Barn. For a great ravine walk, head south through Wilket Creek Park and the winding Don River valley. After hours of walking (or biking or jogging) through almost uninterrupted park, you reach the southern tip of Taylor Creek Park on Victoria Park Avenue, just north of the Danforth. From here you can catch a subway back to your lodgings. ✉ *777 Lawrence Ave. E, entrance at southwest corner of Leslie St. and Lawrence Ave. E, North Toronto* ☎ *416/397–1340, 416/397–4145 tours* 🌐 *www.torontobotanicalgarden.ca.*

🍴 Restaurants

Diwan at the Aga Khan Museum
$$$ | MIDDLE EASTERN | Much like the Aga Khan Museum, Diwan is an architectural wonder that incorporates walls, ceilings, and hanging lamps salvaged from a 19th-century Damascus merchant's home. The menu reflects the museum's mission by incorporating Middle Eastern, Indian, and Persian dishes, with seasonal meat, seafood, and vegetarian dishes. The use of top-notch (and local when possible) ingredients is paramount to executive chef Mark McEwan's mandate. **Known for:** impressive dishes like sweet onion bhaji fritters and kale coconut sambol; eye-popping mix of a modern building and antique details; crisp service. [$] *Average main: C$22* ✉ *Aga Khan Museum, 77 Wynford Dr., North York* ☎ *416/646–4670* 🌐 *diwan.agakhanmuseum.org* 🕓 *Closed Mon., no dinner Thurs.–Tues.*

Edo-ko
$$ | JAPANESE FUSION | FAMILY | Open in one form or another since the 1980s, this neighborhood eatery strives to capture authentic Japanese washoku-style cooking—think tempura, teriyaki, and sushi made with seafood imported from Tokyo's prestigious Tsukiji Market and sushi rice and vinegar expertly made on the premises. Nabe hot pots and udon noodle bowls are a great way to warm up in the colder months. **Known for:** some of the area's best sushi; devoted local following; lovely bar area. [$] *Average main: C$16* ✉ *429 Spadina Rd., Yonge and Eglinton* ☎ *416/482–8973* 🌐 *www.edorestaurants.com* [M] *St. Clair West.*

Pizza Banfi
$$ | ITALIAN | FAMILY | No matter what day or time, there's usually a line at Pizza Banfi for two reasons: it doesn't take reservations, and the classic Italian food is really good. While the decor is slightly cliché, with Renaissance-style wall paintings over light-color bricks, the pizzas

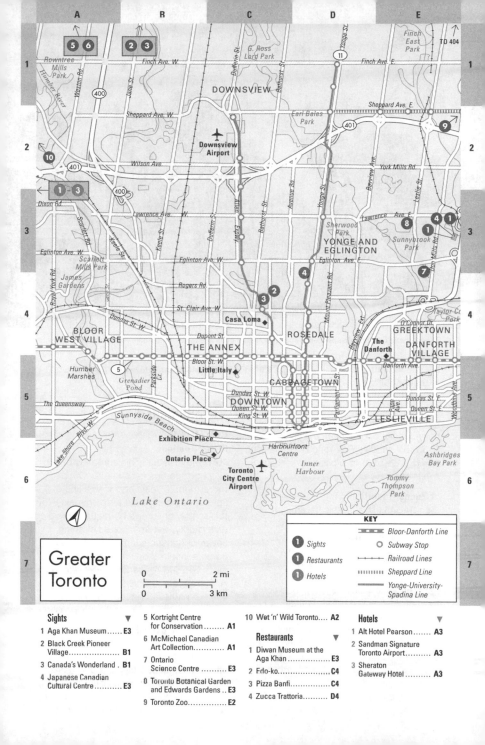

Greater Toronto

0 ___ 2 mi
0 ___ 3 km

KEY
━ ✕ ━ ✕ Bloor-Danforth Line
○ Subway Stop
┼┼┼┼ Railroad Lines
‖‖‖‖‖‖ Sheppard Line
━━━ Yonge-University-
Spadina Line

❶ Sights
❶ Restaurants
❶ Hotels

Sights ▼
1 Aga Khan Museum...... **E3**
2 Black Creek Pioneer
Village.................... **B1**
3 Canada's Wonderland . **B1**
4 Japanese Canadian
Cultural Centre........... **E3**
5 Kortright Centre
for Conservation **A1**
6 McMichael Canadian
Art Collection............. **A1**
7 Ontario
Science Centre **E3**
0 Toronto Botanical Garden
and Edwards Gardens .. **E3**
9 Toronto Zoo.............. **E2**
10 Wet 'n' Wild Toronto.... **A2**

Restaurants ▼
1 Diwan Museum at the
Aga Khan **E3**
2 Edo-ko................... **C4**
3 Pizza Banfi............... **C4**
4 Zucca Trattoria.......... **D4**

Hotels ▼
1 Alt Hotel Pearson....... **A3**
2 Sandman Signature
Toronto Airport.......... **A3**
3 Sheraton
Gateway Hotel **A3**

The futuristic Ontario Science Centre engages visitors of all ages with hands-on exhibits and workshops.

are the real attraction. Thin-crust pies are tossed in full view of the appreciative crowd, then baked to perfection. **Known for:** one of the neighborhood's favorites; generous servings of pasta; good-priced daily specials. [$] *Average main: C$15* ✉ *333B Lonsdale Rd., Yonge and Eglinton* ☎ *416/322–5231* ⏲ *Closed Sun.* [M] *Eglinton West.*

★ Zucca Trattoria

$$$ | **ITALIAN** | This classic Italian joint delivers the purest made-from-scratch Italian food in a modern, sleek, and friendly room. The wine list of more than 150 labels, all Italian varieties, is beautifully paired with the pasta, all handmade and hand-rolled. In addition to meat dishes like braised rabbit and muscovy duck, grilled fish is a specialty. Finish your night with an Amaretto crème caramel. **Known for:** seafood dishes like squid-ink pasta and grilled octopus; dining room is always full, so book in advance; complimentary chickpea bread. [$] *Average main: C$30* ✉ *2150 Yonge St., Yonge and Eglinton* ☎ *416/488–5774* 🌐 *www.zuccatrattoria.com* ⏲ *No lunch* [M] *Eglinton.*

Shopping

CLOTHING

Hatley Boutique

CLOTHING | **FAMILY** | This company began as a cottage business in rural Québec more than 25 years ago with a line of aprons depicting cute farm animals. Now this mainly children's boutique is stocked with quirky, nature-inspired clothing covered in insects, animals, trees, and flowers inspired by the Canadian wilderness. ✉ *2648 Yonge St., at Craighurst Ave., Yonge and Eglinton* ☎ *416/486–4141* 🌐 *www.hatley.com* [M] *Lawrence or Eglinton.*

OUTDOOR EQUIPMENT

Sporting Life

SPORTING GOODS | The first off the mark with the latest sportswear trends, this is the place to get hip, outdoorsy labels like Moncler, Canada Goose, and Dale of Norway—or to snag ski and snowboard gear, and poll the staff for advice on where to use it. ✉ *2665 Yonge St., north of Eglinton Ave., Yonge and Eglinton* ☎ *416/485–1611* ⊕ *www.sportinglife.ca* Ⓜ *Eglinton.*

Northern and Eastern Suburbs

Toronto is rich in culture, even beyond the city limits with pockets accessible deep in the GTA (Greater Toronto Area). The McMichael Canadian Art Collection, in the quaint suburb of Kleinburg, houses the stellar collection of Group of Seven pieces. Just minutes outside of downtown Toronto, Black Creek Pioneer Village is a living-history museum that is extremely kid-friendly. Nearby is the enormous theme park, Canada's Wonderland. The sprawling Toronto Zoo, set in the beautiful Rouge River Valley, is the perfect destination for a day trip, as is the Kortright Centre for Conservation … if you've got wheels.

◉ Sights

Black Creek Pioneer Village
MUSEUM VILLAGE | FAMILY | Less than a half-hour drive from downtown is this mid-19th-century living-history-museum village that makes you feel as though you've gone through a time warp. Black Creek Pioneer Village is a collection of 40 buildings from the 19th century, including a town hall, a weaver's shop, a printing shop, a blacksmith's shop, and a one-room schoolhouse. The mill dates from the 1840s and has a massive wooden waterwheel that can grind up to a hundred barrels of flour a day. As people in period costumes go about the daily routine of mid-19th-century Ontario life, they explain what they're doing and answer questions. Visitors can see farm animals; take wagon rides, Victorian dance classes, and 19th-century baseball lessons; and explore a hands-on

discovery center. ✉ *1000 Murray Ross Pkwy., near intersection of Jane St. and Steeles Ave., North York* ☎ *416/736–1733* ⊕ *www.blackcreek.ca* ✉ *C$15, parking C$7* ⊘ *Closed Jan.–Apr.*

Canada's Wonderland
AMUSEMENT PARK/WATER PARK | FAMILY | Canada's first theme park, filled with more than 200 games, rides, restaurants, and shops, includes favorite attractions like KidZville, home of Snoopy, Charlie Brown, and the rest of the Peanuts gang; Windseeker, which features 32 301-foot swings; and Skyhawk, where riders take control of their own cockpit. But Wonderland isn't just for the smallest members of the family; the Bat roller coaster takes riders forward, and then back, through stomach-churning corkscrews and loops. Bring swim gear to take advantage of Splash Works, the 20-acre on-site water park. ■ TIP→ Order tickets online in advance for discount prices. ✉ *9580 Jane St., Vaughan* ☎ *905/832–7000, 905/832–8131* ⊕ *www.canadaswonderland.com* ✉ *C$67* ⊘ *Closed Nov.–late May and weekdays in Sept. and Oct.*

Kortright Centre for Conservation
NATURE PRESERVE | Only 10 minutes north of the city, this delightful conservation center has more than 16 km (10 miles) of hiking trails through forest, meadow, and marshland, as well as a Bee Space where kids can see them up close and taste their honey, and an Innovation Trail that demonstrates how technology can reduce our impact on the wild. In the magnificent woods there have been sightings of foxes, coyotes, rabbits, deer, and a wide array of birds. Seasonal events include a spring sugar bush maple syrup festival and a honey harvest festival. To get here, drive 3 km (2 miles) north along Highway 400, exit west at Major Mackenzie Drive, and continue south 1 km (½ mile) on Pine Valley Drive to the gate. ✉ *9550 Pine Valley Dr., Woodbridge* ☎ *905/832–2289* ⊕ *www.kortright.org* ✉ *From C$9, parking C$4 on weekends.*

Canada's Wonderland is the country's first theme park.

McMichael Canadian Art Collection

MUSEUM | On 100 acres of lovely woodland in Kleinburg, 30 km (19 miles) northwest of downtown, the McMichael is the only major gallery in the country with the mandate to collect exclusively Canadian art. The museum holds impressive works by Tom Thomson, Emily Carr, and the Group of Seven landscape painters, as well as their early-20th-century contemporaries. These artists were inspired by the wilderness and sought to capture it in bold, original styles. First Nations art and prints, drawings, and sculpture by Inuit artists are well represented. Strategically placed windows help you appreciate the scenery as you view art that took its inspiration from the vast outdoors. Inside, wood walls and a fireplace set a country mood. Free guided tours are offered from Wednesday to Sunday at 12:30 and 2. ⊠ *10365 Islington Ave., west of Hwy. 400 and north of Major Mackenzie Dr., Kleinburg* ☎ *905/893–1121* ⊕ *www.mcmichael.com* ✉ *C$18, parking C$7.*

Toronto Zoo

ZOO | **FAMILY** | With terrain ranging from river valley to dense forest, the Rouge Valley was an inspired choice of site for this 710-acre zoo in which 5,000 different mammals, birds, reptiles, and fish are grouped according to their natural habitats. Enclosed, climate-controlled pavilions have botanical exhibits, such as the Africa pavilion's giant baobab tree. Daily activities might include chats with animal keepers and animal and bird demonstrations. An "Around the World Tour" takes approximately three hours and includes the Africa, Americas, Australasia, Indo-Malayan, and Canadian Domain pavilions. From late April through early September, the Zoomobile can take you through the outdoor exhibit area. The African Savanna is the country's finest walking safari, a dynamic reproduction that brings rare and beautiful animals and distinctive geological landscapes to the city's doorstep. Reserve ahead and you can dine in the Savanna's Safari Lodge and camp overnight in the Serengeti Bush Camp. ⊠ *Meadowvale Rd., Exit 389 off*

Hwy. 401, Scarborough ☎ 416/392–5929, 416/392–5947 for Serengeti Bush Camp reservations 🌐 www.torontozoo.com 🎟 C$28, parking C$10 🕒 Closed Jan.–Apr.

Wet 'n' Wild Toronto

AMUSEMENT PARK/WATER PARK | **FAMILY** | The largest park of its kind in Canada, Wet 'n' Wild has huge waterslides, a lazy river, giant outdoor hot tubs, a fantastic wave pool, and Bear Footin' Bay, a delightful area for younger children to splash around in. If water's not your thing, splurge on a group cabana, hang out at the Coconut Cove Bar, or go for a ziplining experience through the trees. ✉ *7855 Finch Ave. W, off Hwy. 427, Brampton ☎ 416/369–0123 🌐 www.wetnwildtoronto.com 🎟 C$45, parking C$15.*

Pearson International Airport Area

If you have an early-morning departure or late-night arrival at Pearson International Airport, staying nearby might be the best option, considering the drive from downtown Toronto can take up to two hours when traffic is at its worst.

Hotels

Alt Hotel Pearson

$$ | **HOTEL** | Not your average airport hotel, this hip boutique lodging offers plush digs at affordable prices. **Pros:** minutes from all airport terminals; rooms have lots of high-tech touches; modern and minimalist decor. **Cons:** some noise from hallways; minimal breakfast service; location on the highway. [$] *Rooms from: C$169 ✉ 6080 Viscount Rd., Mississauga ☎ 905/362–4337, 855/855–6080 🌐 www.althotels.com/en/torontoairport 🛏 153 rooms 🍴 No meals.*

Sandman Signature Toronto Airport

$$ | **HOTEL** | **FAMILY** | Reasonable prices, an indoor swimming pool and hot tub, and quiet, modern rooms are the advantages of this property just down the road from Pearson International Airport. **Pros:** roomy fitness center; excellent service; free Internet access. **Cons:** restaurant gets extremely busy; poll area feels a bit closed in; some rooms need a refresh. [$] *Rooms from: C$159 ✉ 55 Reading Ct., Mississauga ☎ 416/798–8840 🌐 www.sandmanhotels.com 🛏 256 rooms 🍴 No meals.*

Sheraton Gateway Hotel

$$$ | **HOTEL** | For quick layovers, it's hard to beat the location of this chain hotel right inside the main terminal of Pearson International Airport. **Pros:** you can't get closer to your gate than this; totally soundproof rooms; attractive restaurant. **Cons:** fitness center is on the small side; pricey compared to nearby options; some dated furnishings. [$] *Rooms from: C$264 ✉ Terminal 3, Toronto AMF, Mississauga ☎ 905/672–7000 🌐 www.starwoodhotels.com 🛏 474 rooms 🍴 No meals.*

Chapter 12

SIDE TRIPS FROM TORONTO

Updated by
Jesse Ship

◉ Sights	🍴 Restaurants	🛏 Hotels	🛍 Shopping	🍸 Nightlife
★★★★★	★★★★☆	★★★★☆	★★★☆☆	★★☆☆☆

WELCOME TO
SIDE TRIPS FROM TORONTO

TOP REASONS TO GO

★ **Take in Niagara Falls:** The Falls' amazing display of natural power is Ontario's top attraction. See them from both the U.S. and Canadian sides.

★ **Enjoy Shakespeare and Shaw:** A couple of long-dead British playwrights have managed to make two Ontario towns boom from May through October with the Shakespeare Festival in Stratford and the Shaw Festival in Niagara-on-the-Lake.

★ **Tour Award-Winning Wineries:** The Niagara Peninsula has an unusually good microclimate for growing grapes; most of the more than 60 wineries have tastings.

★ **Explore the Great Outdoors:** Ski at resorts north of Toronto; canoe backcountry rivers in Algonquin Provincial Park; hike or bike the Niagara-to-Lake-Huron Bruce Trail or the Niagara Parkway along the Niagara River.

★ **Taste a Little of Ontario:** Niagara-on-the-Lake and Stratford are both renowned for their skilled chefs who serve culinary masterpieces created with farm-fresh ingredients.

1 Niagara Falls. South of Toronto near the U.S. border, the thundering falls are an impressive display of nature's power. Taking a boat ride to the bottom of the falls is a thrilling experience, and one that's guaranteed to leave you soaked.

2 The Niagara Wine Region. The temperate Niagara region bordering Lake Ontario is the ideal growing climate for all kinds of produce, including grapes. Wineries stretch along the shores of Lake Ontario south of Toronto to the pretty Victorian-style town of Niagara-on-the-Lake, at the junction of Lake Ontario and the Niagara River.

3 Stratford. An acclaimed Shakespeare Festival brings this rural town alive from April through October. Overwhelmingly popular, it has become Stratford's raison d'être, with a multitude of inns and locavore restaurants growing up around it. Frequent outdoor music and arts festivals color the squares and parks all summer.

4 Southern Georgian Bay. The southern shores of Lake Huron's Georgian Bay are home to waterfront towns and beaches that are popular getaways for Torontonians in summer. Ski resorts—Blue Mountain is the most popular—draw city folk as well once the snow falls and they become biking and adventure resorts in summer.

5 Muskoka. This area north of the city is known for its lakes and vacation cottages. Tackle the four-hour drive to Algonquin Provincial Park and you're rewarded with pristine forested land for canoeing, camping, and moose-spotting.

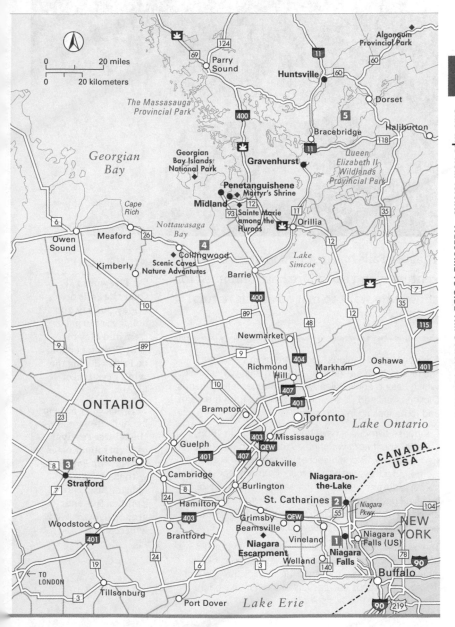

0 20 miles
0 20 kilometers

124
69
Parry Sound
Huntsville 60
11
60
Algonquin Provincial Park
Dorset

The Massasauga Provincial Park
400
Bracebridge 118
5
11
Haliburton
35

Georgian Bay
Georgian Bay Islands National Park
Gravenhurst
Queen Elizabeth II Wildlands Provincial Park

Cape Rich
Penetanguishene
Martyr's Shrine
Midland 12
93 Sainte Marie among the Hurons
11 Orillia
12

Owen Sound 6
Meaford 26
Nottawasaga Bay
Collingwood
4
Lake Simcoe
35

Kimberly
Scenic Caves Nature Adventures
Barrie
400
7

10
89
89
Newmarket
9
48
12

9
6
10
Richmond Hill
404
Markham
Oshawa 401
115

ONTARIO
Brampton
407
401
Toronto Lake Ontario

23
Guelph
403 Mississauga
401 407 QEW
Oakville

8 3
Kitchener
Stratford
Cambridge
8
Burlington
Niagara-on-the-Lake

7
24
Hamilton
St. Catharines 2
55
Niagara Pkwy
NEW YORK 104

Woodstock
403
Brantford
Grimsby
Beamsville
QEW
Vineland
Niagara Falls (US)

401
24
Niagara Escarpment
Welland 140
Niagara Falls 1
Buffalo
78
90

19
Tillsonburg
3
6
3
Port Dover
Lake Erie
90 219

CANADA
USA

TO LONDON

Niagara Falls has inspired visitors for centuries, and the allure hasn't dimmed for those who want to marvel at this natural wonder.

Missionary and explorer Louis Hennepin described the falls in 1678 as "an incredible Cataract or Waterfall which has no equal." Nearly two centuries later, Charles Dickens declared, "I seemed to be lifted from the earth and to be looking into Heaven."

Countless daredevils have been lured here. In 1859, 100,000 spectators watched as the French tightrope walker Charles Blondin successfully crossed Niagara Gorge, on a three-inch-thick rope. From the early 18th century, dozens went over in boats and barrels. Nobody survived until 1901, when schoolteacher Annie Taylor emerged from her barrel and asked, "Did I go over the falls yet?" Stunts were outlawed in 1912.

The depiction of the thundering cascades in the 1953 Marilyn Monroe film *Niagara* is largely responsible for creating modern-day tourism. And though the lights of the souvenir shops and casinos shine garishly bright for some, views of the falls are unspoiled.

NIGHT LIGHTS

See **Fireworks Over the Falls** on Friday, Sunday, and holidays at 10 pm from mid-May to early September (and on Friday during the Winter Festival of Lights).

Between early November and late January, the **Winter Festival of Lights** illuminates the Niagara Parkway, with 125 animated lighting displays and 3 million tree and ground lights. ⊕ *www.wfol.com.*

WAYS TO EXPLORE

BY AIR:

National Helicopters. National Helicopters has 20-minute tours over the falls and wine country, plus romance and other specialty tours. ✉ *Niagara District Airport, 468 Niagara Stone Rd., Niagara-on-the-Lake* ☎ *905/641–2222, 800/491–3117* ⊕ *www.nationalhelicopters.com.*

Niagara Helicopters. This company does 12-minute sightseeing flights over the whirlpool, gorge, and all three falls, plus winery trips. ✉ *3731 Victoria Ave., Niagara Falls* ☎ *905/357–5672, 800/281–8034* ⊕ *www.niagarahelicopters.com* ✉ *C$139/person* ☞ *C$149.*

The **Whirlpool Aero Car** cable car crosses the gorge over the Niagara River whirlpool.

BY BOAT:

The **Maid of the Mist** is an oldie but a goodie, and still pulls in huge crowds. Adrenaline-fueled Whirlpool Jet Boat Tours in Niagara-on-the-Lake plow headfirst into the Class-V Niagara River rapids on an hour-long ride.

BY BUS:

Double Deck Tours Take an authentic, red London double-decker bus tour with Double Deck Tours. Fares include admission to Journey Behind the Falls, *Maid of the Mist,* and the Whirlpool Aero Car; the four-hour tour also includes the Floral Clock and Niagara Glen. ✉ *5900 Falls Ave., Niagara Falls* ☎ *905/374–7423* ⊕ *www.doubledecktours.com* ✉ *C$86.*

BY FOOT:

Stroll the Niagara Parkway promenade, stand on the Table Rock Centre terrace, and walk over the Rainbow Bridge. The **White Water Walk** is the closest you'll get to the rapids from land; **Journey Behind the Falls** is a walk through tunnels behind the falls.

IN ONE DAY

If you have only a day in Niagara Falls, walk the waterfront promenade and go on a *Maid of the Mist* tour. (Plan for wet shins and shoes.) Also consider the Whirlpool Aero Car, a cable-car ride over the whirlpool, or the Whitewater Walk, to see the rapids up close. Dinner within view of the falls, which are colorfully lit at night, is a relaxing end to a full day.

THE AMERICAN SIDE

Canada has the superior views and a more developed waterfront, with better restaurants. In contrast, the American waterfront is lined with parks, ideal for hiking and picnicking. Because you're behind the falls here, rather than facing them, views are limited. Stick to Canada for most of your visit, but if you have more time, cross the Rainbow Bridge on foot to get close to Bridal Veil Falls on a Cave of the Winds tour from Goat Island.

Ontario may not be famed for its wines—yet—but the Niagara Peninsula alone has around 75 wineries and has been producing wine commercially since the early 1970s. Four decades on, the region is coming into its own with some of the world's best wines of origin.

The position of the Niagara appellation, wedged between Lake Ontario and the Niagara Escarpment, creates a microclimate that regulates ground and air temperature and allows for successful grape growing (today more than 30 varietals) in an otherwise too-cold province. Winds off Lake Ontario are directed back by the escarpment, preventing cold air from settling. Heat stored in lake waters in summer keeps ground temperatures warmer longer into winter. In spring, the cold waters keep the grounds from warming too fast, protecting buds from late-spring frosts. Some say that the slightly colder climate means a more complex-tasting grape. Indisputably it *does* provide perfect conditions for producing some of the world's best ice wine.

WHAT'S IN A VQA

Canadian wine is regulated by the Vintners Quality Alliance. Many Niagara wineries proudly declare their vintages VQA; in fact, 65% of all VQA wines in Ontario are Niagara wines. To be deemed VQA is no small honor: wines must meet rigorous standards—including being made entirely from fresh, quality-approved Ontario-grown grapes (no concentrates) and improved grape varieties, passing laboratory testing, and approval by an expert tasting panel prior to release. Look for the VQA stamp on the label.

NIAGARA WINE TOURING BASICS

THE ONTARIO WINE ROUTE

Niagara Grape & Wine Festival. The Niagara Grape & Wine Festival group organizes three big events in Niagara. The largest, with an annual half-million attendees, is the eponymous, 10-day **Niagara Wine Festival**, in September, celebrating the grape harvest. The three-week **Niagara Ice Wine Festival**, in January, is a nod to Niagara's specialty, ice wine. The three-weekend **Niagara New Vintage Festival**, in June, is a wine-and-culinary event. ⊠ *Montebello Park, 64 Ontario St., St. Catharines* ☎ *905/688–0212* ⊕ *www.niagarawinefestival.com.*

TIMING AND COSTS

Most wineries are open year-round, with limited hours in winter. Tastings begin between 10 and noon. Reservations may be needed for tours in summer.

Tastings usually cost C$1–C$2 per wine, or up to C$7 for more expensive wines. The larger wineries do regular public tours; at smaller operations you may be able to arrange a tour in advance. Tasting and/or tour fees are often waived if you buy a bottle of wine.

ORGANIZED TOURS

Crush on Niagara. Crush on Niagara wine-tour packages include overnight stays, meals, and winery tours. ⊠ *4101 King St., Beamsville* ☎ *905/562–3373, 866/408–9463* ⊕ *www.crushtours.com.*

Grape and Wine Tours. Grape and Wine Tours runs day trips and one- or two-night wine-tour packages from Toronto and Oakville. Pickup and drop-off at Niagara-on-the-Lake and Niagara Falls hotels is included. ⊠ *758 Niagara Stone Rd., Niagara-on-the-Lake* ☎ *905/562–4920, 855/682–4920* ⊕ *www.niagaragrapeandwinetours.ca.*

ONTARIO'S ICE WINES: SWEET SIPPING

Ontario is the world's leading producer of ice wine. It's produced from ripe grapes left on the vine into the winter. When grapes start to freeze, most of the water in them solidifies, resulting in a fructose-laden, aromatic, and flavorful center. Ice-wine grapes must be picked at freezing temperatures before sunrise and basket-pressed immediately. By nature ice wine is sweet, and when well made it smells of dried fruits, apricots, and honey and has a long, refreshing finish.

Vidal grapes are ideal for ice wine, due to their thick skin and resistance to cracking in sub-zero temperatures. The thin-skinned Riesling yields better results but is susceptible to cracking and ripens much later than Vidal.

Drink ice wine after dinner, with a not-too-sweet dessert, or alongside a strong cheese. Here in Niagara it also appears in unexpected places such as tea, martinis, chocolate, ice cream, French toast, and glazes for meat and seafood.

The rush of 700,000 gallons of water a second. The divinely sweet, crisp taste of ice wine. The tug of a fish hooked under a layer of ice. Sure, the big-city scene in Toronto delivers the hustle and bustle you came for, but escaping the city can transport you to another world. The struggle is choosing which world to visit first.

There's Niagara Falls, acres of local vineyards in Niagara-on-the-Lake and the surrounding wine region, or the whimsical "cottage country," with its quiet towns, challenging ski slopes, and lakefront resorts. Or you can hit the outdoors on Bruce Trail, Canada's oldest and longest footpath, which winds from Niagara Falls to Tobermory 885 km (550 miles) north.

If superlatives are what you seek, the mesmerizing and deservedly hyped Niagara Falls, one of—or more technically, three of—the most famous waterfalls in the world, is Ontario's most popular attraction. Worth seeing at least once, it is truly beautiful (say what you will about the showy town behind it).

Oenophile trailblazers should consider Niagara's rapidly developing wine trail. The Niagara Escarpment, hugging Lake Ontario's western shores, is one of the most fertile growing areas in Canada. A lakeshore drive southwest of Toronto yields miles of vineyards and farm-to-table restaurants, culminating in the Victorian white-picket-fence town of Niagara-on-the-Lake, known for its amazing five-star restaurants and hotels and nearly as luxurious B&Bs.

Nourish your appreciation for the arts in and around Stratford. Two major theater events, the Stratford Festival and the Shaw Festival (in Niagara-on-the-Lake), have long seasons with masterfully orchestrated plays by William Shakespeare and George Bernard Shaw.

Both outdoors enthusiasts who want to rough it and soft-adventure seekers who yearn for a comfortable bed with the glow of a fireplace at night feel the lure of the nearly 3,000-acre Algonquin Provincial Park. Sunday drivers find solace near Georgian Bay and in the Muskokas, part of Ontario's lake-smattered cottage country.

Planning

When to Go

With the exception of destinations like wineries and ski resorts, June through September is prime travel season: Stratford and Shaw festivals are in full swing, hours of operation are longer for most attractions, the mist coming from Niagara Falls is at its most refreshing, and patios are open almost everywhere, not to mention the obvious abundance of water activities and amusement parks.

That said, there's fun to be had in wintertime as well. While Muskoka cottage country, Stratford, and some parks in Algonquin become inaccessible ghost towns between November and April (the time most resorts schedule renovations and maintenance), ski resorts and wineries offer many packages and activities. Enjoy tours on and tastings of one of Ontario's most prized exports during Niagara's Ice Wine Festival, or enjoy the Canadian winter by snowboarding, skiing, ice fishing, and snowmobiling. Travel around the holiday season to take in the beautiful decorations, lights, and special events.

Getting Here and Around

AIR
Toronto's Pearson International Airport, 30 km (18 miles) north of downtown, is the obvious choice. Downtown Toronto's smaller Billy Bishop Toronto City Airport serves mostly Porter Airlines; it gets you Niagara-bound on the Gardiner Expressway in a matter of minutes. Hamilton International Airport is about halfway between Toronto and Niagara Falls. Buffalo Niagara International Airport is 30 miles from Niagara Falls, Ontario, but border crossings can add time to your trip.

CONTACTS Billy Bishop Toronto City Airport. ⊠ 1 Island Airport, Harbourfront ☎ 416/203–6942 ⊕ www.billybishopairport.com. **Buffalo Niagara International Airport.** ⊠ 4200 Genesee St., Buffalo ☎ 716/630–6000 ⊕ www.buffaloairport.com. **Hamilton International Airport.** ⊠ 9300 Airport Rd., Hamilton ☎ 905/679–1999 ⊕ flyhamilton.ca. **Toronto Pearson International Airport.** ⊠ 6301 Silver Dart Dr., Mississauga ✥ Best accessed by UPX, direct train from Union subway station

☎ 866/207–1690, 416/247–7678 ⊕ v torontopearson.com.

CAR
Ontario's only toll road is the east–west Highway 407, north of Toronto. It's expensive (22¢–25¢ per kilometer) and has no tollbooths; you will be billed via mail if the system has your state's license plate information on file. Avoid Toronto-area highways during weekday rush hours (6:30 to 9:30 am and 3:30 to 6:30 pm). Traffic between Toronto and Hamilton might crawl along at any hour.

You can get by without a car in downtown Niagara Falls and Stratford if you book a hotel close to the action.

The Ministry of Transportation has updates for roadwork and winter road conditions.

CONTACTS Ministry of Transportation. ☎ 416/235–4686, 800/268–4686 ⊕ www.mto.gov.on.ca.

TRAIN
VIA Rail connects Toronto with Niagara Falls and Stratford. GO Transit, Toronto's commuter rail, has summer weekend service to Niagara Falls. Ontario Northland's Northlander line travels between Toronto and Bracebridge, Gravenhurst, Huntsville, and other northern points.

CONTACTS GO Transit. ☎ 416/869–3200, 888/438–6646 ⊕ www.gotransit.com. **Ontario Northland.** ☎ 705/476–5598, 800/363–7512 ⊕ www.ontarionorthland.ca. **VIA Rail.** ☎ 888/842–7245 ⊕ www.viarail.ca.

Hotels

Make reservations well in advance during summer and at ski areas in winter. Prices are higher in peak season and nearer to the tourist centers. In Niagara Falls, for example, hotel rates are determined by proximity to the falls. Taxes are seldom included in quoted prices, but rates sometimes include food, especially in

Toronto is a great base to begin your explorations of Ontario.

One Day: In a long day you could see a matinee at the Shakespeare festival, hit a ski resort north of Toronto, visit a few Niagara Escarpment wineries, or—with some stamina—see Niagara Falls. All these destinations require about four hours of driving time round-trip, not accounting for rush-hour traffic jams.

Two Days: A couple of days are sufficient to get a feel for Niagara Falls, Niagara-on-the-Lake, Stratford, or a Muskoka town or two. Alternatively, head up to Collingwood for an overnight snowboarding or skiing trip.

Four Days: You can decide between an intensive outdoorsy trip in the Algonquin area hiking, biking, camping, canoeing, and exploring; or, a relaxing tour of Niagara Falls and Niagara-on-the-Lake, with some time spent at spas and wineries, biking, and hitting culinary hot spots.

One Week: Combine Stratford and Niagara, or really delve into the Niagara region. (A week is probably too much for just Niagara Falls or just Niagara-on-the-Lake.) Alternatively, you could spend some serious time communing with nature in Algonquin Park and meandering through quaint Muskoka and Georgian Bay towns.

more remote areas such as Muskoka, where many resorts offer meal plans. *Hotel reviews have been shortened. For full information, visit Fodors.com.*

What it Costs in Canadian Dollars			
$	**$$**	**$$$**	**$$$$**
RESTAURANTS			
under C$12	C$12–C$20	C$21–C$30	over C$30
HOTELS			
under C$125	C$125–C$175	C$176–C$250	over C$250

Restaurants

The dining in Stratford and Niagara-on-the-Lake is enough to boost a whole other genre of tourism, as there are a number of outstanding restaurants thanks to the area's many chefs being trained at the area's reputable culinary schools, and impeccably fresh ingredients from local farms. Produce, meats, cheeses, beers, and wine are all produced in Ontario, and some restaurants even have their own gardens, vineyards, or farms. In the immediate areas surrounding Niagara Falls, the dining is a little more lackluster, as views, convenience, and glamour take precedence over food, but there are some great pubs and upscale restaurants to be found among the tourist traps. Reservations are always encouraged, if not essential.

Visitor Information

CONTACTS Niagara Falls Tourism. ☎ 800/563-2557 ⊕ www.niagarafallstourism.com. **Ontario Parks.** ☎ 888/668-7275, 519/826-5290 ⊕ www.ontarioparks.com. **Ontario Snow Resorts Association.** ☎ 705/443-5450 ⊕ www.skiontario.ca. **Ontario Tourism.** ☎ 800/668-2746, 905/754-1958 ⊕ www.ontariotravel.net. **Tourism Niagara.** ☎ 289/477-5344 ⊕ www.tourismniagara.com.

Clifton Hill's food, shopping, games, rides, and other attractions will keep the whole family entertained.

Niagara Falls

130 km (81 miles) south of Toronto.

Niagara Falls has inspired artists for centuries. English painter William H. Bartlett, who visited here in the mid-1830s, noted that "you may dream of Niagara, but words will never describe it to you." Although cynics have called it everything from "water on the rocks" to "the second major disappointment of American married life" (Oscar Wilde)—most visitors are truly impressed. Henry James recorded in 1883 how one stands there "gazing your fill at the most beautiful object in the world."

WHEN TO GO

Water-based falls tours operate only between mid-May and mid-September, and the summer weather combats the chilly falls mist. Fewer events take place in other seasons, and it's too cold in winter to linger on the promenade along the parkway next to the falls, but it's much easier to reserve a window-side table for two at a falls-view restaurant. Clifton Hill and most indoor attractions are open year-round. At any time of year it feels a few degrees cooler on the walkway near the falls.

GETTING HERE AND AROUND

Niagara Falls is easily accessible by car, bus, and train. VIA Rail and GO (summer only) trains serve Niagara Falls, both stopping at the main rail station, not far from the falls. WEGO is a Niagara region bus system with four lines designed for tourists. The nearest airports are in Toronto, Hamilton, and Buffalo, New York.

If you want to explore on your own, a car is by far the best choice. The four- to eight-lane Queen Elizabeth Way—better known as the QEW—runs from the U.S. border at Fort Erie through the Niagara region to Toronto.

BORDER CROSSINGS

Everyone—including children and U.S. citizens—must have a passport or other approved travel document (e.g., a New York State–issued "enhanced" driver's

:ense) to enter the United States. The Department of Homeland Security website (⊕ *www.dhs.gov*) has the latest information. Avoid crossing the border at high-traffic times, especially Friday and Saturday nights. The Canada Border Agency and the U.S. Customs and Border Protection list border wait times into Canada and into the U.S., respectively, online at ⊕ *www.cbsa-asfc.gc.ca/bwt-taf* and ⊕ *apps.cbp.gov/bwt*. Crossings are at the Peace Bridge (Fort Erie, ON–Buffalo, NY), the Queenston–Lewiston Bridge (Queenston, ON–Lewiston, NY), and the Rainbow Bridge (Niagara Falls, ON–Niagara Falls, NY).

PARKING
In Niagara Falls, parking prices increase closer to the falls. It can be triple the price to park along the Niagara Parkway (C$26.55 per day) than it is up the hill near Victoria Street (usually C$5 per day). If you park up top, know that the walk down to the falls is a steep one. You might want to take a taxi back up, or hop aboard the Falls Incline Railway, a funicular that operates between the Table Rock Centre and Portage Road behind the Konica Minolta Tower. The trip takes about one minute and costs C$2.75 (day passes are available for C$7).

SHUTTLE
Available year-round, climate-controlled WEGO buses travel on a loop route on the Niagara Parkway between the Table Rock Centre and the Whirlpool Aero Car parking lot, about 9 km (6 miles) north and as far north as Queenston Heights Park, 15 km (9 miles) downriver. A day pass, available from welcome centers and at any booth on the system, is C$9 per person per day (get the second day free from late October to mid-April). You can get on and off as many times as you wish at well-marked stops along the route, and buses pick up frequently (every 20 minutes).

CONTACTS Niagara Falls VIA Rail Canada Train Station. ✉ *4267 Bridge*

First Things First

Start at the **Table Rock Welcome Centre** (✉ *6650 Niagara Pkwy., about 500 meters south of Murray Hill*) for a close-up of Horseshoe Falls. Here you can buy a Niagara Parks Great Gorge Adventure Pass, tickets for the WEGO buses, and do the Journey Behind the Falls and Niagara's Fury. At the end of the WEGO line, it's easy to hop aboard and do all the falls-front sights in a northward direction. Starting with the *Maid of the Mist* or a Jet Boat Tour when you arrive is also a good way to get your feet wet—literally.

St. ☎ *888/842–7245* ⊕ *www.viarail. ca.* **WEGO.** ☎ *905/356–1179* ⊕ *www. wegoniagarafalls.com.*

DISCOUNTS AND DEALS
Pick up the free Save-A-Buck coupon booklet for discounts on various tours, attractions, and restaurants. ■ TIP→ **Many attractions have significant online discounts and combination tickets.** Bundled passes are available through the tourism board, at welcome centers (foot of Clifton Hill and Murray Hill, near *Maid of the Mist* ticket booth, Table Rock Centre), and at most attractions' ticket windows.

The **Clifton Hill Fun Pass** incorporates entry to six of the better Clifton Hill attractions (including the SkyWheel and the Midway Combo Pass rides) for C$29.95. The Midway Combo Pass (C$9.99) includes two indoor thrill rides: Wild West Coaster Simulator and the Ghostblasters Dark Ride.

Available mid-April to late October, the **Niagara Falls and Great Gorge Pass** (C$65) covers admission to Journey Behind the Falls, *Maid of the Mist,* White Water Walk, and Niagara's Fury, plus a number

Niagara Falls: Past and Future

The story begins more than 10,000 years ago as a group of glaciers receded, diverting the waters of Lake Erie north into Lake Ontario. The force and volume of the water as it flowed over the Niagara Escarpment created the thundering cataracts. Erosion has been considerable since then, more than 7 miles in all, as the soft shale and sandstone of the escarpment have been washed away and the falls have receded. Diversions of the water for power generation have slowed the erosion somewhat, spreading the flow more evenly over the entire crestline of Horseshoe Falls. The erosion is now down to 1 foot or less per year.

At this rate—given effects of power generation and change in riverbed composition—geologists estimate it will be some 50,000 years before the majestic cascade is reduced to rapids somewhere near present-day Buffalo, 20 miles to the south.

of discounts and two days of unlimited use of both the WEGO buses and the Falls Incline Railway. From late October to mid-April, the **Winter Magic Pass** includes Niagara's Fury, the Butterfly Conservatory, Journey Behind the Falls, and discount coupons.

CONTACTS Clifton Hill Fun Pass. ⊕ *www. cliftonhill.com.*

TOURIST INFORMATION

The main Niagara Falls Tourism center is on Robinson Street near the Skylon Tower.

Open June through August, welcome centers are run by Niagara Parks and have tickets for and information about Niagara Parks sights, including WEGO and Falls Incline Railway passes and the Niagara Falls and Great Gorge Adventure Pass. Welcome Centre kiosks are at the foot of Clifton Hill, foot of Murray Hill, and near the *Maid of the Mist* ticket booth; a welcome center booth is inside the Table Rock Centre.

CONTACTS Info Niagara - Fallsview Tourist Area. ⊠ *5400 Robinson St.* ☎ *905/356–6061, 800/563–2557* ⊕ *www. niagarafallstourism.com.* **Niagara Parks.**

☎ *905/356–2241, 877/642–7275* ⊕ *www. niagaraparks.com.* **Niagara Parks Commission.** ☎ *905/371–0254, 877/642–7275* ⊕ *www.niagaraparks.com.* **Ontario Trails Council.** ☎ *877/668–7245, 613/389–7678* ⊕ *www.ontariotrails.on.ca.*

Sights

Battle Ground Hotel Museum

MUSEUM | The region's only surviving example a 19th-century tavern, this clapboard building originally opened to serve early visitors to the battleground of the War of 1812. There are displays of the lives of settlers during the war, native artifacts, and military attire. ⊠ *6137 Lundy's Lane* ☎ *905/358–5082* ⊕ *niagarafallsmuseums.ca/visit/battle-ground-hotel-museum.aspx* ⊠ *Donation.*

Bird Kingdom

ZOO | **FAMILY** | A tropical respite from the crowds and Las Vegas–style attractions, Bird Kingdom is the world's largest indoor aviary, with more than 400 free-flying birds and more than 80 bird species from around the world in the 50,000-square-foot complex. For creepy-crawly lovers, there are also ers, lizards, and snakes—including 00-pound python that you can hold. arking is an additional C$2 per half hour, but there's a public lot on nearby Hiram Street that is C$5 per day. ✉ *5651 River Rd.* ☎ *905/356–8888, 866/994–0090* ⊕ *www.birdkingdom.ca* 🖼 *C$18.*

Casino Niagara

CASINO—SIGHT | Smaller and more low-key than Fallsview, Casino Niagara has slot machines, video-poker machines, and gambling tables for blackjack, roulette, and baccarat. There are also several lounges, a sports bar, a Yuk Yuk's comedy club, and an all-you-can-eat buffet restaurant. ✉ *5705 Falls Ave.* ☎ *905/374–3598, 888/946–3255* ⊕ *www.casinoniagara.com.*

Clifton Hill

NEIGHBORHOOD | **FAMILY** | This is undeniably the most crassly commercial district of Niagara Falls, with haunted houses, more wax museums than one usually sees in a lifetime, and fast-food chains galore (admittedly, the Burger King here is unique for its gigantic Frankenstein statue towering above). For kids the entertainment is endless, especially kids who enjoy arcade games. Attractions are typically open late (as late as 2 am in summer, 11 pm the rest of the year), with admission ranging from about C$10 to C$16. One of the most popular attractions is the 175-foot **SkyWheel** (C$10.99) with enclosed, climate-controlled compartments. Next door, **Dinosaur Adventure Golf** (C$9.99) combines minigolf, ferocious mechanical dinosaurs, and an erupting minivolcano. The **Great Canadian Midway** is a 70,000-square-foot entertainment complex with arcade games, a bowling alley, air hockey, and food. **Ripley's Believe It or Not! Museum** is creepily fascinating, while **Movieland Wax Museum** has such lifelike characters as Harry Potter and Barack and Michelle Obama. **Hershey's Chocolate World** is 7,000 square feet of truffles, fudge, and the trademark Kisses, marked by a six-story chocolate bar at the base of the hill, on the other

side of Casino Niagara. ✉ *Clifton Hill* ☎ *905/358–3676* ⊕ *www.cliftonhill.com.*

Fallsview Casino Resort

CASINO—SIGHT | Canada's largest gaming and resort facility crowns the city's skyline, overlooking the Niagara Parks with picture-perfect views of the falls. Within the 30-story complex are Canada's first casino wedding chapel, a glitzy theater, spa, shops, and plenty of restaurants. For the gaming enthusiasts, more than 100 gaming tables and 3,000 slot machines on one of the wolrd's largest casino gaming floors. The Las Vegas–style Avalon Ballroom showcases a wide array of talents, from Al Pacino to Jon Stewart. ✉ *6380 Fallsview Blvd.* ☎ *888/325–5788, 905/371–7505* ⊕ *www.fallsviewcasinoresort.com.*

★ Hornblower Niagara Cruises

TOUR—SIGHT | **FAMILY** | Operating since 1846, when they were wooden-hulled, coal-fired steamboats, the misty tour boats are now run by Hornblower. Double-deck steel vessels tow fun-loving passengers on 20-minute journeys to the foot of the falls, where the spray is so heavy that ponchos must be distributed. From the observation areas along the falls, you can see those boarding the boats in their blue slickers. The very similar *Maid of the Mist* boat tours operate from the American side. ■**TIP**➜ **Unless you cower in the center of the boat, your shoes and pants will get wet: wear quick-drying items or bring spares.** ✉ *5920 Niagara Pkwy.* ⊕ *www.niagaracruises.com/voyage-to-the-falls-boat-tour* 🖼 *C$29* ⊗ *Closed Nov.–Apr.*

Journey Behind the Falls

VIEWPOINT | This 30- to 45-minute tour starts with an elevator ride down to an observation deck that provides an eye-level view of the Canadian Horseshoe Falls and the Niagara River. From there a walk through tunnels cut into the rock takes you behind thunderous waterfalls, and you can glimpse the back side of the crashing water through two portals

Rides on the Maid of the Mist have been thrilling visitors to Niagara Falls since 1846.

cut in the rock face. ✉ *Table Rock Centre, 6650 Niagara Pkwy.* ☎ *905/371–0254, 877/642–7275* ⊕ *www.niagaraparks.com* 🎟 *Mid-Dec.–mid-Apr. C$12, mid-Apr.– Dec. C$22.*

Marineland

AMUSEMENT PARK/WATER PARK | FAMILY | A theme park with a marine show, wildlife displays, and rides—as well as a beluga whale habitat with underwater viewing areas—Marineland is 1½ km (1 mile) south of the falls. The daily marine shows include performing killer whales, dolphins, harbor seals, and sea lions. Children can pet and feed deer at the Deer Park. Among the many rides are Dragon Mountain, the world's largest nonstop roller coaster and tamer fare like Ocean Odyssey for the kids. ✉ *7657 Portage Rd., off Niagara Pkwy.* ☎ *905/356–9565* ⊕ *www.marineland.ca* 🎟 *C$51* ⊘ *Closed mid-Oct.–mid-May.*

★ Niagara Falls

SIGHTS OVERVIEW | One of North America's most impressive natural wonders, the falls are actually three cataracts: the American and Bridal Veil Falls in New York State, and the Horseshoe Falls in Ontario. In terms of sheer volume of water— more than 700,000 gallons per second in summer—Niagara is unsurpassed compared to other bodies of water on the continent.

On the Canadian side, you can get a far better view of the American Falls and a close-up of the Horseshoe Falls. You can also park your car for the day in any of several lots and hop onto one of the WEGO buses, which run continuously to all the sights along the river. If you want to get close to the foot of the falls, the *Maid of the Mist* boat takes you near enough to get soaked in the spray.

After experiencing the falls from the Canadian side, you can walk or drive across Rainbow Bridge to the U.S. side. On the American side you can park in the lot on Goat Island near the American Falls and walk along the path beside the Niagara River, which becomes more and more turbulent as it approaches the big drop-off of just over 200 feet.

The amusement parks and tacky souvenir shops that surround the falls attest to the area's history as a major tourist attraction. Most of the gaudiness is contained on Clifton Hill, Niagara Falls' Times Square. Despite these garish efforts to attract visitors, the landscaped grounds immediately bordering the falls are lovely and the beauty of the falls remains untouched.

One reason to spend the night here is to admire the falls illumination, which takes place every night of the year, from dusk until at least 10 pm (as late as 1 am during the summer). Even the most contemptuous observer will be mesmerized as the falls change from red to purple to blue to green to white, and finally all the colors of the rainbow in harmony. ✉ *Niagara Falls.*

Niagara Falls IMAX Theatre
ARTS VENUE | **FAMILY** | Get the human story behind the falls, from local native tribes' relationship with the waters to the foolhardy folks who went over the edge, with *Niagara: Miracles, Myths, & Magic* on the six-story IMAX screen. The on-site Daredevil Exhibit chronicles the expeditions of those who have tackled the falls and has some of the actual barrels they used on display. ✉ *6170 Fallsview Blvd.* ☎ *905/358-3611, 866/405-4629* ⊕ *www. imaxniagara.com* 🎟 *Movie C$16; exhibit C$10.*

Niagara's Fury
TOUR—SIGHT | **FAMILY** | Learn how Niagara Falls formed over thousands of years on this 20-minute simulation ride. Standing on a mesh platform surrounded by an uninterrupted 360-degree viewing screen, you feel snow falling, winds blowing, the floor rumbling, and waves crashing as you watch glaciers form, collide, and melt, creating the falls as we know them today. ■**TIP→ In certain spots you *will* get wet; ponchos are provided.** ✉ *Table Rock Welcome Centre, 6650 Niagara Pkwy.* ☎ *905/356-2241,*

877/642-7275 ⊕ *www.niagaraparks.com/ visit/attractions/niagaras-fury* 🎟 *C$16.*

Niagara Parks Botanical Gardens
GARDEN | These 100 acres of immaculately maintained gardens are among the most captivating attractions around Niagara Falls. Here you'll find the **Niagara Parks Butterfly Conservatory**, housing one of North America's largest collections of free-flying butterflies—at least 2,000 butterflies from 50 species around the world are protected in a climate-controlled, rain forest–like conservatory. ■**TIP→ Between May and mid-October, for C$25 per person, you can tour the gardens in a horse and carriage.** ✉ *2565 Niagara Pkwy* ☎ *905/356-8119, 877/642-7275* ⊕ *www. niagaraparks.com* 🎟 *Parking C$5.*

Skylon Tower
VIEWPOINT | **FAMILY** | Rising 775 feet above the falls, this is the best view of the great Niagara Gorge and the entire city. The indoor-outdoor observation deck has visibility up to 130 km (80 miles) on a clear day. Other reasons to visit include amusements for children, a buffet restaurant, a revolving dining room, and a 3-D theater that lets you experience the falls up close. ■**TIP→ Admission is free if you're enjoying a meal in the dining room.** ✉ *5200 Robinson St.* ☎ *905/356-2651, 800/814-9577* ⊕ *www.skylon.com* 🎟 *C$17.*

Whirlpool Aero Car
VIEWPOINT | **FAMILY** | In operation since 1916, this antique cable car crosses the Whirlpool Basin in the Niagara Gorge. This trip is not for the fainthearted, but there's no better way to get an aerial view of the gorge, the whirlpool, the rapids, and the hydroelectric plants. ✉ *3850 Niagara Pkwy., 4½ km (3 miles) north of falls* ☎ *905/371-0254, 877/642-7275* ⊕ *www.niagaraparks.com/visit/ attractions/whirlpool-aero-car* 🎟 *C$16* ⊗ *Closed early Nov.–mid-Mar.*

White Water Walk

NATURE SITE | FAMILY | A self-guided route involves taking an elevator to the bottom of the Niagara Gorge, the narrow valley created by the Niagara Falls and River, where you can walk along a 1,000-foot boardwalk beside the Class VI rapids of the Niagara River. The gorge is rimmed by sheer cliffs as it enters the giant whirlpool. ✉ *4330 Niagara Pkwy., 3 km (2 miles) north of falls* ☎ *905/371–0254, 877/642–7275* 🌐 *www.niagaraparks.com* 🎫 *C$14* ⏲ *Closed mid-Nov.–early Apr.*

🍴 Restaurants

Dining in Niagara Falls is still a bit disappointing because of the lack of sophistication that usually comes with a highly touristic area (especially when compared with the neighboring foodie paradise Niagara-on-the-Lake). A view of the falls and convenient location don't come cheap, so prices are rarely what one would consider reasonable. Thankfully, the landscape is slowly changing, and some falls-view restaurants, such as 21 Club, are hiring creative chefs who are stepping up the quality—though still at a pretty penny. But with views like these, it might be worth it.

★ Casa Mia Ristorante

$$$$ | ITALIAN | The best ingredients prepared simply and served in generous portions are what make this off-the-beaten-path restaurant such a find. A free shuttle service from Niagara Falls hotels whisks guests to this labor of love, owned and operated by the Mollica family. Modern Amalfi Coast–inspired decor brings a seaside terrace indoors, and it all feels miles, not 10 minutes, away from the city's tourist attractions. **Known for:** extremely popular with local diners; wine cellar with more than 300 options; relaxed dining experience. [$] *Average main: C$35* ✉ *3518 Portage Rd.* ☎ *905/356–5410, 888/956–5410* 🌐 *www.casamiaristorante.com* ⏲ *No lunch weekends.*

Napoli Ristorante e Pizzeria

$$ | ITALIAN | A five-minute drive from Clifton Hill, this local joint manages to be both casual and refined. Sit in the back room where exposed-brick columns and black-and-white photos of Naples on the walls set the scene for the southern Italian pasta dishes and thin-crust pizzas. The extensive menu includes 10 pizzas with wafer-thin crusts and generous dollops of tomato sauce, and plenty of pasta dishes and hearty meat dishes to choose from. **Known for:** family-operated establishment that's a local favorite; extensive Italian and Niagara-region wine selection; homemade roasted sausage with baked polenta. [$] *Average main: C$16* ✉ *5485 Ferry St.* ☎ *905/356–3345* 🌐 *www.napoliristorante.ca* ⏲ *No lunch.*

Queen Victoria Place

$$$ | CONTEMPORARY | Inside a former refectory building dating from 1904, this gracious second-floor restaurant has a huge veranda overlooking the falls across Niagara Parkway. The kitchen run by celebrated chef Sydney Krick, whose menu reflects high-quality contemporary cuisine like burgers with melted goat cheese, porcini-crusted lamb chops, and maple-brined pork chops. **Known for:** books up in advance for seating on the veranda; focus on locally sourced artisanal ingredients; smart wine and beer pairings. [$] *Average main: C$25* ✉ *6345 Niagara Pkwy.* ✥ *At Morrow st.* ☎ *905/356–2217* 🌐 *www.niagaraparks.com/dining.*

Skylon Tower Revolving Dining Room

$$$$ | AMERICAN | The big draw here is the revolving 360-degree view perched 520 feet above the Horseshoe Falls—it's simply breathtaking. The atmosphere puts it above those serving similar cuisine in the area, drawing an eclectic crowd of couples in cocktail attire and families in casual clothes. The menu revolves as well; prime rib with horseradish sauce and chicken cordon bleu have made appearances. One floor above is

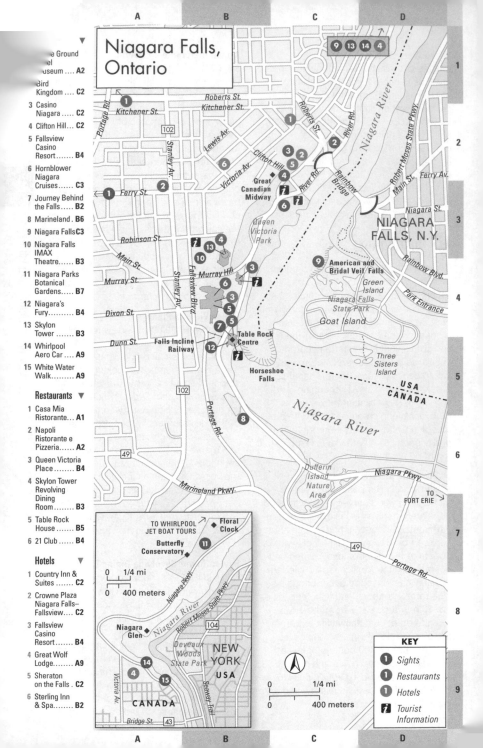

Niagara Falls, Ontario

Roberts St.
Kitchener St.
Kitchener St.
Lewis Av.
Clifton Hill
Roberts St.
River Rd.
Niagara River
Rainbow Bridge
Portage Rd.
102
Stanley Av.
Victoria Av.
Ferry St.
Great
Canadian
Midway
NIAGARA
FALLS, N.Y.
Niagara St.
Robinson St.
Main St.
Murray St.
Queen
Victoria
Park
American and
Bridal Veil Falls
Rainbow Blvd.
Robert Moses State Pkwy.
Main St.   Ferry Av.
Park Entrance
Green
Island
Niagara Falls
State Park
Goat Island
Three
Sisters
Island
USA
CANADA
Murray Hill
Fallsview Blvd.
Stanley Av.
Dixon St.
Dunn St.
Falls Incline
Railway
Table Rock
Centre
Horseshoe
Falls
Niagara River
102
Dufferin
Island
Nature
Area
Niagara Pkwy.
TO
FORT ERIE →
49
Portage Rd.
Marineland Pkwy.
Portage Rd.
49

TO WHIRLPOOL
JET BOAT TOURS
Floral
Clock
Butterfly
Conservatory
Niagara Pkwy.
0   1/4 mi
0   400 meters
Niagara River
Robert Moses State Pkwy.
104
Niagara
Glen
Deveaux
Woods
State Park
NEW
YORK
USA
Victoria Av.
CANADA
Bridge St.
43
Seaway Trail

0   1/4 mi
0   400 meters

KEY

1 Sights
1 Restaurants
1 Hotels
🛈 Tourist
Information

the **Summit Suite Buffet**, an all-you-can-eat option that doesn't revolve, but has comparable views for slightly less money. A reservation at either restaurant includes free admission to the observation deck. **Known for:** best spot for seasonal firework shows; revolving selection of special dishes; award-winning cuisine. $ *Average main: C$55* ✉ *5200 Robinson St.* ☎ *905/356–2651, 888/975–9566* ⊕ *www.skylon.com* ☽ *Closed Nov.–Apr.*

Table Rock House

$$$$ | CONTEMPORARY | White tablecloth service, and an-up-close-and-personal view of the rushing Horseshoe falls rapids amount to a stunning dining experience. Prix-fixe dinners are recommended to take advantage of the hearty menu. **Known for:** crème brûlée with Wayne Gretzky cream whiskey; the closest possible dining experience to the falls; Fogo Island shrimp ciabatta sandwich. $ *Average main: C$45* ✉ *6650 Niagara Pkwy.* ☎ *905/354–3631* ⊕ *www.niagarafallstourism.com/eat/fallsview-dining/table-rock-house-restaurant.*

21 Club

$$$$ | STEAKHOUSE | The best fine-dining-with-a-view in town, 21 Club plays up its casino locale without being kitschy. The high-ceiling modern space is inspired by roulette, in a profusion of red, black, and gold, and juxtaposes the traditional steak-house menu. More secluded seating areas wind around the perimeter next to huge windows overlooking the falls, on a raised, illuminated floor on a patio. Because 21 Club is accessible only via the casino floor, all diners must be at least 19. **Known for:** steak options span the continents; extensive wine list with more than 700 options; on-site sommeliers know their stuff. $ *Average main: C$40* ✉ *Fallsview Casino Resort, 6380 Fallsview Blvd.* ☎ *905/358–3255, 888/325–5788* ⊕ *www.fallsviewcasinoresort.com/dining* ☽ *Closed Tues. and Wed. No lunch.*

Hotels

A room with a view of the falls means staying in a high-rise hotel, usually a chain. Hotels with falls views are clustered near the two streets leading down to the falls, Clifton Hill (and adjacent Victoria Avenue), and Murray Street (and adjacent Fallsview Boulevard). Families gravitate toward Clifton Hill for its range of entertainment options. Murray Street, where the Fallsview Casino is located, is less ostentatious and closer to the falls.

Niagara Falls has plenty of B&Bs, but they're mediocre compared with those in Niagara-on-the-Lake, 20 km (12 miles) north. All the hotels here are within walking distance of the falls.

Country Inn & Suites

$ | HOTEL | If you're on a budget but not willing to stay at a dingy motor lodge, this seven-story hotel is probably your best choice. **Pros:** high-speed Internet is among the amenities; within walking distance of Clifton Hill; breakfast is included. **Cons:** 15-minute walk down to the falls; crowded during peak season; no views. $ *Rooms from: C$110* ✉ *5525 Victoria Ave.* ☎ *905/374–6040, 800/830–5222* ⊕ *www.countryinns.com* ⇴ *108 rooms* ⌑ *Free breakfast.*

Crowne Plaza Niagara Falls–Fallsview

$$ | HOTEL | Since it opened as the Hotel General Brock in 1929, this grande dame of Niagara hotels has hosted royalty, prime ministers, and Hollywood stars—including Marilyn Monroe, who stayed here while filming the potboiler film *Niagara*. **Pros:** central location near Clifton Hill; old-world sophistication; pool and hot tubs. **Cons:** even rooms with views have small windows; some of the decor is a bit tired; charge for Internet access. $ *Rooms from: C$128* ✉ *5685 Falls Ave.* ☎ *905/374–4447, 800/263–7135* ⊕ *www.niagarafallscrowneplazahotel.com* ⇴ *234 rooms* ⌑ *No meals.*

★ Fallsview Casino Resort

$$$$ | **HOTEL** | Thanks to its lofty perch, all 35 stories of the Fallsview Casino Resort overlook the Horseshoe, American, and Bridal Veil falls. **Pros:** the most glamorous address in Niagara Falls; Avalon Ballroom is just steps away; excellent spa and pool. **Cons:** rates are as high-flying as the views; rooms fill up fast in high season; a bit like a shopping mall. $ *Rooms from: C$349 ⊠ 6380 Fallsview Blvd. ☎ 905/358–3255, 888/325–5788 ⊕ www. fallsviewcasinoresort.com ⤲ 374 rooms ⦵ No meals.*

Great Wolf Lodge

$$$$ | **RESORT** | **FAMILY** | Instead of the usual casino-and-slot-machine ambience you find in other area hotels, you'll find a spectacular water park of 12 slides, seven pools, outdoor hot tubs, and other fun amenities at the Great Wolf Lodge. **Pros:** diversions for kids and adults in the water park; delightful themed suites; great for kids. **Cons:** open-concept rooms lack privacy for parents; many of the amenities cost extra; menus lack healthy options. $ *Rooms from: C$320 ⊠ 3950 Victoria Ave. ☎ 905/354–4888 ⊕ www. greatwolf.com ⤲ 406 suites ⦵ No meals.*

Sheraton on the Falls

$$$ | **HOTEL** | Just steps from Niagara Parkway, this 22-story tower at the corner of Clifton Hill is the most polished option in that area. **Pros:** perfect location very close to local attractions; breakfast room overlooks all three falls; nicely renovated rooms. **Cons:** no views from below the sixth floor; expensive Wi-Fi and parking; chain hotel feel. $ *Rooms from: C$239 ⊠ 5875 Falls Ave. ☎ 905/374–4445, 888/229–9961 ⊕ www.sheratononthe-falls.com ⤲ 670 rooms ⦵ No meals.*

Sterling Inn & Spa

$$$$ | **B&B/INN** | Unique among the many options in Niagara Falls is this boutique hotel in a converted 1930s milk facto-ry—hence the unusual bottle-shape tower near the entrance. **Pros:** on-site restaurant known for its locally sourced cuisine; breakfast is included in the rates; the quirky feel of a boutique hotel. **Cons:** low-slung building has no views of the falls; 20-minute walk to Clifton Hill; park-ing costs extra. $ *Rooms from: C$302 ⊠ 5195 Magdalen St. ☎ 289/292–0000, 877/783–7772 ⊕ www.sterlingniagara. com ⤲ 41 rooms ⦵ Free breakfast.*

Activities

HIKING AND BIKING
Niagara Glen Nature Reserve

HIKING/WALKING | The 82.5-acre Niagara Glen nature reserve has 4 km (2½ miles) of hiking trails through forested paths that pass giant boulders left behind as the falls eroded the land away thousands of years ago. Some trails are steep and rough, and the elevation change is more than 200 feet. Guided hiking tours are available. ⊠ *3050 Niagara Pkwy. ⊕ www. niagaraparks.com.*

Niagara River Recreation Trail

BICYCLING | From Fort Erie to Niagara-on-the-Lake, this recreation trail is 56 km (35 miles) of bicycle trails along the Niagara River. The 29-km (18-mile) route between Niagara Falls and Niagara-on-the-Lake is paved. The trail is divided into four sections, each with site-specific history: Niagara-on-the-Lake to Queen-ston; Queenston to the Whirlpool Aero Car; Chippawa to Black Creek; and Black Creek to Fort Erie. ⊠ *Niagara Falls ⊕ www.niagaraparks.com.*

Niagara-on-the-Lake

15 km (9 miles) north of Niagara Falls, 130 km (80 miles) south of Toronto.

The hub of the Niagara wine region is the town of Niagara-on-the-Lake (some-times abbreviated NOTL). Since 1962 this town of 14,000 residents has been considered the southern outpost of fine summer theater in Ontario because of its acclaimed Shaw Festival. As one of the country's prettiest and best-preserved Victorian towns, Niagara-on-the-Lake has architectural sights, shops, flower-lined streets, and plentiful ornamental gardens in summer, quality theater nearly year-round, and some of the best chefs and hoteliers in the country.

WHEN TO GO

The town is worth a visit at any time of the year for its inns, restaurants, and proximity to the wineries (open year-round), but the most compelling time to visit is from April through November, during the Shaw Festival, and when the weather allows alfresco dining. Wine-harvesting tours and events take place in the fall and, for ice wine, in December and January. Be warned that the tiny town can get packed over Canadian and American holiday weekends in summer: parking will be scarce; driving, slow; and you might have to wait for tastings at wineries.

GETTING HERE AND AROUND

From Buffalo or Toronto, Niagara-on-the-Lake is easily reached by car via the QEW. NOTL is about a two-hour drive from Toronto, a bit far for just a day trip. From Niagara Falls or Lewiston, take the Niagara Parkway. There's no public transport in Niagara-on-the-Lake or to Niagara Falls, 15 km (9 miles) south.

Niagara-on-the-Lake is a very small town that can easily be explored on foot. Parking downtown can be nightmarish in peak season. Parking along the main streets is metered, at C$2.25 to C$2.75 per hour. On most residential streets parking is free but still limited.

TOURS

Sentineal Carriages conducts year-round tours in and around Niagara-on-the-Lake. Catch a carriage at the Prince of Wales hotel or make a reservation for a pickup. The private, narrated tours are C$95 for 30 minutes, C$140 for 45 minutes, and C$180 for 1 hour (prices are per carriage).

CONTACTS Sentineal Carriages.
☎ 905/468–4943 ⊕ www.sentinealcarriages.ca.

VISITOR INFORMATION

CONTACTS Niagara-on-the-Lake Chamber of Commerce and Visitor & Convention Bureau. ✉ 26 Queen St. ☎ 905/468–1950 ⊕ www.niagaraonthelake.com.

Sights

Château des Charmes

WINERY/DISTILLERY | Founded in 1978, this is one of Niagara's first wineries, and one of the two largest family-owned wineries in Niagara (Peller is the other). Originally from France, the Bosc family were pioneers in cultivating European varieties of grapes in Niagara. Wines here consistently win awards, and the winery is particularly known for its chardonnay and Gamay Noir Droit, made from a grape variety that was accidentally created through a mutation. The wine is proprietary, and this is the only winery allowed to make it. ✉ 1025 York Rd. ☎ 905/262–4219 ⊕ www.chateaudescharmes.com ⛲ Tasting flights C$10; tours from C$10.

Floral Clock

CLOCK | The 40-foot-in-diameter floral clock, one of the world's largest, is comprised of 16,000 bedding plants. Its "living" face is planted in a different design twice every season—viola in the spring and Alternantheras and Santolina Sage in the summer and fall. ✉ 2405 Niagara Pkwy. ☎ 905/356–8119 ⊕ www.niagaraparks.com ⛲ Free.

★ Fort George National Historic Site

MILITARY SITE | **FAMILY** | On a wide stretch of parkland south of town sits this fort that was built in the 1790s but lost during the War of 1812. It was recaptured after the burning of the town in 1813 and largely survived the war, only to fall into ruins by the 1830s. Thankfully, it was reconstructed a century later, and you can explore the officers' quarters, the

Did You Know?

In addition to fueling tourism with their natural beauty, the falls have also provided power to local residents and industry for more than 270 years. Today, the Niagara Power Plant is the largest producer of electricity in New York State.

barracks rooms of the common soldiers, the kitchen, and more. Staff in period costumes conduct tours and reenact 19th-century infantry and artillery drills. ⊠ *51 Queens Parade* ☎ *905/468–6614* ⊕ *www.pc.gc.ca/en/lhn-nhs/on/fortgeorge* ⊠ *C$12, C$6 parking* ⊗ *Closed weekdays Nov.–Apr.*

Frogpond Farm Organic Winery

WINERY/DISTILLERY | Ontario's first certified-organic winery is a small, family-owned affair with exclusively organic wines. The setting is truly farmlike: sheep and guinea hens mill about outside while you taste. With only eight varieties, all VQA and including a nice ice wine, you can become an expert in this label in one sitting. The wines are available on-site, online, and at selected restaurants in Ontario; many of the labels are available at the Liquor Control Board of Ontario. ⊠ *1385 Larkin Rd.* ☎ *905/468–1079, 877/989–0165* ⊕ *www.frogpondfarm.ca* ⊠ *Free.*

Jackson-Triggs Niagara Estate Winery

WINERY/DISTILLERY | An ultramodern facility, this famous winery blends state-of-the-art wine-making technology with age-old, handcrafted enological savvy, as evidenced by the stainless steel trough by the entrance. A multitude of tours, workshops, and events are offered. The hourly public tour is a great introduction to winemaking and includes three tastings and a mini-lesson in wine tasting. Its award-winning VQA wines can be sipped in the tasting gallery and purchased in the retail boutique. ⊠ *2145 Niagara Stone Rd.* ☎ *905/468–4637, 866/589–4637* ⊕ *www.jacksontriggswinery.com* ⊠ *Tastings C$10, tours C$15.*

Konzelmann Estate Winery

WINERY/DISTILLERY | An easygoing winery with a friendly staff and sociable tasting bar, Konzelmann has garnered praise (and awards) from various authoritative sources for its fruitier wines in particular, and it's known for high-quality ice wines, one of which made *Wine Spectator*'s top 100 wines list, the first Canadian wine ever to make the list. Konzelmann's vineyards border Lake Ontario, and the winery has a viewing platform with vistas of the vines and water. The retail shop is well stocked with wine-related gifts. ⊠ *1096 Lakeshore Rd.* ☎ *905/935–2866* ⊕ *www.konzelmann.ca* ⊠ *Tours from C$10.*

Niagara Apothecary

MUSEUM | Restored to look like a 19th-century pharmacy that opened here in 1869, the apothecary has glass-fronted walnut cabinets that display vintage remedies such as Merrill's System Tonic, which "Purifies the Blood and Builds up the System." Among the boxes and bottles is a rare collection of apothecary flasks. ⊠ *5 Queen St.* ☎ *905/468–3845, 800/220–1921* ⊕ *www.niagaraapothecary.ca* ⊠ *Free* ⊗ *Closed Oct.–May.*

Niagara Historical Society & Museum

MUSEUM | In connected side-by-side buildings—one the 1875 former Niagara High School building and the other the first building in Ontario to have been erected as a museum, in 1906—this extensive collection relates to the often colorful history of the Niagara Peninsula from earliest times through the 19th century. ■ **TIP→ During June, July, and August, the museum offers guided walking tours of the town at 11 am on Thursday, Friday, and Saturday; and Sunday at 2 pm.** ⊠ *43 Castlereagh St.* ☎ *905/468–3912* ⊕ *www.niagarahistorical.museum* ⊠ *C$5* ⊗ *Closed Good Fri., Easter Sun., Thanksgiving day, Dec. 18–Jan. 1.*

Queen Street

NEIGHBORHOOD | You can get a glimpse of the town's rich architectural history walking along this single street. At the corner of Queen and King streets is Niagara Apothecary, a mid-Victorian building that was an apothecary from 1866 to 1964. The Court House situated across the street became the Town Hall in 1862. Presently, it houses a small 327-seat theater during Shaw Festival. At No. 209

is the handsome Charles Inn, formerly known as Richardson-Kiely House, built in 1832 for Charles Richardson, who was a barrister and member of Parliament. ■TIP→ **The 10 or so blocks of shopping includes upscale restaurants and cafés, designer-label boutiques, old-fashioned ice-cream parlors, and a spa. You could easily spend an entire day in this area.** ⊠ Niagara-on-the-Lake.

St. Mark's Anglican Church

RELIGIOUS SITE | One of Ontario's oldest Anglican churches, St. Mark's was built in 1804, and its parish is even older, formed in 1792. The stone church still houses the founding minister's original library of 1,500 books, brought from England. During the War of 1812, American soldiers used the church as a barracks, and still-visible rifle pits were dug in the cemetery. The church is open for concerts, lectures, and weekly services. ⊠ 41 Byron St. ☎ 905/468–3123 ⊕ stmarksnotl.org.

Stratus Vineyards

WINERY/DISTILLERY | Standing out from a vast landscape of single varietal wines, Stratus specializes in assemblage: combining multiple varieties of grapes to create unique blends. Established in 2000, and emerging on the Niagara wine scene in 2005, they continue to perfect what has traditionally been a recipe for disaster for winemakers. A fine example is the Stratus White, a mix of six grape varieties that's complex and unlike anything you've ever tasted (in a good way). Sip all three assemblage wines (white, red, and ice wine) and a handful of single varietals in the modern glass-walled tasting room, installed in the world's first LEED-certified winery. ■TIP→ **Tours must be reserved in advance and can include cheese and charcuterie.** ⊠ 2059 Niagara Stone Rd. ☎ 905/468–1806 ⊕ www.stratuswines. com ⊠ Tastings C$15 (flight of 4).

Trius Winery at Hillebrand

WINERY/DISTILLERY | With more than 300 wine awards, this winery—one of Niagara's first and largest—produces many excellent varieties. Its reds (especially Trius Red and Trius Cabernet Franc) are some of the best in Niagara, consistently taking top prizes at competitions; the Trius Brut is another gold medalist. The half-hour cellar and vineyard tour are set to the tune of bubbly social media-ready installations complete with generous complimentary samplings. Another dozen themed tours and regular events include a seminar where you can blend your own wine and an evening of chef-hosted meals at their terrific restaurant. ■TIP→ **Book in advance for tours.** ⊠ 1249 Niagara Stone Rd. ☎ 905/468–7123, 800/582–8412 ⊕ www.triuswines.com ⊠ Tastings from C$2, tours from C$15.

Whirlpool Jet Boat Tours

TOUR—SIGHT | FAMILY | An hour-long thrill ride, these tours veer around and hurdle white-water rapids that follow Niagara canyons up to the wall of rolling waters, just below Niagara Falls. Children must be at least six years old for the open-boat Wet Jet Tour and four years old for the covered-boat (dry!) Jet Dome Tour; minimum height requirements also apply. Tours depart from Niagara-on-the-Lake or Niagara Falls, Ontario (June to August only) and Lewiston, NY. ⊠ 61 Melville St. ☎ 905/468–4800, 888/438–4444 ⊕ www. whirlpooljet.com ⊠ C$70 ⊘ Closed mid-Oct.–mid-Apr.

🍴 Restaurants

George Bernard Shaw once said, "No greater love hath man than the love of food," and Niagara-on-the-Lake, which hosts a festival devoted to the playwright, is a perfect place to indulge your epicurean desires. Many eateries serve fine produce and wines from the verdant Niagara Peninsula, and the glut of high-end options fosters fierce competition. A

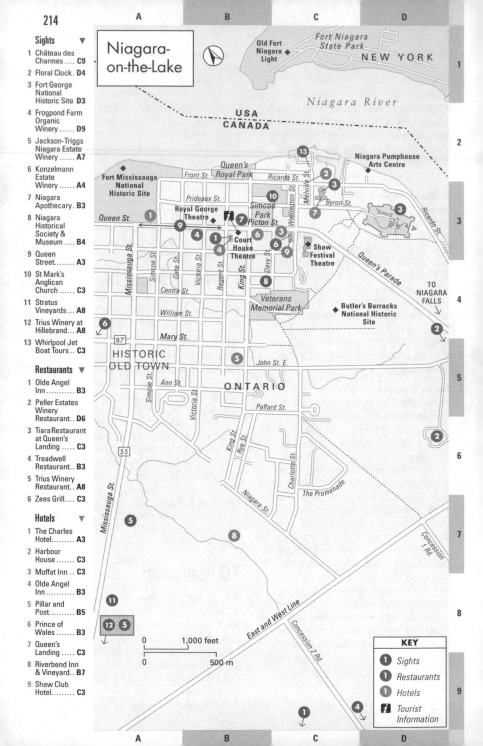

214

Niagara-on-the-Lake

Niagara River

Old Fort Niagara Light
Fort Niagara State Park
NEW YORK

USA
CANADA

Niagara Pumphouse Arts Centre

Queen's Royal Park
Front St.
Ricardo St.
Fort Mississauga National Historic Site
Prideaux St.
Melville St.
Byron St.
Queen St.
Royal George Theatre
Simcoe Park
Picton St.
Wellington St.
Court House Theatre
Davy St.
Shaw Festival Theatre
Queen's Parade

Mississauga St.
Simcoe St.
Gate St.
Victoria St.
Regent St.
King St.

Centre St.
Veterans Memorial Park
Butler's Barracks National Historic Site

William St.

Mary St.

HISTORIC OLD TOWN

John St. E.

Ann St.
ONTARIO

Simcoe St.
Victoria St.
Paffard St.

King St.
Rye St.
Charlotte St.
The Promenade
Niagara St.

Mississauga St.

East and West Line
Concession 2 Rd.
Concession 1 Rd.

TO NIAGARA FALLS

| 0 | 1,000 feet |
| 0 | 500 m |

KEY

❶ Sights
❶ Restaurants
❶ Hotels
🛈 Tourist Information

number of inns and wineries here have restaurants. Especially in summer, make reservations whenever possible. Many restaurants serve dinner only until 9.

Olde Angel Inn

$$ | **BRITISH** | You can request a Yorkshire pudding to accompany any meal at this tavern just off Queen Street, which should tip you off to its British leanings, played out further in the decor: a warren of rooms with creaky floors and worn (or well-loved, depending on how you see it) wooden tables and chairs, low ceilings and exposed beams, and convivial chatter throughout. Ontario's oldest operating inn sets out pub fare such as shepherd's pie, bangers and mash, and steak-and-kidney pie. Entrées change periodically but always include the house specialty, prime rib of beef au jus. **Known for:** 24 domestic and imported brews are on tap; in operation since 1789; live music many evenings. [$] *Average main: C$15* ✉ *224 Regent St.* ☎ *905/468–3411* 🌐 *www.angel-inn.com.*

★ Peller Estates Winery Restaurant

$$$$ | **EUROPEAN** | Frequently cited as the best restaurant in Niagara-on-the-Lake—an impressive feat in a town with so many excellent restaurants—Peller Estates manages refinement without arrogance. The stately Colonial Revival dining room is anchored by a huge fireplace at one end and has windows running the length of the room overlooking a large patio and the estate vineyards. A menu of ever-changing expertly prepared entrées often weaves the Peller Estates wine into modern Canadian cuisine. **Known for:** farm-to-table cooking with locally sourced ingredients; seasonal game entrées; gorgeous views. [$] *Average main: C$35* ✉ *290 John St. E* ☎ *905/468–4678* 🌐 *www.peller.com.*

Tiara Restaurant at Queen's Landing

$$$$ | **FRENCH** | Niagara-on-the-Lake's only waterfront restaurant, the regal Tiara sits beside a marina with a view of the Niagara River beyond the sailboat masts. The elegant, amber-hue Georgian-meets-contemporary dining room is buttoned up but accented by a pretty stained-glass ceiling and near-panoramic windows that give nearly every table a water view. The outdoor tables next to the marina, however, are the ones to request to go with the exquisite French-influenced menu. Round out the meal with homemade ice cream topped with seasonal berries. **Known for:** decadent weekend brunch buffet; prime views from the terrace; prime rib surf-and-turf dinner. [$] *Average main: C$50* ✉ *155 Byron St.* ☎ *905/468–2195, 888/669–5566* 🌐 *www.vintage-hotels.com.*

Treadwell Restaurant

$$$$ | **CANADIAN** | This brainchild of chef-owner Stephen Treadwell (formerly of the prestigious Auberge du Pommier), his chef de cuisine Matthew Payne, and his son, wine sommelier James Treadwell, Treadwell embodies the philosophy of farm-to-table. Sit down for dinner on the sidewalk patio or in the sleek dining room and indulge some of the best that Southern Ontario has to offer. **Known for:** lobster club sandwich rules the brunch menu; prestigious Ontario-focused wine list; bread from nearby Treadwell Bakery. [$] *Average main: C$41* ✉ *114 Queen St.* ☎ *905/934–9797* 🌐 *www.treadwellcuisine.com.*

★ Trius Winery Restaurant

$$$$ | **INTERNATIONAL** | Niagara-on-the-Lake's first winery restaurant is still one of its best. After a complimentary winery tour and tasting, you can continue to indulge in the spacious, light-filled dining room with big double doors framing vineyards almost as far as the eye can see. The menu of locally inspired cuisine changes every six weeks. Tasting menus are available to try such culinary masterpieces as wild sockeye salmon with asparagus and fennel slaw. **Known for:** excellent seasonal dinner selections; the bar has its own tasting menu; farm-to-table cooking. [$] *Average main: C$55*

Niagara-on-the-Lake, in the heart of the Niagara wine region, has gained fame for its fine wines and food, beautiful setting, and the annual summer Shaw Festival.

✉ *1249 Niagara Stone Rd., at Hwy. 55* ☎ *905/468–7123, 800/582–8412* 🌐 *www.triuswines.com.*

Zees Grill

$$$ | **ECLECTIC** | For alfresco dining, it's hard to beat Zees Grill for its huge wraparound patio with heat lamps across from the Shaw Festival Theatre. More informal than most similarly priced restaurants in town, it has a seasonal menu that brings panache to homegrown comfort foods such as grilled swordfish with purple potato hash and buttered baby bok choy or beef ribs with shallot, garlic, and fingerling potato hash. Appetizers follow a similarly elegant, yet whimsical, philosophy. **Known for:** brined turkey breast sandwich with cranberry-infused aioli is a great lunch; don't pass up the banana bread French toast for breakfast; one of the best local places for outdoor dining. [$] *Average main: C$30* ✉ *92 Picton St.* ☎ *905/468–5715* 🌐 *www.zees.ca* 🕑 *No lunch Dec.–mid-Apr.*

Hotels

Niagara-on-the-Lake may be Canada's B&B capital, with more than 100 to its name. Their service and quality can rival some of the priciest hotels. In terms of superior lodging, you're spoiled for choice in Niagara-on-the-Lake and it's hard to go wrong with any of the properties within the town's historic center. Prices are high, but hotels sometimes offer significant deals online.

The Charles Hotel

$$$ | **B&B/INN** | An air of old-fashioned civility permeates this 1832 Georgian gem, with a nice location on the main street. **Pros:** historic design updated with modern touches; highly lauded restaurant; cozy building. **Cons:** some quirks like variable water temperature; some verandas are shared with neighbors; rooms are smaller than you'd expect. [$] *Rooms from: C$245* ✉ *209 Queen St.* ☎ *905/468–4588, 866/556–8883* 🌐 *www.niagarasfinest.com* 🛏 *12 rooms* 🍴 *Free breakfast.*

★ **Harbour House**

$$$ | **HOTEL** | The closest hotel to the waterfront is this luxurious and romantic boutique hotel with a gently sloping gambrel roof and handsome cedar shingles. **Pros:** it's the ideal spot to pamper yourself; luxury without a stuff feel; full breakfast included. **Cons:** virtually no public spaces; gym and spa are off-site; some rooms lack water views. [$] *Rooms from: C$225* ✉ *85 Melville St.* ☎ *905/468–4683, 866/277–6677* 🌐 *www.harbourhousehotel.ca* 🛏 *31 rooms* 🍴 *Free breakfast.*

Moffat Inn

$$$ | **HOTEL** | A central location, reasonable prices, and expert management make this 1835 stucco inn a real find. **Pros:** perfect location on Picton Street; reasonable rates; free Wi-Fi access. **Cons:** not as posh as other area hotels; dated decor and worn carpets; no elevator. [$] *Rooms from: C$240* ✉ *60 Picton St.* ☎ *905/468–4116, 888/669–5566* 🌐 *www.vintage-hotels.com* 🛏 *24 rooms* 🍴 *No meals.*

Olde Angel Inn

$$ | **B&B/INN** | Steeped in military history, the Olde Angel is one of the oldest lodgings in Ontario. **Pros:** excellent price for a hotel in the heart of town; on-site English-style tavern; perfect for history buffs. **Cons:** poor soundproofing, which is a problem for rooms over the pub; dedicated parking for cottages only; no housekeeping in cottages. [$] *Rooms from: C$169* ✉ *224 Regent St.* ☎ *905/468–3411* 🌐 *www.angel-inn.com* 🛏 *7 rooms* 🍴 *No meals.*

★ **Pillar and Post**

$$$ | **HOTEL** | A two-story hotel six blocks from the heart of town, this building has been a cannery, barracks, and basket factory in its 100-plus-year history. **Pros:** unaffected mix of historic and modern; free parking and high-speed Internet; excellent service. **Cons:** not as central as some other hotels; no elevator to second-floor rooms; resort fee for outdoor pool. [$] *Rooms from: C$219* ✉ *48 John St.* ☎ *905/468–2123, 888/669–5566* 🌐 *www.vintage-hotels.com* 🛏 *122 rooms* 🍴 *No meals.*

Did You Know?

The moderate climate of the Niagara region doesn't benefit only grapes: about 40% of Canada's apples and 70% of its peaches, as well as berries, cherries, and pears, are grown in this area smaller than Rhode Island.

Prince of Wales

$$$$ | **HOTEL** | A visit from the Prince of Wales in 1901 inspired the name of this venerable hostelry that still welcomes the occasional royal guest or film star. **Pros:** over-the-top-elegant public spaces; relaxing array of spa treatments; highly trained staff. **Cons:** some views of the parking lot; rabbit warren of corridors; breakfast not included. [$] *Rooms from: C$279* ✉ *6 Picton St.* ☎ *905/468–3246, 888/669–5566* 🌐 *www.vintage-hotels.com* 🛏 *110 rooms* 🍴 *No meals.*

Queen's Landing

$$$ | **HOTEL** | About half of the rooms at this Georgian-style mansion have knockout views of the fields of historic Fort George or the placid waters of the marina—ask for one when making a reservation. **Pros:** service is taken seriously and staff goes above and beyond to please; the tropical indoor pool has a lovely skylight; five-minute walk to city center. **Cons:** historic feel is only skin deep; thin walls between rooms; breakfast not included. [$] *Rooms from: C$250* ✉ *155 Byron St.* ☎ *905/468–2195, 888/669–5566* 🌐 *www.vintage-hotels.com* 🛏 *142 rooms* 🍴 *No meals.*

Peller Estates Winery, known for its award-winning Rieslings and ice wines, provides visitors an elegant experience, from winery tours to tastings to fine dining.

Riverbend Inn & Vineyard

$$$$ | **B&B/INN** | Surrounded by its own private vineyard, this beautifully restored, green-shuttered 1820 mansion is formal in style: it's fronted by a grand portico with four massive columns, and an enormous original 19th-century crystal chandelier greets you in the lobby. **Pros:** five rooms have private balconies over the vineyards; great location for wine lovers; inexpensive breakfasts. **Cons:** furnishings could use an upgrade; far from downtown attractions; no elevator. [$] *Rooms from: C$295* ✉ *16104 Niagara Pkwy.* ☎ *905/468–8866, 888/955–5553* 🌐 *www.riverbendinn.ca* 🛏 *21 rooms* 🍴 *No meals.*

Shaw Club Hotel

$$$ | **HOTEL** | In a town that's largely Georgian or Victorian in style, modern elements like steel and glass give the Shaw Club an edgy and hip vibe. **Pros:** ideal location near the Shaw Festival Theatre; contemporary style in a handsome building; easygoing staff. **Cons:** annex rooms lack the main building's wow factor; some plastic room furnishings; little local charm. [$] *Rooms from: C$250* ✉ *92 Picton St.* ☎ *905/468–5711, 800/511–7070* 🌐 *www.shawclub.com* 🛏 *30 rooms* 🍴 *Free breakfast.*

Performing Arts

ARTS FESTIVALS

★ Shaw Festival

FESTIVALS | Niagara-on-the-Lake remained a sleepy town until 1962, when local lawyer Brian Doherty organized eight weekend performances of two George Bernard Shaw plays, *Don Juan in Hell* and *Candida*. The next year he helped found the festival, whose mission is to perform the works of Shaw and his contemporaries, including Noël Coward, Bertolt Brecht, J. M. Barrie, J. M. Synge, and Anton Chekhov. Now, the festival has expanded to close to a dozen plays, running from April to October, including some contemporary plays by Canadian playwrights, and one or two musicals. All are staged in one of four theaters within a few blocks of one another. The

handsome **Festival Theatre**, the largest of the three, stands on Queen's Parade near Wellington Street and houses the box office. The **Court House Theatre**, on Queen Street between King and Regent streets, served as the town's municipal offices until 1969 and is a national historic site. At the corner of Queen and Victoria streets, the **Royal George Theatre** was originally built as a vaudeville house in 1915. The **Studio Theatre**, the smallest of the four, hosts mostly contemporary performances. The festival is one of the biggest events in the summer.
■TIP→ **Regular-price tickets cost C$28 to C$152, but discounts abound.** ⊠ *10 Queen's Parade* ☎ *905/468–2172, 800/511–7429* ⊕ *www.shawfest.com.*

🛍 Shopping

Niagara-on-the-Lake's historic Queen Street is lined with Victorian storefronts with everything from art galleries to gourmet food stores selling olives, marinades, and vinaigrettes.

FOOD

Greaves Jams & Marmalades
FOOD/CANDY | This shop has been making jams, jellies, and marmalades from mostly local produce using family recipes, since the company began in 1927. The spreads are free from preservatives, pectin, or additives. The jams are often served for afternoon tea in upscale hotel restaurants. ⊠ *55 Queen St.* ☎ *905/468–3608* ⊕ *www.greavesjams.com.*

Harvest Barn Country Markets
FOOD/CANDY | There are many fruit stands and produce markets along the streets of Niagara-on-the-Lake, but just outside of the area is the mother lode that dwarfs the others. Harvest Barn Country Markets, in a barn with a red-and-white-striped awning, sells regional fruits and vegetables and tempts with its fresh-baked goods: sausage rolls, bread, and fruit pies. ⊠ *1822 Niagara Stone Rd* ☎ *905/468–3224* ⊕ *www.harvestbarn.ca.*

The Niagara Escarpment

102 km (63 miles) southeast of Toronto, 41 km (25 miles) west of Niagara-on-the-Lake.

The Niagara Peninsula north of St. Catharines is known as Niagara Escarpment or the Twenty Valley, for the huge valley where the region's main towns of Jordan, Vineland, and Beamsville are. This area is much less visited than Niagara-on-the-Lake, and the wineries more spread out. Peach and pear trees, hiking trails, and long stretches of country road are the lay of the land. Aside from wine tasting, you can also visit the cute-as-a-button town of Jordan.

WHEN TO GO
Unlike Niagara-on-the-Lake, this area doesn't get overcrowded in summer, the ideal season for puttering along the country roads. Many restaurants, cafés, and shops have abbreviated hours between mid-September and late May. Most wineries do open for tastings in winter, but call ahead to be sure and to check on driving conditions, as some of these spots are on steep or remote rural roads.

GETTING HERE AND AROUND
Aside from booking a structured winery tour, getting behind the wheel yourself is the only way to visit the attractions in this region. This area is about 75 minutes from Toronto and 45 minutes from Niagara-on-the-Lake and is a feasible day trip.

VISITOR INFORMATION
CONTACTS Twenty Valley Tourism Association. ⊠ *4890 Victoria Ave. N, Jordan* ☎ *905/562–3636* ⊕ *www.twentyvalley.ca.*

Sights

★ Cave Spring Cellars
WINERY/DISTILLERY | On Jordan's Main Street, Cave Spring is one of the leading wine producers in Canada, with Ontario's oldest wine cellars, in operation since 1871. Go for the Riesling, Chardonnay,

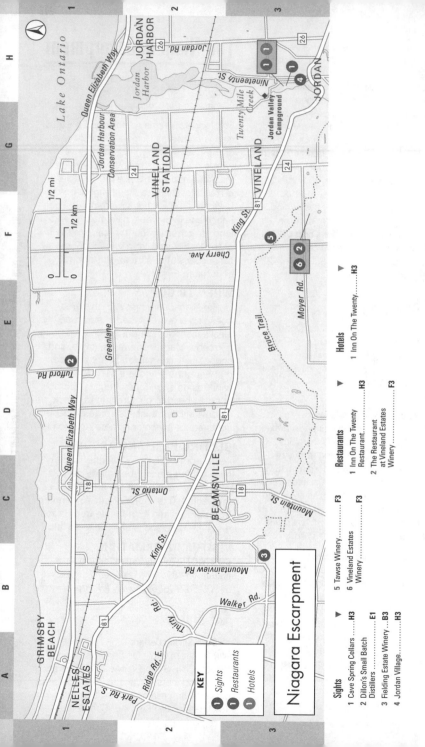

Niagara Escarpment

KEY

- ① Sights
- ① Restaurants
- ① Hotels

Sights ▶

1 Cave Spring Cellars **H3**
2 Dillon's Small Batch
   Distillers **E1**
3 Fielding Estate Winery ...**B3**
4 Jordan Village............**H3**

5 Tawse Winery............**F3**
6 Vineland Estates
   Winery **F3**

Restaurants ▶

1 Inn On The Twenty
   Restaurant...............**H3**
2 The Restaurant
   at Vineland Estates
   Winery **F3**

Hotels ▶

1 Inn On The Twenty.......**H3**

and ice wine. It shares ownership with Inn on the Twenty and On the Twenty restaurant (next door) and produces custom blends for the latter. ■TIP➜ There are public tours every day at 1:30 pm between June and September (only Friday and weekends the rest of the year). ✉ 3836 Main St., Jordan ☎ 905/562–3581 ⊕ www.cavespring.ca ☲ Tastings from C$1.

★ Dillon's Small Batch Distillers
WINERY/DISTILLERY | A nice break from the steady pace of Niagara-area wineries, Dillon's set up its celebrated small batch gin and spirits operation in the Beamsville area, prized for its clean water sources and high-quality produce. But they can't get away from grapes completely, which make up the base of the distinctly flavored gins and vodkas (rosehip, strawberry, cherry, and more). Take a tour (C$15) for an in-depth understanding of the distillation process that includes apothecarian exotics like cassis, bitters, and absinthe. The gift and liquor store could double as a design museum. Outdoor picnic tables are used for summer Sunday food-truck brunches. ✉ 4833 Tufford Rd., Beamsville ☎ 905/563–3030 ⊕ www.dillons.ca.

Fielding Estate Winery
WINERY/DISTILLERY | Muskoka chairs beside the cedar-framed entrance set the tone for the warm and charming winery within. Inside the modern West Coast–style cedar building with a corrugated tin roof and massive stone chimney, Fielding Estate has envious views of vineyards and Lake Ontario from huge picture windows and a big stone fireplace for chilly days. A young team—husband-and-wife owners and two winemakers—has been making quick strides here. The mostly Chardonnay and Riesling producing vineyard has a low yield that enables flavors to be concentrated. ✉ 4020 Locust La., Beamsville ☎ 888/778–7758, 905/563–0668 ⊕ www.fieldingwines.com ☲ Tastings C$5 (3 wines); tours C$15.

Jordan Village
NEIGHBORHOOD | Charming Main Street Jordan, also known as Jordan Village, is a small enclave of cafés and shops selling everything from antiques to artisanal foods. The Inn on the Twenty, the On the Twenty Restaurant, and Cave Spring Cellars are also here. Just a few blocks long, Jordan Village can be fully explored in a morning or afternoon. Home store **CHIC by Janssen** is worth a wander to gawk at items like Siberian fox throws, a bronze bear the size of an actual bear cub, and a C$4,000 cedar canoe. **Irongate Garden Elements** is a favorite with gardeners. ✉ Jordan Rd., off QEW Exit 55, Jordan ⊕ www.jordanvillage.ca.

Tawse Winery
WINERY/DISTILLERY | Eco-friendly Tawse Winery is so committed to producing top-notch Pinot Noir that it installed a six-level gravity-flow system to avoid overhandling the delicate grapes. The investment seems to be paying off, especially considering it's been voted "Winery of the Year" multiple years at the Canada Wine Awards. The rural hillside winery is modern, its big stainless-steel vats visible from the tasting room. ■TIP➜ Don't leave empty handed because tasting fees are waived if you buy two or more bottles. ✉ 3955 Cherry Ave., Vineland ☎ 905/562–9500 ⊕ www.tawsewinery.ca ☲ Tastings C$8 (3 wines), tour $15.

Vineland Estates Winery
WINERY/DISTILLERY | One of Ontario's most beautiful wineries occupies 75 acres that were once a Mennonite homestead established in 1845. The original buildings have been transformed into the visitor center and production complex. Several tour and tasting options are available, including packages that include chocolate, ice wine, and specialty cocktails. The excellent restaurant on-site serves lunch and dinner, and you can find a guesthouse and a B&B on the property. ✉ 3620 Moyer Rd., Vineland ⊕ 40 km (25 miles) west of Niagara-on-the-Lake

Did You Know?

Numerous waterfalls
trickle along the Niagara
Escarpment's beloved
Bruce Trail. At more than
890 km (550 miles) long, it
is the longest footpath in
Canada.

☎ *905/562–7088, 888/846–3526* 🌐 *www.vineland.com* 🎫 *Tastings C$15.*

🍴 Restaurants

★ Inn on the Twenty Restaurant

$$$$ | EUROPEAN | The huge windows framing the Twenty Valley conservation area are reason enough to dine at this restaurant, regarded as one of the best around Toronto, on Jordan's boutique-lined Main Street. Regional specialties and local and organic produce are emphasized on a seasonal menu that has included Wellington County boneless rib-eye steak served with mushroom-and-onion fricassee and blue cheese butter. The dining room, reminiscent of the French and Italian countryside, is lovely, with a soaring ceiling, whitewashed beams, and a view of the gardens. Cave Spring Cellars, which has a shop next door, provides many of the wines. **Known for:** special menus that highlight local produce; unbeatable views of the countryside; try the Québec foie gras on brioche. [$] *Average main: C$32* ✉ *3836 Main St., off QEW Exit 55 or 57, Jordan* ☎ *905/562–7313* 🌐 *www.innonthetwenty.com.*

★ The Restaurant at Vineland Estates Winery

$$$$ | CANADIAN | Exquisite progressive Canadian food and venerable wines are served by an enthusiastic staff on this bucolic property with three 19th-century Mennonite stone buildings. Sit on the large outdoor patio overlooking vineyards and Lake Ontario beyond or in the glassed-in restaurant, where many of the tables have a similar panoramic view. The menu is locally sourced and seasonal: think venison haunch with heirloom beets, torchon, smoked cauliflower purée, and blackberry reduction. Desserts, like spiced pumpkin cheesecake served with mascarpone gelato, are the perfect demonstration of simplicity and innovation. **Known for:** desserts are the perfect demonstration of simplicity and innovation; daily five-course table d'hote menu show off local dishes; artisanal charcuterie and cheese platters. [$] *Average main: C$35* ✉ *3620 Moyer Rd., Vineland* ☎ *905/562–7088, 888/846–3526* 🌐 *vineland.com/the-restaurant.*

🛏 Hotels

Inn on the Twenty

$$$$ | B&B/INN | Seven of the 24 suites in the main building of this Main Street Jordan inn are two story affairs with plenty of space, but the rooms to book—in nice weather at least—are the five ground-level suites with very private garden patios. **Pros:** top-notch cuisine at the sophisticated On the Twenty restaurant; impeccably decorated rooms; central location for wineries. **Cons:** not as much to do in Jordan as in surrounding areas; rooms lack amenities like TVs; breakfast a little lackluster. [$] *Rooms from: C$270* ✉ *3845 Main St., off QEW Exit 55 or 57, Jordan* ☎ *905/562–5336, 800/701–8074* 🌐 *www.innonthetwenty.com* 🛏 *28 suites* 🍴 *Free breakfast.*

🏃 Activities

HIKING

Bruce Trail

BICYCLING | Canada's oldest and longest footpath, the Bruce Trail stretches 890 km (550 miles) along the Niagara Escarpment, with an additional 400 km (250 miles) of side trails. It takes in scenery from the orchards and vineyards of the Niagara Escarpment—one of Canada's 15 UNESCO World Biosphere Reserves—to the craggy cliffs and bluffs at Tobermory, 370 km (230 miles) north of Niagara-on-the-Lake. You can access the hiking trail at just about any point along the route; the main trail is marked with white blazes, the side trails with blue blazes. Northern parts of the trail are remote. ✉ *14184 Niagara Pkwy, Niagara-on-the-Lake* ☎ *905/529–6821, 800/665–4453* 🌐 *brucetrail.org.*

Stratford, Ontario

KEY
- 🔵 Sights
- 🔴 Restaurants
- 🟤 Hotels
- ℹ️ Tourist Information

Sights ▼
1. Gallery Stratford **D1**
2. Stratford Perth Museum **A4**

Restaurants ▼
1. Bentley's **C4**
2. Bijou **C4**
3. Boomer's Gourmet Fries **B4**
4. Keystone Alley **C4**
5. Mercer Kitchen + Beer Hall **C4**
6. Pazzo Taverna and Pizzeria **C4**
7. The Planet Diner **C4**
8. The Prune **C3**
9. Revival House **C4**
10. York Street Kitchen **B4**

Hotels ▼
1. Avery House **D3**
2. Birmingham Manor B&B **B5**
3. Festival Inn **E2**
4. Foster's Inn **C4**
5. Queen and Albert B&B **D3**
6. Stewart House Inn **A4**
7. Swan Motel **E5**
8. The Three Houses Bed & Breakfast Inn **C4**

Stratford

145 km (90 miles) west of Toronto.

In July 1953 Alec Guinness, one of the world's greatest actors, joined with Tyrone Guthrie, probably the world's greatest Shakespearean director, beneath a hot, stuffy tent in a quiet town about a 90-minute drive from Toronto. This was the birth of the Stratford Shakespeare Festival, which now runs from April to late October or early November and is one of the most successful and admired festivals of its kind.

Today Stratford is a city of 32,000 that welcomes more than 500,000 visitors annually for the Stratford Shakespeare Festival alone. But Shakespeare is far from the only attraction. The Stratford Summer Music Festival (July and August) is another highlight, shopping in the enchanting city core is a favorite pastime, and with more amazing restaurants than you could hope to try in one visit, dining out in Stratford could be a reason to return.

WHEN TO GO

The festival runs from mid-April through late October or early November. Most visitors choose their travel dates based on the plays they want to see. About half of the city's restaurants and B&Bs close off-season; the city is quiet in the colder months, but shops and art galleries stay open, hotels have reduced rates, and you'll rub elbows with locals rather than visitors.

GETTING HERE AND AROUND

Ontario's main east–west highway, the 401, which traverses the province all the way from Michigan to Québec, is the main route from Toronto to Kitchener-Waterloo; from there, Highway 7/8 heads to Stratford. Traffic-free driving time is about two hours. VIA Rail has daily service to downtown Stratford from Toronto's Union Station; the trip is about two hours.

Stratford Walking Tours

The Stratford Tourism Alliance (⊕ *www.visitstratford.ca*) produces several themed, self-guided walking tours, such as the Bacon and Ale Trail (C\$30, including six coupons that can be redeemed along the way), Historic Downtown, Local Landmarks, and Shakespearean Gardens. Pick one up from the tourism office at 47 Downie Street.

CONTACTS Stratford VIA Rail Train Station. ✉ *101 Shakespeare St.* ☎ *888/842–7245.*

VISITOR INFORMATION
CONTACTS Stratford Tourism Alliance. ✉ *47 Downie St.* ☎ *519/271–5140, 800/561–7926* ⊕ *www.visitstratford.ca.*

Sights

Gallery Stratford
MUSEUM | Operating since 1967 in a historic pump house, Gallery Stratford exhibits high-profile Canadian visual artists all year and, in summer, local up-and-coming artists. ✉ *54 Romeo St.* ☎ *519/271–5271* ⊕ *www.gallerystratford.on.ca.*

Stratford Perth Museum
MUSEUM | You can brush up on Stratford and Perth County history with permanent displays and changing exhibits that cover such topics as hockey in Stratford, the city's railroad, and the settlement of the area in the early 1800s. There are hiking trails and picnic areas on the property. ✉ *4275 Huron Rd.* ☎ *519/393–5311* ⊕ *www.stratfordperthmuseum.ca* 🎫 *C\$7.*

Bringing the Bard to Ontario

The origins of Stratford are modest. After the War of 1812, the British government granted a million acres of land along Lake Huron to the Canada Company, headed by a Scottish businessman. Surveyors came to a marshy creek surrounded by a thick forest and named it "Little Thames," noting that it might make "a good mill-site." It was Thomas Mercer Jones, a director of the Canada Company, who renamed the river the Avon and the town Stratford. The year was 1832, 121 years before the concept of a theater festival would take flight and change Canadian culture.

For years Stratford was considered a backwoods hamlet. Then came the first of two saviors of the city, both of them also Thomases. In 1904 an insurance broker named Tom Orr transformed Stratford's riverfront into a park. He also built a formal English garden, where flowers mentioned in the plays of Shakespeare—monkshood to sneezewort, bee balm to bachelor's button—bloom grandly to this day.

Next, Tom Patterson, a fourth-generation Stratfordian born in 1920, looked around; saw that the town wards and schools had names like Hamlet, Falstaff, and Romeo; and felt that some kind of drama festival might save his community from becoming a ghost town. The astonishing story of how he began in 1952 with C$125 (a "generous" grant from the Stratford City Council), tracked down Tyrone Guthrie and Alec Guinness, and somehow, in little more than a year, pasted together a long-standing theater festival is recounted in his memoirs, *First Stage: The Making of the Stratford Festival.*

Soon after it opened, the festival wowed critics worldwide with its professionalism, costumes, and daring thrust stage. The early years brought giants of world theater to the tiny town of some 20,000: James Mason, Alan Bates, Christopher Plummer, Jason Robards Jr., and Maggie Smith. Stratford's offerings are still among the best of their kind in the world—the next-best thing to seeing the Royal Shakespeare Company in mother city Stratford-upon-Avon, in England—with at least a handful of productions every year that put most other Canadian summer arts festivals to shame.

🍴 Restaurants

For a tiny town, Stratford is endowed with an unusual array of excellent restaurants. Perth County is a locavore's dream of farmers' markets, dairies, and organic farms. The proximity of the Stratford Chefs School (who also offer day courses to visitors) supplies a steady stream of new talent, and the Shakespeare festival ensures an appreciative audience.

Bentley's

$$ | CANADIAN | The well-stocked bar at this casual pub with booth and patio seating divides the room into two equal halves, with the locals converging on the east side. The pub fare includes quintessentials such as fish-and-chips, grilled steak and fries, burgers, and finger food. Salads, pasta, and sandwiches are also available. **Known for:** roast prime rib draws a crowd on Friday; easygoing staff and clientele; 20 beers on tap. [$] *Average main: C$15* ✉ *99 Ontario St.* ☎ *519/271–1121* 🌐 *www.bentleysbarinn.com.*

★ Bijou

$$$ | **EUROPEAN** | A husband-and-wife team, both Stratford Chefs School grads, operates this small, self-professed "culinary gem." The chalkboard menu changes daily, and nearly everything on it is locally sourced. Two- or three-course prix-fixe dinners have French, Italian, and Asian influences. The other dining options are shared tapas-style "food flights" with a choice of four to six dishes to share among couples are highly encouraged as they showcase the chef's creativity; roast Muscovy duck with mushrooms, beluga lentils, and carrot puree may be an option for your main course. The global dim sum Sunday brunch, with Asian small plate delicacies such as Korean braised beef cheek buns and spicy Chinese omelets, is a must-try. **Known for:** desserts like ricotta cheesecake with seabuckthorn sauce and orange sorbet; farm-to-table cooking at its finest; caters to dietary restrictions. [$] *Average main: C$27* ✉ *74 Wellington St.* ☎ *519/273–5000* 🌐 *www.bijourestaurant.com* 🕒 *Closed Mon.*

Boomer's Gourmet Fries

$ | **ECLECTIC** | The humble potato rises to become a star at Boomer's Gourmet Fries, equipped with a take-out window, a colorful chalkboard menu, and a handful of stools at a counter. Toppings of every kind can be found here, like vegetarian chili, hickory sticks, and salsa. The imaginative pairings apply to the homemade burgers as well. Try one of the many traditional versions of fries topped with cheese curds and gravy. **Known for:** fish-and-chips done simply with blue cod; unique and delicious takes on poutine; done up in comic-book colors. [$] *Average main: C$12* ✉ *26 Erie St.* ☎ *519/275–3147* 🌐 *www.boomersgourmetfries.com.*

Keystone Alley

$$$ | **CANADIAN** | Located on the site of the Keystone Bakery, this local favorite offers contemporary dishes made with fresh, locally sourced ingredients in a minimalist and modern environment. The alley, partially covered against the elements, is the perfect spot for an intimate meal. Keystone is also a microbrewery, offering seasonal, small batch suds on-site. **Known for:** hippie rice bowl with fried chickpeas and tahini; don't miss the South African influenced dishes; tucked away terrace filled with greenery. [$] *Average main: C$23* ✉ *34 Brunswick St.* ☎ *519/271–5645* 🌐 *www.keystonealley.com* 🕒 *Closed Mon.*

★ Mercer Kitchen + Beer Hall

$$$ | **ASIAN FUSION** | In an elevated French bistro setting, Mercer Kitchen engages chefs who have no interest in doing anything that's been done before. Wash down the innovative pan-Asian cuisine—think whole fried fish with charred scallions and soy tartar sauce—with a pint from one of a dozen rotating local craft beer taps. The kitchen welcomes posttheater snackers with a tasty late-night menu. The menus change every few months, so expect something new every visit. **Known for:** rotating seasonal selection of banh mi sandwiches; delicious smoked meat yaki soba noodles; dim sum brunch on weekends. [$] *Average main: C$22* ✉ *104–108 Ontario St.* ☎ *519/271–9202* 🌐 *www.mercerhall.ca.*

Pazzo Taverna and Pizzeria

$$$ | **ITALIAN** | Located where several important streets come together, Pazzo Taverna and Pizzeria is home to one of the city's best and most convivial Italian restaurants. Have a drink and people-watch at the bar or on the patio. The kitchen creates hearty regional Italian mains—like chicken scaloppine with mushrooms, balsamic braised shallots, and wild arugula—that make good use of locally sourced produce, meat, and sustainable fish. It's a popular meeting place after a play, the decor is soothing and modern, and the service is quick and friendly. **Known for:** locals flock to the downstairs pizzeria; lasagna with lobster, shrimp, and crab; streetside seating. [$] *Average main: C$22* ✉ *70 Ontario*

St. ☎ *519/273–6666* 🌐 *www.pazzo.ca* ⏲ *Closed Mon.*

The Planet Diner

$$ | **DINER** | Don't be surprised if you end up licking your fingers or reaching for a fork and knife to polish off your burger at this polka-dotted eatery. The vegan-friendly favorites are made messy, saucy, and decadent, a respite for plant eaters who have forsaken meats but still crave the soothing comfort that only items like a creamy mac and cashew cheese can bring. While true vegans might call foul, heritage country bacon and real pulled pork can be had as well. The brightly decorated vegan doughnuts and cinnamon buns on display at the counter are hard to ignore. **Known for:** brightly decorated vegan doughnuts and cinnamon buns; gluten-free buns available for most dishes; great cashew ice-cream banana split. [$] *Average main: C$20* ✉ *118 Downie St.*

The Prune

$$$$ | **CANADIAN** | A handsome house dating from 1905 holds a number of charming dining rooms leading to a tidy courtyard. Chef Bryan Steele, who is also senior cookery instructor at Stratford Chefs School, coaxes fresh local ingredients into innovative dishes with the best of what's available globally. Dishes change with the harvest, but have included Lake Huron whitefish meunière with asparagus and cinnamon cap mushrooms; and spring risotto with Parmesan, crispy egg, and wild leek pesto. The owners proudly source their meat from small family-owned farms. **Known for:** elaborate dishes that vary on the harvest season; sommelier oversees extensive Ontario-grown wine list; desserts made by in-house pastry chef. [$] *Average main: C$40* ✉ *151 Albert St.* ☎ *519/271–5052* 🌐 *theprune.com* ⏲ *Closed Nov.–mid-May and Mon.*

Revival House

$$$ | **FRENCH** | Constructed in 1873 as a congregational church, the building has most of the original architecture in place, but today snowy white table linens gleam in the afternoon light that pours through the stained-glass windows. Reimagined French classics like the steak frites with root vegetables are hearty production numbers created, of course, with local ingredients. The upstairs Belfry Bar (an actual belfry) is one of the most unique places you'll ever dine on brunch creations. **Known for:** lively summertime patio; French comfort food; Sunday brunch is fantastic. [$] *Average main: C$28* ✉ *70 Brunswick St.* ☎ *519/273–3424* 🌐 *www.revival.house* ⏲ *Church closed Mon. and Jan.–Mar. Belfry closed Sun. and Mon. and Jan.–Mar.*

York Street Kitchen

$$ | **CAFÉ** | Locals come to this casual spot across from the waterfront for the signature generously portioned and juicy sandwiches and, for dinner, homemade comfort dishes, such as meat loaf with Yukon Gold mashed potatoes. But the daily breakfast is a special treat; favorites are the French toast with homemade apple compote and the Mennonite sandwich with homemade summer sausage, cheddar, corn relish, and honey mustard. **Known for:** decorated with vibrant-patterned tablecloths; brilliant build-your-own-sandwich menu; some outdoor seating. [$] *Average main: C$15* ✉ *24 Erie St.* ☎ *519/273–7041* 🌐 *www.yorkstreetkitchen.com.*

🛏 Hotels

Stratford has a wide range of atmospheric B&Bs, motels on the outskirts of downtown, and inns around the center. Room rates are discounted substantially in winter, sometimes by more than 50%.

Avery House

$$$ | **B&B/INN** | This 1874 Gothic Revival home has been transformed into an impeccably decorated B&B with an eclectic interior. **Pros:** continually updated decor; affable host loves her job; big

breakfasts. **Cons:** communal dining not everyone's cup of tea; located on a busy road; ground-floor unit's bathroom isn't en suite. [$] *Rooms from: C$189* ✉ *330 Ontario St.* ☎ *519/273–1220, 800/510–8813* 🌐 *www.averyhouse.com* 🕒 *Closed Nov.–May* 🛏 *6 rooms* 🍴 *Free breakfast.*

★ Birmingham Manor B&B

$$$ | B&B/INN | This gorgeous Victorian home is filled with museum-like artifacts that reference theater ranging from Italian commedia dell'arte to Shakespearean histories. **Pros:** breakfast made with herbs and vegetables picked fresh from the garden; snack on an endless supply of home-baked biscotti; the garden attracts lots of butterflies and birds. **Cons:** some noise from street; uneven flooring upstairs; breakfast coffee a little weak. [$] *Rooms from: C$215* ✉ *240 Birmingham St.* ☎ *519/273–6545* 🌐 *birminghammanor.com* 🛏 *5 rooms* 🍴 *Free breakfast.*

Festival Inn

$$ | HOTEL | Stratford's largest hotel—about 10 minutes by car east of town—offers an unusually wide range of accommodations, from motel-style rooms to beautifully decorated suites with their own jetted tubs. **Pros:** breakfast is served every morning; modern rooms with many amenities; exceptional staff. **Cons:** except for the swooping annex building, architecture is bland; uninspired location on a commercial strip; dated decor. [$] *Rooms from: C$145* ✉ *1144 Ontario St.* ☎ *519/273–1150, 800/463–3581* 🌐 *www.festivalinnstratford.com* 🛏 *169 rooms* 🍴 *Free breakfast.*

Foster's Inn

$$$ | B&B/INN | Two doors down from the Avon and Studio theaters, this brick storefront building dates back to 1906 and has an interesting bit of history—it once housed the International Order of Odd Fellows, a fraternal organization that started in the United Kingdom. **Pros:** excellent location in downtown Stratford; the most delicious steaks in town; great deals in winter. **Cons:** fills up fast in the summer season; two-night minimum stay often required; lobby attached to restaurant. [$] *Rooms from: C$179* ✉ *111 Downie St.* ☎ *519/271–1119, 888/728–5555* 🌐 *www.fostersinn.com* 🛏 *9 rooms* 🍴 *No meals.*

Queen and Albert B&B

$$ | B&B/INN | A 1901 storefront enlivened with a striped awning is the unique facade of this residential-neighborhood B&B. **Pros:** ginger-mango crepes and other delights served in the sunny breakfast room; large rooms with fun and funky decor; two rooms share a balcony. **Cons:** decor is a bit of a hodgepodge; no elevator to upstairs rooms; cramped parking lot. [$] *Rooms from: C$175* ✉ *174 Queen St.* ☎ *519/272–0589* 🌐 *www.queenandalbert.com* 🕒 *Closed Nov.–Apr.* 🛏 *4 rooms* 🍴 *Free breakfast.*

Stewart House Inn

$$$$ | B&B/INN | The interior of this elegant 1870s home retains a Victorian feel but is filled with modern conveniences. **Pros:** exceptional service; outdoor swimming pool; complimentary espresso. **Cons:** not as central as some other inns; ground-floor room available only in summer; not recommended for families with young kids. [$] *Rooms from: C$289* ✉ *62 John St. N* ☎ *519/271–4576, 866/826–7772* 🌐 *stewart-house-inn.ontariocahotel.com* 🛏 *6 rooms* 🍴 *Free breakfast.*

Swan Motel

$ | HOTEL | The original 1960s motel sign still marks this single-story motel 3 km (2 miles) south of downtown. **Pros:** little extras like muffins set out in the morning; quiet location backed by farmland; best deal in town. **Cons:** basic rooms with parking-lot views; not walkable to downtown; motor-lodge layout. [$] *Rooms from: C$110* ✉ *960 Downie St.* ☎ *519/271–6376* 🌐 *www.swanmotel.ca* 🕒 *Closed Nov.–May* 🛏 *24 rooms* 🍴 *No meals.*

The award-winning Festival Theatre, the largest of the Stratford Shakespeare Festival's four venues, has been staging great drama for theater lovers since 1957.

The Three Houses Bed & Breakfast Inn
$$$ | B&B/INN | On a quiet residential street, this elegant and tastefully decorated trio of Edwardian and Victorian homes has been frequented by movie stars like Julie Andrews and Christopher Plummer. **Pros:** popular with couples on honeymoons; exquisite decorative taste; heated saltwater pool. **Cons:** irregular hours in the winter; often rented out to film crews; some steps to climb. $ *Rooms from: C$225* ✉ *100 Brunswick St.* ☎ *519/272–0722* ⊕ *www. thethreehouses.com* ⏎ *6 suites* ❍ *Free breakfast.*

⊕ Performing Arts

ARTS FESTIVALS
★ Stratford Festival
FESTIVALS | FAMILY | One of the two largest classical repertory companies in the world—England's Royal Shakespeare Company is the other—the Festival presents not only Shakespeare plays, but also works by other dramatists (including

new plays) and popular musicals and musical revues in its four theaters.

The 1,800-seat **Festival Theatre** (*55 Queen Street*), with its hexagonal wooden thrust stage and permanent wooden stage set, is the largest and oldest of the theaters—in its first incarnation in 1953 it was just a stage under a tent. The 1,100-seat **Avon Theatre** (*99 Downie Street*) has a traditional proscenium stage, while the **Tom Patterson Theatre** (*111 Lakeside Drive*) has a long, runway-style thrust stage and 600 seats. The petite **Studio Theatre** (*34 George Street E*), with only 260 seats, is the go-to space for experimental and new works. It has a modern appearance and a hexagonal thrust stage.

Throughout the season, 12 to 16 productions are mounted, always with at least a couple of family-friendly productions. At the height of the festival in July and August you may be able to choose from among eight performances. The festival also offers numerous concerts, workshops, tours, lectures, and talks, such as Meet the Festival, where the public can ask questions of actors and artists. The festival has both matinees and evening performances (and many visitors do see two plays per day). ⊠ *55 Queen St.* ☎ *519/273–1600, 800/567–1600* ⊕ *www. stratfordfestival.ca.*

★ Stratford Summer Music

FESTIVALS | For five weeks in July and August, Stratford Summer Music brings musicians—from elegant string quartets to folky bluegrass bands—to indoor and outdoor venues around town. Outdoor performances, like those sounding from a barge on the Avon River, are free. Series may include Saturday-night cabaret at the Church restaurant and classical-music lunches at Rundles. Some performances sell out, so get tickets in advance. ⊠ *Stratford* ☎ *519/271–2101* ⊕ *www.stratfordsummermusic.ca.*

Activities

BIKING
Totally Spoke'd
BICYCLING | Stratford is an ideal town for cruising via bicycle. Totally Spoke'd rents cruisers, mountain bikes, and tandem bikes. Rates are C$35 to C$47 per day. ⊠ *29 Ontario St.* ☎ *519/273–2001* ⊕ *www.totallyspoked.ca* ☉ *Oct.–Apr. closed Mon.*

◯ Shopping

GIFTS
Stratford Festival Shop
GIFTS/SOUVENIRS | In two locations (at the Avon and Festival theaters), this is the place for Shakespeare finger puppets, every Shakespeare play ever written, original costume sketches, soundtracks to the musicals, quotable aprons, and Bard-theme children's books. ⊠ *Avon Theatre, 99 Downie St.* ☎ *519/271–0055* ⊕ *store.stratfordfestival.ca.*

Watson's Chelsea Bazaar
GIFTS/SOUVENIRS | At this brimming curio shop you might find a cat curled up

Discount Tickets

Regular Stratford Festival tickets are around C$55 to C$110, but there are many ways to pay less. Spring previews and some fall performances are heavily discounted. Savings of up to half off can be had for students and seniors, and theatergoers aged 16 to 29 can buy seats online for C$25 for select performances two weeks prior. Also available are early-ordering discounts, rush seats, half-price Tuesday, and family and group discounts.

among the reasonably priced china, glassware, French soaps, kitchen gadgets, and other bric-a-brac. The Bradshaw family has owned a store at this location in various forms (it used to be a high-end china hall) since the 1800s. ⊠ *84 Ontario St.* ☎ *519/273–1790* ⊕ *www.watsonsofstratford.com.*

Midland and Penetanguishene

150 km (90 miles) north of Toronto.

Southern Georgian Bay's largest city is Barrie, but much more interesting are the quiet towns of Midland and Penetanguishene (also called Penetang by locals), occupying a small corner of northern Simcoe County known as Huronia, on a snug harbor at the foot of Georgian Bay's Severn Sound. These are docking grounds for trips to the Georgian Bay Islands National Park. To the west, the attractive harbor town of Collingwood, on Nottawasaga Bay, is at the foot of Blue Mountain, the largest ski hill in the province.

WHEN TO GO

After Labour Day and before Victoria Day weekend (late May), few tourist attractions apart from ski resorts are open.

GETTING HERE AND AROUND

Georgian Bay towns and attractions are west of Highway 400, either via Highway 26 toward Collingwood or well-marked off Highway 400 north of Barrie. These towns and regions are 2½ to 4 hours from Toronto and are generally long weekend or even weeklong trips from the city.

■ TIP→ **If you are heading here in winter, go with a four-wheel-drive vehicle.** Resorts, especially, are usually well off the highway and may require navigating twisting backcountry routes.

VISITOR INFORMATION

CONTACTS Georgian Bay Coastal Route. ⊕ *www.visitgeorgianbay.com*. **Visit Southern Georgian Bay.** ☎ *705/445–7722, 888/227–8667* ⊕ *www.visitsouthgeorgianbay.ca.*

 Sights

Georgian Bay Islands National Park

NATIONAL/STATE PARK | A series of 63 islands in Lake Huron's Georgian Bay, the park can be visited only via boat. Organized boat tours with the park or private companies operate from the weekend closest to May 24 through mid-October, weather permitting. The only way to explore one of the islands on foot is to book a trip on the park's Daytripper boat, bring your own boat, or take a water taxi in Honey Harbour (contact the park for details).

The park's own boat, the Daytripper (C$15.70 June–early October), makes the 15-minute trip to Beausoleil Island, which has hiking trails and beaches, from Honey Harbour, 15 km (9 miles) north of Port Severn at Highway 400 Exit 156.

Two companies do cruises through the Georgian Bay but don't allow you to disembark on any of the islands. The 300-passenger *Miss Midland,* operated by Midland Tours (C$36), leaves from the Midland town dock and offers 2½-hour sightseeing cruises daily at 2 pm mid-May to mid-October. The company can arrange departures from Toronto, which includes time to explore the town of Midland. From the Penetanguishene town dock, Penetanguishene 30,000 Island Cruises takes passengers on Penetanguishene Harbour and the Georgian Bay islands tours, including 1½- and 2½-hour cruises of Penetanguishene Harbour and 3½-hour cruises of the 30,000 islands of Georgian Bay, on the 200-passenger *MS Georgian Queen.* Lunch (C$55) and dinner (C$63) cruises are available with reservations. Captain Steve Anderson, the owner and your tour guide, has operated these tours—a family business—since 1985. Cruises depart one to three times daily in July and August; less frequently (but usually Saturday, Sunday, and Wednesday) in May, June, September, and October. ⊠ *2611 Honey Harbour Rd., off Hwy. 400 Exit 153 or 156, Port Severn* ☎ *705/526–9804* ⊕ *www.pc.gc.ca/en/pn-np/on/georg* 🖾 *C$6* ⊗ *Closed early Oct.–late May.*

Huronia Museum and Huron Ouendat Village

NATIVE SITE | Nearly 1 million artifacts on native and maritime history are on display at the museum building, and there's also a replica Native American village. Visitors can expect contemporary art and extensive photography pieces, in addition to native art and archaeological collections. ⊠ *549 Little Lake Park, Box 638, Midland* ☎ *705/526–2844, 800/263–7745* ⊕ *huroniamuseum.com* 🖾 *C$12.*

Martyrs' Shrine

RELIGIOUS SITE | On a hill overlooking Sainte-Marie among the Hurons, a twin-spired stone cathedral was built in 1926 to honor the eight missionaries stationed in Huronia who were martyred between 1642 and 1649. In 1930, all eight were canonized by the Roman Catholic Church.

The shrine is still active as a pilgrimage site and has daily services. ✉ *16163 Hwy. 12 W, Midland* ☎ *705/526–3788* ⊕ *www. martyrs-shrine.com* 🗟 *C$4* ⊙ *Closed mid-Oct.–mid-May.*

Sainte-Marie among the Hurons
MUSEUM | FAMILY | A Jesuit mission was originally built on this spot in 1639. The reconstructed village, which was once home to a fifth of the European population of New France, was the site of the first European community in Ontario; it had a hospital, farm, workshops, and a church. Workers also constructed a canal from the Wye River. A combination of disease and Iroquois attacks led to the mission's demise. More than 20 structures, including two native longhouses and two wigwams, have been faithfully reproduced from a scientific excavation. Staff members in period costume demonstrate 17th-century trades, share native stories and legends, and grow vegetables—keeping the working village alive. ✉ *16164 Hwy. 12 W, 5 km (3 miles) east of Hwy. 93, Midland* ☎ *705/526–7838* ⊕ *www.saintemarieamongthehurons. on.ca* 🗟 *C$12* ⊙ *Closed Nov.–Mar.*

Scenic Caves Nature Adventures
CAVE | FAMILY | Explore ancient caves, hike along craggy hilltop trails, get a thrill on zipline rides, or brave the suspension footbridge, 25 meters (82 feet) above the ground with amazing views of the bay, 300 meters (985 feet) below. Hiking boots or sneakers are required. ✉ *260 Scenic Caves Rd., Collingwood* ☎ *705/446–0256* ⊕ *www.sceniccaves. com* 🗟 *From C$27* ⊙ *Closed Nov.–late Apr.*

 Hotels

Horseshoe Resort
$$ | RESORT | Modern accommodations at this lodge on a 1,600-acre property come in a variety of shapes and sizes: choose from two-level lofts, spacious hotel rooms, or condos. **Pros:** nearly endless

list of outdoor activities; lots of different lodging options; suites with amazing amenities. **Cons:** scenic but isolated location; uncomfortable sofa beds; off-season dining options limited. ⑨ *Rooms from: C$169* ✉ *1101 Horseshoe Valley Rd., Barrie* ☎ *705/835–2790, 800/461–5627* ⊕ *www.horseshoeresort.com* ⇪ *101 rooms* ⦾ *No meals.*

★ Westin Trillium House
$$$$ | RESORT | FAMILY | Whether you're looking for a luxurious winter ski getaway or a summer escape into the biking and hiking trails of the Niagara Escarpment, the Westin Trillium House really does have something for every season and for everyone, (including your four-legged friends, who get beds in every unit). **Pros:** dozens of dining options outside your door; in-room gas fireplaces keep things cozy; plenty of nearby activities. **Cons:** some rooms have parking lot views; free parking is a long walk from resort; a bit of a chain hotel feeling. ⑨ *Rooms from: C$339* ✉ *220 Gord Canning Dr., Blue Mountains* ☎ *705/443–8080* ⊕ *www. marriott.com/hotels/travel/yyzth-the-wes-tin-trillium-house-blue-mountain* ⇪ *227 rooms* ⦾ *No meals.*

 Activities

SKIING AND SNOWBOARDING
★ Blue Mountain Ski Resort
SKIING/SNOWBOARDING | The largest ski resort in Ontario, and only getting bigger, this huge property near Collingwood revolves around its brightly painted Scandinavian-style alpine "village" with several blocks of shops, restaurants, bars, a grocery, and a plaza with live music. Ontario's most extensively developed and frequented ski area has 42 trails, 22 of which are available after dark for night skiing, served by high-speed six-person lifts; quad, triple, and double lifts; and magic carpets. Aside from the slopes, it has an outstanding 18-hole golf course, mountain biking, a lakeside beach, an aquatic park, and even a roller

coaster that winds down the mountain. ⊠ *108 Jozo Weider Blvd., Blue Mountains* ☏ *705/445–0231, 416/869–3799 from Toronto* ⊕ *www.bluemountain.ca.*

Mount St. Louis Moonstone
SKIING/SNOWBOARDING | **FAMILY** | Skiers and snowboarders can take advantage of 40 runs at Mount St. Louis Moonstone, 26 km (16 miles) north of Barrie. The majority of slopes are for beginner and intermediate skiers, though there's a sprinkling of advanced runs. The resort's Kids Camp, a day-care and ski-school combination, attracts families. Inexpensive cafeterias within the two chalets serve decent meals. ∎**TIP→ No overnight lodging is available.** ⊠ *24 Mount St. Louis Rd., off Hwy. 400 Exit 131, Coldwater* ☏ *705/835–2112, 877/835–2112* ⊕ *www.mountstlouis.com.*

Gravenhurst

74 km (46 miles) north of Barrie.

Outcroppings of pink and gray granite, drumlins of conifer and deciduous forest, and thousands of freshwater lakes formed from glaciers during the Ice Age characterize the rustic Muskoka region north of Toronto. Called Muskoka for Lake Muskoka, the largest of some 1,600 lakes in the area, this region is a favorite playground of those who live in and around Toronto. Place names such as Orillia, Gravenhurst, Haliburton, Algonquin, and Muskoka reveal the history of the land's inhabitants, from Algonquin tribes to European explorers to fur traders.

Gravenhurst is a town of approximately 10,000 and the birthplace of Norman Bethune, a surgeon, inventor, and political activist who is a Canadian hero. The heart of town is the colorful Muskoka Wharf, with its boardwalk along the water, restaurants, steamship docks, vacation condos, and plaza that hosts festivals and a Wednesday farmers'

market from mid-May to early October. Still, Gravenhurst is a tiny town and can be seen in a day or even an afternoon.

WHEN TO GO
As with everywhere in Muskoka, Gravenhurst comes alive in the summer months, with many attractions opening only after Victoria Day and closing between Labour Day and mid-October, as the weather dictates. Nevertheless, area resorts do plan winter activities—snowshoeing, sleigh rides, and the like—and restaurants are open (with shorter off-season hours) year-round.

GETTING HERE AND AROUND
From Toronto, take Highway 400 north, which intersects with the highly traveled and often congested Highway 11. Gravenhurst is about 70 km (40 miles) north of the junction on Highway 11. Driving time in good traffic is a bit over two hours. Ontario Northland buses and trains operate six days a week between Toronto's Union Station and downtown Gravenhurst; travel time is 2 hours 10 minutes.

CONTACTS Gravenhurst Bus and Railway Station. ⊠ *1–150 2nd St. S* ☏ *705/687–2301* ⊕ *ontarionorthland.ca/en/station/gravenhurst.* **Ontario Northland.** ☏ *800/461–8558* ⊕ *www.ontarionorthland.ca.*

VISITOR INFORMATION
CONTACTS Haliburton County Tourism. ☏ *705/286–1333, 800/461–7677* ⊕ *www.haliburtoncounty.ca.* **Muskoka Tourism.** ☏ *705/689–0660, 800/267–9700* ⊕ *www.discovermuskoka.ca.*

 Sights

Bethune Memorial House
MUSEUM | An 1880-vintage frame structure, this National Historic Site honors the heroic efforts of field surgeon and medical educator Henry Norman Bethune (1830–1939), who worked in China during the Sino-Japanese War in the 1930s and

trained thousands to become medics. There are rooms that evoke the period and an exhibit tracing the highlights of his life. ✉ *235 John St. N* ☎ *705/687–4261* 🌐 *www.pc.gc.ca/en/lhn-nhs/on/bethune* 🎟 *C$4* 🕒 *Closed Nov.–May.*

Casino Rama

CASINO—SIGHT | The largest First Nations–run gambling emporium in Canada, Casino Rama lures visitors to the Orillia area. A short jaunt from the ski resort areas around Barrie, the 192,000-square-foot complex has 2,500 slot machines, more than 110 gambling tables, eight restaurants, a lounge, and an adjoining 300-room all-suites luxury hotel. Catch acts like Foreigner, Jerry Seinfeld, and Dolly Parton here. ✉ *5899 Rama Rd., Rama* ☎ *705/329–3325, 800/832–7529* 🌐 *www.casinorama.com.*

Muskoka Discovery Centre

MUSEUM | Learn about steamboat history in this museum with a rotating collection of historic boats that have included a 1924 propeller boat, a 30-foot 1894 steamboat, and gleaming wooden speedboats. ✉ *Muskoka Wharf, 275 Steamship Bay Rd.* ☎ *705/687–2115, 866/687–6667* 🌐 *realmuskoka.com* 🎟 *C$12* 🕒 *Closed Sun. and Mon. in late Oct.–mid-June.*

Muskoka Steamships

TOUR—SIGHT | **FAMILY** | In warm weather, the best way to experience Muskoka Lake is aboard one of these historic vessels. The restored 128-foot-long, 99-passenger *RMS Segwun* (the initials stand for Royal Mail Ship) is North America's oldest operating steamship, built in 1887, and is the sole survivor of a fleet that provided transportation through the Muskoka Lakes. The 200-passenger *Wenonah II* is a 1907-inspired vessel with modern technology. Reservations are required. ✉ *Muskoka Wharf, 185 Cherokee La.* ☎ *705/687–6667, 866/687–6667* 🌐 *realmuskoka.com* 🎟 *Sightseeing cruises C$34* 🕒 *Closed weekends Nov.–May.*

Stephen Leacock Museum

MUSEUM | Readers of Canada's great humorist Stephen Leacock may recognize Orillia as "Mariposa," the town he described in *Sunshine Sketches of a Little Town.* Leacock's former summer home is now the Stephen Leacock Museum, a National Historic Site. Among the rotating exhibits are books, manuscripts, and photographs depicting Leacock, his family, and the region that inspired his writings. In the Mariposa Room, characters from the book are matched with the Orillia residents who inspired them. ✉ *50 Museum Dr., off Hwy. 12B, Orillia* ☎ *705/329–1908* 🌐 *www.leacockmuseum.com* 🎟 *C$5* 🕒 *Closed weekends.*

🍴 Restaurants

Blue Willow Tea Shop

$$ | **CAFÉ** | The dozen or so petite tables are set with blue-willow-pattern china in this quaint restaurant serving traditional English fare on the Muskoka Wharf. Afternoon tea—a three-tier platter of shortbread, scones with Devonshire cream, and savory finger sandwiches, plus a pot of tea per person—is served every afternoon. Crepes and other favorites are available at breakfast, with sandwiches, such as grilled bacon and Brie, are among the offerings for lunch. Popular items on the short dinner menu include baked fish and chips and classic bangers and mash. The attached shop sells loose-leaf teas and other take-home gifts. $ *Average main: C$15* ✉ *900 Bay St., Muskoka Wharf* ☎ *705/687–2597* 🌐 *www.bluewillowteashop.ca* 🕒 *Closed Mon.*

Boathouse Restaurant

$$$ | **CONTEMPORARY** | Consistent with the aesthetics of Taboo Resort, the Boathouse offers luxurious and contemporary international cuisine in a subdued dining room with sleek furnishings, hardwood floors, and a wall of lakefront windows. The kitchen has oriented the menu to

The Muskoka region north of Toronto is a popular destination for people wanting to escape the faster pace of city life.

appeal to a health-conscious crowd. **Known for:** waterfront barbecues with roast pork and lamb; lovely views of the water; fresh seafood dishes. [$] *Average main: C$24* ✉ *Taboo Musckoka, 1209 Muskoka Beach Rd.* ☎ *866/369–9672* 🌐 *www.taboomuskoka.com/dine/boathouse-restaurant.*

Hotels

Bayview-Wildwood Resort
$$$ | **RESORT** | **FAMILY** | A 20-minute drive south of Gravenhurst, this all-inclusive lakeside resort dates to 1898 and is particularly geared to outdoor types and active families. **Pros:** for privacy there are cottages with decks; casual, carefree atmosphere; free activities for kids. **Cons:** noisy trains pass by day and night; rustic feel isn't for everyone; strict meal times. [$] *Rooms from: C$250* ✉ *1500 Port Stanton Pkwy., Severn Bridge* ☎ *705/689–2338, 800/461–0243* 🌐 *www.bayviewwildwood.com* 🛏 *73 rooms* 🍴 *All-inclusive.*

★ **Taboo Muskoka**
$$$ | **RESORT** | A magnificent 1,000-acre landscape of rocky outcrops and evergreen trees typical of the Muskoka region surrounds this alpine lodge–style resort. **Pros:** fantastic golf course; forest and lake views; excellent spa. **Cons:** expensive rates in high season; no bar or food service at the pool; lots of corporate events. [$] *Rooms from: C$225* ✉ *1209 Muskoka Beach Rd.* ☎ *705/687–2233, 800/461–0236* 🌐 *www.tabooresort.com* 🛏 *62 rooms* 🍴 *Free breakfast.*

Shopping

BEER

Muskoka Brewery
WINE/SPIRITS | It's a real treat to visit this brewery, tasting room, and retail store for one of the most popular beers in Ontario, especially if you come for the free tour. While you're here, taste beers like the cream ale and Mad Tom IPA, or seasonal ales like the Summer Weiss or the Double Chocolate Cranberry Stout. It's half-way between Gravenhurst and

Bracebridge, off Highway 11. ⊠ *1964 Muskoka Beach Rd., Bracebridge* ☎ *705/646–1266* ⊕ *www.muskokabrewery.com.*

Huntsville

51 km (32 miles) north of Gravenhurst.

Muskoka's Huntsville region is filled with lakes and streams, stands of virgin birch and pine, and deer—and no shortage of year-round resorts. It is usually the cross-country skier's best bet for an abundance of natural snow in Southern Ontario. All resorts have trails.

Huntsville is a major gateway to Algonquin Provincial Park. Most people go to Algonquin in the summer, but the many winter attractions—ice fishing, cross-country skiing, dogsled tours—make it a popular destination in cold months as well. The only time to avoid is the notorious blackfly season, usually sometime in May. The mosquito population is healthy all summer, so pack repellent, pants, and long-sleeved shirts. Algonquin Provincial Park can be done in a weekend, but four days is the average stay; the park is huge and there's a lot of ground to cover.

WHEN TO GO
Summer is high season for vacationers in Huntsville, but the town is also ideal for cross-country skiing, ice fishing, and other backcountry winter adventures.

GETTING HERE AND AROUND
From Toronto, take Highway 400 north just past Barrie and then take Highway 11 north about 120 km (75 miles). Without traffic, the trip is about three hours. At least four Ontario Northland buses operate between Toronto's Union Station and Huntsville daily; travel time is four hours, and the station is in the north of the city, a short walk to Main Street. From Gravenhurst, Huntsville is about

55 km (35 miles) north on Highway 11, a 45-minute drive.

A good four-hour drive from Toronto, Algonquin Provincial Park is most readily reached via Highway 400 north to Highway 60 east. The huge park has 29 different access points, so call to devise the best plan of attack for your visit based on your interests. The most popular entry points are along the Highway 60 corridor, where you'll find all the conventional campgrounds. If you're heading into the park's interior, spring for the detailed Algonquin Canoe Routes Map (C$4.95), available from the park's website. The visitor centers, at the park gates, or on the Highway 60 corridor, 43 km (27 miles) east of the west gate, have information on park programs, a bookstore, a restaurant, and a panoramic-viewing deck. ■**TIP**➜ **In winter, go with a four-wheel-drive vehicle.**

CONTACTS Huntsville Bus Station. ⊠ *225 Main St. W* ☎ *705/789–6431* ⊕ *ontarionorthland.ca/en/station/huntsville.*

VISITOR INFORMATION
CONTACTS Huntsville/Lake of Bays Chamber of Commerce. ⊠ *37 Main St. E* ☎ *705/789–4771* ⊕ *www.lakeofbays.on.ca.*

Sights

★ Algonquin Provincial Park
NATIONAL/STATE PARK | Stretching across 7,650 square km (2,954 square miles) and containing nearly 2,500 lakes, Algonquin Provincial Park logs 272 bird species, 45 species of mammals, and 50 species of fish. The typical visitor is a hiker, canoeist, camper, or all three. But don't be put off if you're not the outdoorsy sort. About a third of Algonquin's visitors come for the day to walk one of the 17 well-groomed and well-signed interpretive trails or to enjoy a swim or a picnic. Swimming is especially good at the Lake of Two Rivers, halfway between the west and east gates along Highway 60. Spring,

Highway 60 takes drivers on a scenic route through Ontario's famed Algonquin Provincial Park.

when the moose head north, is the best time to catch a glimpse of North America's largest land mammal. Getting up at the crack of dawn gives you the best chance of seeing the park's wildlife. Park naturalists give talks on area wildflowers, animals, and birds, and you can book a guided hike or canoe trip. Expeditions to hear wolves howling take place in late summer and early autumn. The park's **Algonquin Logging Museum** (late-June–mid October, daily 9–5) depicts life at an early Canadian logging camp. The east gate is west of town of Whitney, and the west gate is east of town of Dwight ✉ *Hwy. 60, Algonquin Provincial Park* ☎ *705/633–5572* 🌐 *www.algonquinpark.on.ca* 🎟 *C$18 per vehicle.*

🍴 Restaurants

★ Arowhon Pines Restaurant

$$$$ | CANADIAN | A meal at this breathtaking hexagonal restaurant in the heart of Algonquin Provincial Park is the highlight of many visits. A view of the lake is a great accompaniment to the food, but a towering stone fireplace in the center of the log-walled dining room is an attraction, too. Menus change daily, but you can expect hearty Canadian dishes with local and seasonal ingredients. Bring your own wine for no corkage fee. **Known for:** children's menus and babysitting service; limited seating for nonresort guests; weekend lunch buffet. [$] *Average main: C$80* ✉ *Algonquin Provincial Park West Entrance, 8 km (5 miles) north of Hwy. 60, Algonquin Provincial Park* ☎ *705/633–5661, 866/633–5661* 🌐 *www.arowhon-pines.ca* 🕓 *Closed mid-Oct.–late May.*

Bartlett Lodge Restaurant

$$$$ | CANADIAN | In the original 1917 lodge building, this small lakeside pine dining room offers an ever-changing prix-fixe menu of contemporary Canadian cuisine, which might kick off with fennel and mustard-rubbed pork belly and move on to pistachio and cherry-crusted Australian rack of lamb or the house specialty, beef tenderloin. Fish and vegetarian options, such as sweet-potato gnocchi with shaved Gruyère, are always available. Desserts, included with the meal, always include some variation of crème brûlée (perhaps a chocolate-chili version), and homemade pie. **Known for:** you have to bring your own wine; four-course prix-fixe dinners; complimentary water taxi pickup. $ *Average main: C$72* ✉ *Boat from Algonquin Provincial Park Cache Lake Landing, south of Hwy. 60* ☎ *705/633–5543, 866/614–5355* ⊕ *www. bartlettlodge.com* ◷ *Closed late Oct.– mid-May. No lunch.*

Hotels

★ Arowhon Pines

$$$$ | **RESORT** | The stuff of local legend, Arowhon is a family-run wilderness retreat deep in Algonquin Provincial Park known for unpretentious rustic atmosphere and superb dining. **Pros:** all-inclusive rate includes a wide range of activities; excellent restaurant worth a trip; secluded feel. **Cons:** pricey considering its lack of frills; road can be tricky at night; limited cell phone service. $ *Rooms from: C$410* ✉ *Algonquin Provincial Park West Entrance, 8 km (5 miles) north of Hwy. 60, Algonquin Provincial Park* ☎ *705/633–5661, 866/633–5661* ⊕ *www. arowhonpines.ca* ◷ *Closed mid-Oct.–late May* ⇲ *50 rooms* ⦿ *All-inclusive.*

Bartlett Lodge

$$$ | **RESORT** | Smack in the center of Algonquin Provincial Park, this impressive 1917 resort is reached by a short boat ride across Cache Lake. **Pros:** completely quiet and peaceful; cabins have plenty of privacy; some rooms have wood stoves. **Cons:** expensive restaurant offers only dinner; no phones or TVs in the cabins; lots of mosquitoes in the summer. $ *Rooms from: C$200* ✉ *From Algonquin Provincial Park Cache Lake Landing, south of Hwy. 60, Algonquin Provincial Park* ☎ *705/633–5543, 905/338–8908* ⊕ *www.bartlettlodge.com* ◷ *Closed late Oct.–early May* ⇲ *14 rooms* ⦿ *Free breakfast.*

Deerhurst Resort

$$$ | **RESORT** | This golf-focused resort along Peninsula Lake is a 780-acre, self-contained community with restaurants and lodgings to fit every budget and style, from weddings to corporate events. **Pros:** resort arranges various Algonquin Park tours; summer and winter activities for everyone; affordable hike-and-stay packages. **Cons:** size can sometimes be overwhelming; busy check-in and checkout lines; getting enough towels can be a challenge. $ *Rooms from: C$219* ✉ *1235 Deerhurst Dr., south of Rte. 60* ☎ *705/789–6411, 800/461–4393* ⊕ *www.deerhurstresort. com* ⇲ *400 rooms* ⦿ *No meals.*

Walker Lake Resort

$$ | **RESORT** | **FAMILY** | Rustic two- and three-bedroom furnished cottages overlook Walker Lake at this resort, and many come with whirlpool tubs and fireplaces. **Pros:** very peaceful setting; free fishing boat rentals; easy access to Algonquin Park. **Cons:** no on-site restaurant; cottages require weekly rentals; bring your own bottled water. $ *Rooms from: C$175* ✉ *1040 Walker Lake Dr.* ☎ *705/635–2473, 800/565–3856* ⊕ *www.walkerlakeresort. com* ⇲ *7 cottages* ⦿ *No meals.*

Activities

SKIING AND SNOWBOARDING
Hidden Valley Highlands Ski Area
SKIING/SNOWBOARDING | The ski area has 35 skiable acres with 13 hills and three quad lifts. It's great for beginner and intermediate skiers, with a couple of black-diamond runs for daredevils. ✉ *1655 Hidden Valley Rd., off Hwy. 60* ☎ *705/789–1773, 800/398–9555* ⊕ *www. skihiddenvalley.on.ca.*

SPORTS OUTFITTERS
Algonquin Outfitters
CAMPING—SPORTS-OUTDOORS | The most well-known outfitter in the area has multiple locations in and around the park, specializing in canoe trip packages and

Adventure Tours Near Algonquin

If planning an Algonquin Provincial Park adventure seems daunting, leave it to the pros. Transport from Toronto, meals, and accommodations are included. You might, for example, do a multiday paddle-and-portage trip, catered with organic meals. Most companies have cabins, some quite luxurious, in Algonquin Park for tour participants; other tours may require backcountry tent camping.

Call of the Wild Call of the Wild offers guided trips of different lengths— dogsledding and snowmobiling in winter, canoeing and hiking in summer—deep in the park away from the more "touristy" areas. The tour company's in-park Algonquin Eco Lodge is powered only by waterfall. A popular package is a four-day canoe trip and three days relaxing at the lodge. ✉ *Algonquin Eco Lodge, 3594 Elephant Lake Rd., Algonquin Provincial Park* ☎ *905/471–9453, 800/776–9453* ⊕ *www.callofthewild.ca.*

Northern Edge Algonquin Northern Edge Algonquin eco-adventure company provides adventurous learning vacations and retreats with themes such as moose tracking (via canoe), sea kayaking, and women-only weekends. Home-cooked comfort food is local and organic; lodging ranges from new cabins to tents. ✉ *Algonquin Park Access Point #1, Algonquin Provincial Park* ☎ *888/383–8320* ⊕ *www.northernedgealgonquin.com.*

Voyageur Quest Voyageur Quest has a variety of adventure wilderness canoe trips year-round in Algonquin Provincial Park and throughout northern Ontario, including a number of family-geared vacations. ✉ *Round Lake, Algonquin Park Access Point #1, Algonquin Provincial Park* ☎ *416/486–3605, 800/794–9660* ⊕ *www.voyageurquest.com.*

Winterdance Dogsled Tours Winterdance Dogsled Tours takes you on half-day, full-day, multiday, and moonlight husky-led dogsledding adventures in and near Algonquin Provincial Park. Canoe tours are available in summer, as are kennel visits with the sled dogs. ✉ *6577 Haliburton Lake Rd., Haliburton* ☎ *705/457–5281* ⊕ *www.winterdance.com.*

rentals, outfitting and camping services, sea kayaking, and a water-taxi service to the park's central areas. Stores are at Oxtongue Lake (the main store—near the west Highway 60 park entrance), Huntsville, Opeongo Lake, Bracebridge, Haliburton, and Brent Base on Cedar Lake. ✉ *Oxtongue Lake store, 1035 Algonquin Outfitters Rd., R.R. 1, just north of Hwy. 60, Dwight* ☎ *705/635–2243, 800/469–4948* ⊕ *algonquinoutfitters.com.*

★ **Portage Store**

CAMPING—SPORTS-OUTDOORS | If you plan to camp in the park, contact the Portage Store, which provides extensive outfitting services and guided canoe trips. It rents canoes and sells self-guided canoe packages that include all the equipment you need for a canoeing-and-camping trip in the park. Also available are bike rentals, maps, detailed information about routes and wildlife, and an on-site general store and casual restaurant. ✉ *Hwy. 60, Canoe Lake, Algonquin Provincial Park* ☎ *705/633–5622 in summer, 705/789–3645 in winter* ⊕ *www.portagestore.com.*

Index

Photo Credits

Front Cover: Brady Baker / EyeEm [Description: Illuminated Buildings In Toronto.]. **Back cover, from left to right:** Vadim Rodnev/Shutterstock, Javen/Shutterstock, Canadapanda/Shutterstock. **Spine:** jiawangkun/Shutterstock. **Interior, from left to right:** Steven_Kriemadis/iStockphoto (1). Elijah-Lovkoff/iStockphoto (2). **Chapter 1: Experience Toronto:** James William Smith/Shutterstock (6-7). Aqnus Febriyant/Shutterstock (8). Kiev.Victor/Shutterstock (9). Diego Grandi/Shutterstock (9). Jesse Milns/Tourism Toronto (10). JHVEPhoto/Shutterstock (10). Philip Lange/Shutterstock (10). Royal Ontario Museum (11). Spiroview Inc/Shutterstock (12). typhoonski/iStockphoto (12). EQRoy/Shutterstock (13). Opticalmealfinder/Koi Koi (16). Jo-Anne McArthur/Village of Dreams Productions (16). Fuwa Fuwa (16). Barb Simkova/Patois (17). Pai (17). Finn O'Hara c/o Mahjong Bar (18). Jonathan Friedman (19). **Chapter 3: Harbourfront, Entertainment District, and the Financial District:** Jon Bilous/Shutterstock (51). Jon Bilous/Shutterstock (52). Tourism Toronto (53). Loozrboy/Flickr, [CC BY 2.0] (53). Roy Rainford / age fotostock (59). 2010 Getty Images/iStock (65). Shawn Goldberg/Shutterstock (71). 416style/Flickr, [CC BY 2.0] (73). Marc Bruxelle (76). **Chapter 4: Old Town and the Distillery District:** Tourism Toronto (83). Peter Mintz/agefotostock (86). Tourism Toronto (91). **Chapter 5: Yonge-Dundas Square Area:** Tourism Toronto (93). Oleksiy Maksymenko/agefotostock (98). Alan Marsh/agefotostock (101). **Chapter 6: Chinatown, Kensington Market, and Queen West:** mikecphoto/Shutterstock (103). jphilipg/Flickr, [CC BY 2.0] (106). Angelo Cavalli / age fotostock (110). Alastair Wallace/Shutterstock (114). Courtsy of Toronto Eaton Centre (119). **Chapter 7: West Queen West, Ossington, and Parkdale:** Tom Arban (121). Emily Sheff (126). diegograndi/iStockphoto (131). **Chapter 8: Leslieville, Greektown, Little India, and The Beaches:** Cedric Swaneck/Radical Road Brewing (133). OTMP (140). Amalia Ferreira Espinoza/Shutterstock (143). **Chapter 9: Queen's Park, The Annex, and Little Italy:** Liberty Group (145). Oleksiy Maksymenko/agefotostock (151). Cafe Diplomatico (157). **Chapter 10: Yorkville, Church and Wellesley, Rosedale, and Cabbagetown:** Tourism Toronto (159). 2008 George Pimentel (160). Jesse Milns/Tourism Toronto (161). Joshua Jensen/Flickr, [CC BY 2.0] (161). Nest Redux/David Hou (177). **Chapter 11: Greater Toronto:** TRphotos/Shutterstock (179). Courtesy of Ontario Science Centre (184). Jay Thaker/Shutterstock (186). **Chapter 12: Side Trips from Toronto:** JANIFEST/iStockphoto (189). Nitin Sanil/iStockphoto (192). Courtesy of Niagara Falls Tourism (193). Willem Dijkstra/iStockphoto (193). Henry Georgi / age fotostock (194). Craig Hatfield/Flickr, [CC BY 2.0] (195). Elena Elisseeva/Shutterstock (195). JTB Photo/agefotostock (199). JANIFEST/iStockphoto (203). Dennis MacDonald / age fotostock (210-211). JTB Photo/agefotostock (216). Tourism Toronto (218). Klaus Lang/agefotostock (222). Kerry Hayes/Stratford Shakespeare Festival (230). Design Pics/agefotostock (236). Glenn Davy/agefotostock (238). **About Our Writers:** All photos are courtesy of the writers except for the following: Natalia Manzocco, courtesy of Yuli Scheidt.

Every effort has been made to trace the copyright holders, and we apologize in advance for any accidental errors. We would be happy to apply the corrections in the following edition of this publication.

Notes

Notes

Notes

Notes

Notes

Notes

Notes

Fodor's TORONTO

Publisher: Stephen Horowitz, *General Manager*

Editorial: Douglas Stallings, *Editorial Director*; Jill Fergus, Jacinta O'Halloran, Amanda Sadlowski, *Senior Editors*; Kayla Becker, Alexis Kelly, Rachael Roth, *Editors*

Design: Tina Malaney, *Director of Design and Production*; Jessica Gonzalez, *Graphic Designer*; Mariana Tabares, *Design & Production Intern*

Production: Jennifer DePrima, *Editorial Production Manager*; Carrie Parker, *Senior Production Editor*; Elyse Rozelle, *Production Editor*; Jackson Pranica, *Editorial Production Assistant*

Maps: Rebecca Baer, *Senior Map Editor*; Mark Stroud (Moon Street Cartography), David Lindroth, *Cartographers*

Photography: Viviane Teles, *Senior Photo Editor*; Namrata Aggarwal, Ashok Kumar, Carl Yu, *Photo Editors*; Rebecca Rimmer, *Photo Intern*

Business & Operations: Chuck Hoover, *Chief Marketing Officer*; Robert Ames, *Group General Manager*; Devin Duckworth, *Director of Print Publishing*; Victor Bernal, *Business Analyst*

Public Relations and Marketing: Joe Ewaskiw, *Senior Director Communications & Public Relations*; Esther Su, *Senior Marketing Manager*

Fodors.com: Jeremy Tarr, *Editorial Director*; Rachael Levitt, *Managing Editor*; Teddy Minford, *Editor*

Technology: Jon Atkinson, *Director of Technology*; Rudresh Teotia, *Lead Developer*; Jacob Ashpis, *Content Operations Manager*

Writers: Jennifer Foden, Natalia Manzocco, Jesse Ship

Editors: Mark Sullivan, Caroline Trefler

Production Editor: Elyse Rozelle

26th Edition

ISBN 978-1-64097-240-7

ISSN 1044–6133

All details in this book are based on information supplied to us at press time. Always confirm information when it matters, especially if you're making a detour to visit a specific place. Fodor's expressly disclaims any liability, loss, or risk, personal or otherwise, that is incurred as a consequence of the use of any of the contents of this book.

SPECIAL SALES

This book is available at special discounts for bulk purchases for sales promotions or premiums. For more information, e-mail SpecialMarkets@fodors.com.

PRINTED IN CANADA

10 9 8 7 6 5 4 3 2 1